*Biting the Bullet*

JENNY SIMPSON

# BITING THE BULLET

**Living with the SAS**

HarperCollins*Publishers*

HarperCollins*Publishers*
77–85 Fulham Palace Road,
Hammersmith, London W6 8JB

This paperback edition 1997
1  3  5  7  9  8  6  4  2

First published in Great Britain by
HarperCollins*Publishers* 1996

A catalogue record for this book is
available form the British Library

ISBN 0 00 638826 4

Set in Linotype Minion

Printed and bound in Great Britain by
Caledonian International Book Manufacturing Ltd, Glasgow

FOR PAUL AND VANDA

At length did cross an Albatross,
Thorough the fog it came;
As if it had been a Christian soul,
We hailed it in God's name.

. . .

The many men, so beautiful;
And they all dead did lie:
And a thousand thousand slimy things
Lived on, and so did I.

I looked upon the rotting sea,
And drew my eyes away;
I looked upon the rotting deck,
And there the dead men lay.

. . .

I closed my lids, I kept them close,
And the balls like pulses beat;
For the sky and the sea, the sea and the sky
Lay like a load on my weary eye,
And the dead were at my feet.

Extract from the *Rime of the Ancient Mariner*,
SAMUEL TAYLOR COLERIDGE, 1798

# Contents

# Illustrations

*My love to the man I married,*
*and to the man who gave me the pen*

# 1 | From This Day Forward

THEY SAY AN ALBATROSS may have caused the accident. They believe the huge seabird might have flown into the rotor blades of the Sea King and caused it to ditch in the South Atlantic that Wednesday evening in May.

Bloodstained feathers were found floating on the waves near to where the twenty men on board had drowned. When I heard about the albatross later I thought of the *Rime of the Ancient Mariner* and reread Coleridge's famous lines.

The Sea King had been carrying thirty men. It had been on a routine five-minute hop across the mile of rough seas separating two ships, HMS *Intrepid* and HMS *Hermes*. On its second approach to *Intrepid*, 500 foot above sea-level, there was a loud bang and the helicopter suddenly lost all power before plunging into the waves in the darkness. It capsized and sank almost immediately.

Only ten men managed to escape. There was blind panic in the cold, dark water, as the survivors pushed past flailing limbs and floating equipment to find their way to the surface. Those who didn't find their way out were lost, and nineteen of them came from 22 Special Air Service. It was the forty-eighth day of the Falklands Conflict and the greatest single loss to the Regiment since it was founded more than forty years earlier.

The news of the accident didn't filter through immediately. Journalists travelling with the Task Force were initially told only that the helicopter had crashed and later that those who had died were Royal Marines.

At Stirling Lines, the SAS camp in Hereford, less than a mile from my home, Pat Dawson, the Families Officer, received a phone call on the Thursday night. By mid-morning on Friday, he had started to compile a list of the dead.

Ian and I'd been married for just a few months. He had been so excited about going to the Falklands. As a relative newcomer to the Regiment he had not yet seen a 'war' although he had completed a couple of tours of duty in Northern Ireland as a regular soldier before he joined the SAS in 1979.

The day the Argentinians invaded, Friday 2 April 1982, he was due to have parachute training but the weather was so bad it was cancelled, so he waited around the camp all day for news. I heard about the invasion at work when a colleague rushed in to tell me the news and to ask me if Ian would be going. Sitting at my desk and with the eyes of my colleagues upon me, I told them I honestly didn't know. It simply didn't occur to me at that moment that my new husband might soon become part of a huge British invasion force being sent half-way round the world.

Unbeknown to me, Lieutenant-Colonel Michael Rose had put Ian's D Squadron (one of the four main squadrons of the SAS, A,B,D and G, each consisting of sixty-four men) on standby the minute he learned of the invasion from a BBC newsflash. At first there was uncertainty as to who the invaders were but it quickly became apparent to the British inhabitants of the remote islands that some at least were soldiers.

I managed to get off work early and rushed home, anxious to speak to Ian and ask him the question I was almost afraid to utter. When I walked in through the front door of our little Victorian house and saw the fire in his eyes as he stood in the hallway, laden with packing for his bergen (backpack), I knew the answer.

I felt frightened and bewildered. I didn't know whether to be happy for him or sad for myself. I hadn't a clue what to say or how to react. But his enthusiasm for the mission was so apparent that I realised instinctively that what he needed more than anything right then was my support and encouragement. It wasn't a time for theatrics.

I helped him pack and we spent the evening quite happily,

laughing, joking and fooling around. He was pumping adrenaline, I could almost smell it on him. He was young and fit and preparing to do what he had been trained for and he liked the way it felt. There was no time to feel sorry for myself or wish that things could be any different. This was the man I had married, the SAS soldier who had stolen my heart and to see him then set my own pulse racing with attraction and excitement.

We went to bed early and finally fell asleep in each other's arms. At five the next morning, he suddenly sat bolt upright in bed. His thick black hair wild and unkempt, his eyes blazing, he looked for all the world like the half-gypsy that he was. Recently returned from two months' exercises in Kenya, he had a fearsome tan and was in peak condition, twenty-six years old and determined to set the world alight.

'It's going to happen today. We're definitely going today,' he said and jumped out of bed. I'd never seen him so fired up before. I leaned on my elbow and watched him standing stark naked in front of me, in a state of great excitement. I told him to shut up and come back to bed, but he didn't and then I couldn't get back to sleep myself.

By lunchtime he was packed. His bergen was in the hall, and his belt-kit containing his water bottle, rations and spare ammunition was laid out neatly on the new floral duvet I had recently bought for our double bed. His combat gear, socks and other clothes were always washed, ironed and rolled up in the pine chest of drawers next to the bed in case he had to move suddenly and grab a handful, but this time he had grabbed the lot and I kept tripping over piles of clothes and kit on the landing and in the hall.

We had arranged to visit my mum that day and when we got there and I told her about the invasion and the possibility that Ian might be going, she and I made light of it all. Sitting around her kitchen table, we laughed and joked about how many sandwiches he would need. I was so young and naive, I knew less than my mother about world affairs and we both genuinely believed that the Falkland Islands were somewhere off the coast of Scotland. When Ian asked me why I kept referring to Scotland and told me that the islands were 8,000 miles away, near Argentina, I was speechless. I still couldn't quite believe my husband would be going all that way to fight what seemed to me like a few foreign whalers.

Ian was totally channelled. 'I will be off', he kept saying. 'I'll be going any day now, you'll see.' He and his mates were all phoning each other up, asking if anyone had heard when they would be leaving. They were even getting calls from ex-members of the Regiment determined to get in on the war who said they were going to try to sneak on board some of the Task Force ships. One even made it as far as the *Canberra*, only to be hauled off unceremoniously by the Military Police after his wife telephoned and tipped them off.

I spoke to a few of the other wives and they told the same story. Their men were poking around in attics and at the bottom of cupboards, trying to find kit to take with them, looking for maps and books and wet weather gear. I wasn't alone in feeling that I was just getting in the way, and that we wouldn't even have time to discuss what it all meant. Ian kept saying there would be time enough to talk just as soon as he was packed. He was on a high, psyching himself up to go, willing the telephone to ring with the call and I knew that he wouldn't find the time.

That night I prepared his favourite meal, steak salad. I lit candles and dressed up, thinking that this was how I wanted him to remember me when he was away. We drank some wine and went to bed early and held each other tight. It was like a dream. My head felt like it was bursting with all the things I wanted to say and yet we lay silently in each other's arms, neither of us able to voice our innermost fears. His eyes were distant and glazed. When I leaned over him and looked into them I knew that in his mind he was already gone.

The phone rang at eleven p.m. and my heart sank. Ian was given his instructions to be in the camp the next day to be briefed for their departure on Monday. 'You know this is something I've got to do,' he told me, as he put the receiver down and reached out with his finger to catch the single tear rolling down my cheek. I nodded and pressed my eyelids shut against the flood. I knew that, for both our sakes, I had to let him go.

The next day, a Sunday, seemed especially long. He was at camp all day for a briefing at which he learned that the Argentinian military junta led by General Leopoldo Galtieri was planning a full-scale invasion of the Falklands. As I wandered around and around the house, aimlessly rearranging the furniture and ornaments, dusting, plumping cushions and tidying needlessly, Ian was going through his usual preparatory routines with his fellow troopers, studying maps of the islands and discussing tactical approaches, only this time it was for real and not just an exercise. The primary mission the SAS were to attempt, he and his men were told, was to retake South Georgia, already occupied by an unknown force of several thousand hostile Argentinian troops. As simple as that.

All day I waited at home for news. By the evening I was sitting on the stairs next to the telephone, looking at the bergen I was already beginning to resent. Ian eventually rang at six p.m. and I was so pleased to hear his voice. All I wanted was for him to come home, for a last quiet night together, just him and me, for a chance to talk about all the things that were spinning around in my head, to tell him how much I loved him and how proud I was that he was going off to war.

But he had other plans. He told me he had arranged for us to go out that night for a few drinks in town with a couple of close friends, Paul Bunker and his wife Vanda. I was disappointed but I knew I couldn't say anything. It was probably just his way of keeping the blood pumping. Maybe it was best that we didn't talk too deeply about how we felt. Maybe he couldn't handle that right now. I wasn't even sure I could.

I was pleased that of all the people Ian could have chosen to spend that last night with, he had picked Paul and Vanda. Paul was in the Regiment, a quiet, considerate man who was one of Ian's closest friends and who would be travelling with him to the Falklands.

They had met the previous year when they were both studying Arabic as part of their training and after their classes they would sit together in our local pub, The Swan. The landlords, our friends Mandy and Terry, would pour them a few pints and leave them gabbling away all afternoon, testing each other on their vocabulary.

Paul was also twenty-six, a real gem with a lovely smile and a very dry sense of humour. Originally from the West Country, he had a 'yokel' accent that Ian used to mimic brilliantly. Ian also used to rib him mercilessly about being a 'blanket stacker' because he came from the Royal Ordnance Corps (who deal with logistics, supply, maintenance of provisions and artillery) and was not an infantryman like most of the men in the SAS. But he was a good soldier and had passed the infamous Selection process with flying colours, joining Mountain Troop while Ian joined the Air Troop. The pair of them hit it off from the start and remained firm friends.

Vanda, Paul's wife, was someone I had known for years in Hereford, where she worked in Marks & Spencer as a shop assistant. Tall and pretty, slim and quite pixie-like, she was the spitting image of Shirley MacLaine. She was great fun, the life and soul of the party and a great leveller who never, ever let anyone get away with anything. Almost from the day we first met, she referred to me as 'old fruit'. They were a pretty special couple.

We met them in The Swan, and stayed well after closing time, all having a few drinks too many. The evening was spent laughing, joking, playing darts and generally having a great time. Vanda and I were joking about all the fun we would have while our men were away and Paul and Ian were teasing us about all the dusky Argentinian beauties they had heard about. Everything was very upbeat until about midnight when Mandy, who was polishing glasses behind the bar, suddenly burst into tears. We all stopped laughing and looked at her in silence.

'What are you crying for?' I asked. 'They're only going away for a few weeks. There's nothing to worry about.'

She blinked at me through her tears and said, 'No, Jenny, no. This time it's no good, I just know that it's no good. I can feel it.'

I didn't want to hear. 'Give over and pour us all a drink,' I said, grinning a little too broadly. 'They'll be back before we can even get our hands on their credit cards.'

Mandy wandered off, sniffing, to set up another few bottles. I looked up and met Paul's eyes across the bar. We stared at each other for a moment but said nothing. There was nothing we could say, the silence said it all. Vanda caught my eye and we also examined each other momentarily. I could feel tears pricking at the back of my eyes. Ian watched the three of us uneasily and was the first to break the silence.

'Come on you lot, this is meant to be a jolly send-off, not a bloody wake. Whose round is it anyway?'

Vanda responded to his request by slapping a five pound note on the bar. Then she slid down from her stool and started to tap dance in the corner, hitching her skirt up around her knees. Ian was laughing so much he nearly fell off his bar stool and Paul joined in, easing the atmosphere. I blinked hard several times and then started clapping in time. It was going to be all right. Everything was going to be all right.

Having drunk far too much that night, we staggered home together in the early hours, singing. We left our car in the pub car park overnight and decided to pick it up early the next morning. When we got down there after mid-day, feeling terrible, Mandy was nowhere to be seen and we were grateful for that.

That last day was one of saying little but feeling so much. Ian took me out to lunch at the steak bar at the Imperial Hotel in town. He fetched me a drink, a 'hair of the dog' he said, but it wasn't just my hangover that was making me feel so wretched. This was the first time I had ever had to be truly brave and I found it very hard. How could I laugh and eat and drink and pretend it was just a normal, happy day out when I knew the only man I ever loved was about to leave for the other side of the world and God knows what?

Almost everywhere we looked there were other guys from the Regiment with their wives and children around town, buying portable hi-fis and other toys to while away the time on their long hitchhike south, treating their loved ones to flowers and meals and presents. I nodded at the other wives we passed, our eyes meeting only fleetingly but the emotion that lay behind them flashing with recognition and we half-smiled in acknowledgement of it.

Many of the eyes were red-rimmed, some were unashamedly watery, mine were determinedly dry. None of us knew how long our men would be gone, whether it would be weeks or months, or if they would be coming back at all. But I told myself repeatedly that it didn't matter how long Ian was away because he would be coming back. I knew he would. He had to.

This was going to be our first opportunity to test a promise I had made him when he went to Northern Ireland the previous year. In my first letter to him I wrote that, from that moment on, if we couldn't be together physically, then we would be together in our hearts and minds through the letters we wrote and the love we sent across the airwaves. We called it 'fluencing', a phrase used by his gypsy mother. 'If we write to each other every day or speak to each other each night, then our long separations will become bearable,' I wrote. 'We'll fluence each other from across the miles and then we'll always be together.'

We got home from town and Ian went through his final packing list. David, his troop commander, called round to tell him what time he would be leaving that evening. He had to be at camp for a final briefing by the Regiment's brigadier, Peter de la Billière, before being flown in a VC10 directly to Ascension Island, to be boarded on ships bound for the Malvinas, as the Argentinians referred to the Falkland Islands.

I made tea and stood in the kitchen with Ian, watching the second hand on the wall clock ticking away the few minutes we had left. Rinsing his mug and placing it on the draining board, he turned stiffly to say his farewells. I tightened my grip around my mug and struggled with my emotions.

'You know I'll be back,' he told me. 'I promise you that.'

Putting my mug down, I reached up and threw my arms around his shoulders, burying my face in his neck, breathing in the smell of his skin.

'I know you will. And I'll be brave, I promise,' I told him. I vowed in my heart at that moment that I would be strong, whatever. He held me for a moment and then released my grip with his hands and left the room. As he packed the last items into his bergen, I chatted on about how I would telephone everyone to tell them he had gone and promised to attend to a few domestic matters that needed attention.

'I'll sort out those bills and go and see the bank manager next week,' I continued, hoping that the mundane nature of my conversation would defuse the atmosphere.

His jacket over his arm, his bergen on his back, he turned to look at me as he stood in the doorway. Neither of us spoke, I standing barefoot in the kitchen in jeans and a T-shirt, a tea towel in my hand, my blonde hair still tousled from the afternoon's breeze; he kitted to the teeth and laden with gear, all in black and with the fire still burning in his eyes.

I opened my mouth to speak but nothing came out. He half-smiled, blew me a kiss and then suddenly he was gone, out of the door and out of my life. That was it. He didn't even give me a chance to say goodbye.

The men of the SAS have their own ways of dealing with death, which quite often seem strange or even disrespectful to outsiders. They are known as pilgrims after a quotation from a poem by James Elroy Flecker, written in the early part of this century. The lines which are inscribed above the memorial clock tower at Stirling Lines, read:

> We are the Pilgrims, master; we shall go
> Always a little further, it may be
> Beyond the last blue mountain barred with snow
> Across that angry or that glimmering sea.

When one of the pilgrims is killed, the others hold a high-spirited auction for his kit at a sort of Regimental wake. They all gather together at the camp, have a few beers and then start bidding ridiculously large sums of money for articles of kit or clothing they have no need for, and often don't really want. It is their way of expressing their grief and giving a donation to the widow.

The wives know about the auctions but are not involved. We try to joke about the insurance pay-outs and thank our lucky stars that our pilgrim wasn't the one who was killed. We even have our own parody of the Regimental motto 'Who Dares Wins'. We say, 'Who

Cares Who Wins?' and we might add, 'Win or Lose, Come Home Safe'.

An SAS wife who weeps and wails is pretty rare. We have evolved a sense of humour similar to the men's which makes light of danger and almost mocks death. When you deal with death every day, either the threat of it or the direct result of it, you simply can't allow yourself to be swamped with feelings of fear or sadness unless it happens to someone very close to you. If you did you would either go mad or kill yourself.

Humour is not always enough and in my weakest moments I think of the words of one of the favoured readings at SAS memorial services, from Sir Fitzroy Maclean, 'Death is only a horizon and a horizon is nothing more than the limit of our sight.'

More poignant perhaps is the final part of the Flecker poem, which is rarely quoted and has never become as well known as the section adopted by the Regiment.

Just as the pilgrims are about to leave for yet another glimmering sea, the women lament their imminent departure. In words which could have been written specifically for anyone who chooses to marry into the SAS, one women turns to the weeping crowd and tells them:

> What would ye? ladies. It was ever thus
> Men are unwise and curiously planned
> They have their dreams
> And do not think of us.

Once Ian was out of the door, there was almost no information about where he was or what he was doing. For security reasons, the men are not allowed to contact their wives directly and the camp officials give little away for much the same reasons. It is only long after the event that we learn what really happened. I tried very hard to imagine where Ian was as I got up to go to work each day, I tried to estimate the time difference and think about what he might be doing at that particular moment. Most of the time, as I learned a lot later, I didn't even come close.

After leaving me standing in the kitchen, Ian arrived at the camp that Monday evening for the briefing by de la Billière, which turned out to be a classic in Regimental history. The brigadier's advice to the dozens of special services soldiers about to go off to war consisted of, 'Keep your bergen weight below forty pounds and don't throw away your biscuits from your twenty-four-hour ration pack.' As their bergens seldom weighed less than eighty pounds and some of them were later so hungry in the severe mountain conditions that they were almost reduced to eating the soles of their boots, the brilliance of the advice was rather lost on them. They also noticed that their commander was wearing his sweater back to front. Terrific, they thought.

They flew to Ascension Island before hitchhiking a series of long boat rides to the Exclusion Zone, a 200-mile radius of the Falkland Islands patrolled by British ships. Ian was very ill at ease on the huge naval vessels transporting him to the other side of the world. With little to do but exercise or play cards, he felt he was not in control of his own destiny. To keep himself occupied he and a few mates trained daily on the deck in shorts, until the captain warned them that they were over-exciting the crew. This was their first exposure to the Merchant Navy and they made sure they dressed up to the neck and down to the toes after that.

They also encountered considerable hostility from some of the naval ratings who had already been at sea for several months and who failed to share in the enthusiasm for the war. One unidentified crewman even sabotaged his ship's guns during a drill in the hope that the vessel would have to return to England for a refit. Surrounded by such antipathy, Ian couldn't wait to reach dry land.

By the time they reached the Exclusion Zone the weather was appalling. They and their kit were ferried between vessels by Wessex helicopters in high seas. Once on board they were 'hot-bedding' – sleeping where they could, often on the floor in heavy rolling seas, or jumping into beds recently vacated by the night shifters.

My bed at home seemed far too big without Ian, and I found myself unable to sleep or waking restlessly at dawn. I couldn't settle to anything. My mind was with him, wondering what he was doing. I yearned to hear his voice, feel his touch or see his smiling face.

I knew that I had to try to get into some sort of routine while he was away and I tried to keep myself as busy as I could. Work was a welcome distraction. It meant I had to get up at a set time each morning, no matter how little I had slept the night before, and put on a brave face. I was the only SAS wife at my office, a large company of several hundred people in Hereford. Most of my immediate colleagues knew what Ian did for a living and were supportive and kind, but the rest did not and had no idea how hurtful some of their casual comments about the war were.

'Did you see the Task Force set sail?' one young man in personnel asked me excitedly one morning, not long after Ian had left. 'Those Argies won't know what's hit them, once we get our boys over there. All these pacifists go on about how many lives could be lost in the process, but what really matters is that Britain is showing the rest of the world what's what.' I looked at his fresh young face and recognised the fire in his eyes. Was Ian that naive? I wondered.

After work I would occasionally go out for a drink with friends, or to the cinema, or out for a meal. Then it would be home to bed and the nightly ritual of letter-writing and making up packages and parcels for Ian, which would be dropped off at the special mail collection point at the camp on my way to work. I would kiss each parcel goodbye and wish it speedily on its way. If I could have wrapped myself up in brown paper and string and sent myself, then I would have done.

After what seemed like forever at sea, but which was actually less than two weeks, Ian and his squadron were transferred to HMS *Endurance*, the Royal Navy's Arctic Survey ship. There waiting for him were dozens of my letters and parcels, which had been flown on ahead. He opened them excitedly and started to write back to me in earnest, almost every day, telling me his news. His letters were collected by helicopter and flown to mother ships on the edge of the Exclusion Zone, before being sent back to Ascension Island and home. They took weeks to get to me and often arrived in batches of three or four, crumpled and crushed from spending so long in the bottom of huge mail sacks.

I read every word and savoured their sentiments. I relished the glimpse into Ian's days and nights that they gave me. When he said in his letters that he was permanently tuned to the BBC World Service to follow the latest developments, I asked a friend at work to tune in the little short-wave radio I had at home so that I could listen to it with him. I would curl up under our duvet each night, the radio crackling away quietly on my bedside table, writing my letters until the distinctive World Service News music would strike up its nursery-rhyme beat and I would turn up the volume.

It was through the BBC that we both learned of the main Argentinian invasion after the junta's initial foray into British territory. The following day, 15 April, a Nimrod aircraft flew close to Ian's ship and dropped a canister into the sea. It contained an encoded Flash Message (top priority) requiring 'Immediate Action', giving him and his fellow soldiers the order to go in and start to destroy the enemy bases. Ian was delighted. He would soon be on dry land at last.

Vanda and I kept in close touch. We were both trying to be brave for our men and for each other. Each suspected that at nights the other was crying herself to sleep, but neither of us ever let our guard slip enough for the other to know it. I filled my days with work, my evenings on the phone to her or some of the other wives, and my nights writing letters. I watched all the television news coverage, read the newspapers and listened to the opinions of my father, brothers and work mates about when they thought the war would be over and how they thought we were doing.

I wished that I knew more about the place Ian had been sent to, or understood why Margaret Thatcher and her government had despatched him there in the first place. Even when I looked up the Falkland Islands in an atlas at the local library and read about its population and industry, I was largely bewildered by the politics of it all. All I knew was that I wanted my husband home safe.

Over a month passed, and I started to miss Ian pretty badly. I found myself rifling through folders of photographs, looking for pictures of him to carry in my purse. I was angry with myself for not having any really good shots of him and promised I would get some better ones done when he came home. At work when I was daydreaming about him I would suddenly worry that I had forgotten what he really looked like. I would reach into my handbag and pull out a photo and study it hard, memorising every line, the way his nose overshadowed his lip, the curve of his jaw, the cut of his hair.

At night when I got home, I hardly gave myself time to take off my coat before rushing upstairs to his wardrobe. Reaching inside for a favourite jacket, I would pull it around my shoulders and hold a sleeve to my face, feeling its roughness on my skin, inhaling the special way his skin smelled. God, I ached for him.

I doubt he had any time at all to miss me by then, since he was well established off the Falkland Islands and starting to have a bit more fun. On 15 May, almost six weeks after he had left, he was involved in the first successful attack against the Argentinians, an SAS raid on an airfield on Pebble Island. It was an extremely dangerous mission, there was a military garrison nearby with a large number of Argentinian soldiers, air force pilots and crews, and Ian and his fellow soldiers knew they had to make a quick strike – in less than thirty minutes – so as to avoid any prolonged contact with the garrison.

One day before the attack, Ian went down with the flu, he really had it badly – a high temperature and aching limbs – and felt dreadful. He confined himself to sick bay and took medication to try and get his temperature down. He knew of the impending attack and he was desperate to get himself in shape for it. Two hours before the operation, a mate came and gave him the nod and he discharged himself from sick bay, grabbed his kit and jumped on the back of a chopper. He wasn't going to miss this one for the world.

When they got to the drop-off point forty-five of them spilled out of the Sea Kings and split up into small patrols to head towards the airfield. They all had to quickly complete a seven-kilometre tab (march) from hell in freezing cold night-time conditions, laden with more than eighty pounds of kit and weapons. Ian felt dreadful, really ill, yet he still managed to run like hell for more than an hour across unforgiving terrain that gave no cover at all, remembering all the while that once the strike was over he would have to do exactly the same tab back to the RV (rendezvous) point.

As they got near to the desolate airfield on a windswept finger of grassland normally only inhabited by a handful of islanders and more than 100,000 sheep, it became apparent that one troop had got lost on the march in. Well, it was pitch-dark and the whole place looked the same. It was to Ian's great good fortune that they did, however, because as a result of this he was instructed to be in the fire-support team, providing cover for the teams that were to run up to the aircraft, place explosives on them and disable them any way they could, as soon as the diversionary attack started.

This last-minute change of plan diverted him and his troop from having to clear the village house by house to alert local islanders to the forthcoming attack. It was later reported that one of the buildings he would have innocently approached, known locally as the Woolshed, contained more than 200 Argentinians lying in wait.

As the word went up, the attack opened with a massive naval bombardment from the ships Ian and his fellow soldiers had just come from. Then he and his men opened fire, their mortar lighting up the sky. They watched and provided fire cover as two seven-man assault teams went in. Two Argentinians in a bunker to the side of the strip opened fire and were quickly dealt with.

As the assault teams strafed the Argentinian planes with machine gun fire, threw in grenades and, in some cases, ripped the instrument panels out with their bare hands, Ian and his troop provided continuous cover in case the air crews and soldiers started pouring out of their sleeping quarters, guns blazing.

When they saw the assault teams were clear, they continued firing and moving back with them. Fire and manoeuvre, the routines they knew and practised almost daily. But that is when the assault troop realised they were running backwards through a minefield. The mines started to go off all around them – command-detonated by the Argentinian troops - and all hell broke loose. Ian had no time to consider whether or not he was about to be blown up as he provided cover, it was a question of one foot on the ground and one moving, all the men leap-frogging past each other to protect one another as the mortar rounds continued to light up the sky and the whole settlement seemed to be ablaze as the ammunition dump went up.

Thankfully, Ian managed to escape without a scratch, as did the rest of his troop. Paul Bunker was not so lucky. He was hurled ten feet in the air by one of the land mines. Thrown to the ground, he suffered concussion and the man next to him suffered shrapnel wounds to his legs. Both had to be carried back on the seven-mile return tab so that they could be stretchered to the ship. Ian, who is trained as a medic, helped treat them before flying out on the last chopper. He looked back on Pebble Island to see the airfield burning behind him. It was his first taste of action and he felt elated.

It was one of the Regiment's most successful missions ever – eleven Argentinian aircraft and the ammunition dump destroyed by D Squadron. It was carried out in the best traditions of undercover operational attack. The raid was reported in the newspapers back home, but the SAS were never publicly mentioned. As is so often the case with Regiment operations, the Royal Marines were given all the glory.

The camp let us know privately that our men had been involved and that it had been a successful contact, but little further information filtered out. I scanned the newspaper reports and listened to the news bulletins to see if there would be more details of what had happened, but – as usual in matters involving the Regiment – the media machine seemed to have been all but muzzled by the Whitehall mandarins.

Paul had not been having a good war. A few days earlier he had injured his back when the helicopter in which he was being airlifted from Fortuna glacier crashed in a blizzard, tipping over on its side. He had a lucky escape that day and now he was in the sick bay again for the second time in a few weeks. Even there he wasn't safe.

The navy crews who heard what the SAS had achieved at Pebble Island waited on deck for them all to return, clapping, cheering and shouting their encouragement as their helicopters landed one by one. As the last helicopter returned, the over-enthusiastic matelots pressed around the SAS soldiers who were still fully armed, causing one of their rifles to go off by accident. Two rounds were fired straight down through the roof of the sick bay below. The bullets landed a few inches from Paul Bunker's bed.

Vanda was told only that Paul had received a minor head injury. They said he was concussed and in the sick bay but would be all right and would be back at work within a day or two. That night she dropped by unexpectedly to keep me company. She didn't tell me that Paul had been injured because she knew that I would then worry about Ian. I liked to maintain the illusion that Ian wasn't fighting at all, but was safely tucked up in his bunk on board ship, reading my letters. But I could tell that something was on her mind, she couldn't stop talking and was very restless, pacing up and down in my kitchen.

I poured her a drink and asked her what was wrong.

'I don't know, really, old fruit,' she said. 'I guess I'm just worried about Paul. I can't stop thinking about him. He is always on my mind.'

I patted her arm and stood up to make us something to eat. 'Come on now, Vanda,' I said. 'This isn't like you at all. Where's that famous smile? Paul will be fine, they both will. They'll be home soon and we'll all go down The Swan and have a few drinks and you'll wonder why on earth you worried.' My words didn't seem to be reaching her.

'I know, I know,' was all she said, but I could see she wasn't listening. I poured us both another glass of wine and told her we were all in this together and had to be strong for each other.

'We have to be as brave as them,' I reminded her. 'It goes with the territory.'

Some women marry into the Regiment for the prestige and excitement of it all. They enjoy playing the anxious little woman, sitting at home waiting for their heroes, collecting the pay cheques and letting everyone know how much they are suffering. But it is not that simple, as many of them come to realise before they pack their bags and close the door behind them for the last time. It is not just a question of staying the course and expecting a free ride. We have to be as tough as our men when it comes to facing up to various hardships. With the waiting goes the anxiety, the loneliness and –

worst of all – the fear. Vanda, of all people, knew that and it bothered me that she seemed to be handling it worse than I was. I had always thought of her as being so strong.

Maybe I picked up on her unease, there was something very unsettling about her visit and that night was one of many when I couldn't sleep. Ian's mother telephoned me late to say she couldn't sleep either and that bothered me immensely; I worried that she might be sensing something in her gypsy way. I told her not to worry, and that she should lie on the bed and close her eyes, as I did, to give them a rest at least. But after I had put down the receiver I couldn't even close my own eyes.

On the Friday morning of that week I was at work as usual. At my request, my sixteen-year-old niece Lisa had come to stay for a few days to keep me company while Ian was away and I decided to walk home at lunchtime to see her. Lisa was a fresh-faced, pretty young girl who had come to treat me like an older sister. The first-born daughter of my older sister Dotty, she was born when I was only thirteen and I had grown to love her over the years. Having her around would do me good, I told myself. I wouldn't feel so isolated and she would be refreshingly good company for a while.

Just before I left the office at 12.30 that day, Kathy, a colleague and friend, rang me from the main office block. They had been listening to the latest news bulletins on the radio and she asked if I had heard about the Marines who had died in a helicopter crash. I told her I hadn't. As she gave me the details, my eyes welled up for those who had been lost, but I thought, Thank God it's not my husband. When I got home Lisa wasn't in so I made myself a sandwich and turned on the television. The crash was the top story on the one o'clock news but I hardly had time to listen before the telephone rang.

'Are you OK?' It was Karen, the wife of David, Ian's troop corporal.

Gulping down my mouthful, I wiped my lips and said, 'Yes, I am fine. Why?'

She asked me if I was sure, and I laughed and told her that I was all right.

After a brief pause, she said, 'It's not him then?'

My heart skipped a beat as I asked her what she meant.

'The helicopter crash,' she said, 'it's not Ian?'

My heart stopped. I asked her what she was talking about. 'They were all Marines, weren't they?' I said. 'Karen, the news said they were all Marines.'

'Is that why you weren't in camp this morning, because you believed they were all Marines?' she asked.

There was a long pause. I couldn't answer her for all the questions spinning round in my head. What was she on about? Did she mean that the men who died weren't Marines? Was she saying they were SAS? Oh my God.

Sensing my confusion, Karen finally said, 'Jenny, I think you had better come down and see me. I'm at Tanya's. Come right away.'

I was numb. I grabbed my coat and bag, got into the car and started the ten-minute drive to Tanya's house. She was a close friend of Karen's who lived on an estate in Hereford, just 500 yards from Paul and Vanda.

On the way to Tanya's house, I kept repeating to myself, 'It can't be Ian, it isn't him, I would know if anything had happened to him.' Another voice in my head was saying, 'Oh my God, what if it is him? What the hell am I going to do? Please don't let it be him.'

I was on auto-pilot, driving my Toyota Corolla through Hereford like a woman demented. Terry, the landlord of The Swan, passed me going the other way and went home and told Mandy that he thought something must be terribly wrong because of the expression on my face. Reminded of her own premonition on our last night together before the boys had gone, she prayed that her instincts had been wrong.

By the time I got to Tanya's I was a nervous wreck. Half of me was quivering all over and the other half was wondering who should call my office to tell them that I wouldn't be back at work that afternoon. I thought the Regiment had left it to Karen and Tanya to break the news to me. But when I walked in the door and looked at their faces I realised that they didn't know, any more than I did, if Ian was alive or dead. They sat me down and Karen gave me a cigarette. I didn't smoke, I hadn't smoked for five years, but I took it.

'If the Families Officer hasn't called you, then Ian must be all right,' Karen reasoned out loud. 'They would have let you know.'

'But they don't have my work number and anyway, I went home for lunch,' I explained, as much to myself as to them.

She told me how all the other wives had been summoned to the camp that morning and told the news. Pat Dawson had stood up in front of them all and said, 'I am afraid there has been a terrible accident. Those of you here have nothing to worry about, your men are safe. But many lives have been lost and I am afraid that the wives who aren't here with us today are the ones who have suffered losses. I know you will do all you can to help me help them now.' Because I wasn't there, my friends had assumed that I was one of the widows.

Karen told me the names of those who had died, many of whom were close friends. A friend, Carole, had lost her husband Paddy Armstrong whom the men had nicknamed 'Pucara Paddy' after his skill in placing explosives on the Pucara planes in Pebble Island a few days earlier.

Bill Begley, a friend of Ian's from Selection days, had been killed. I had met Bill and his wife and thought they were a charming couple. He was a short, sturdy Irishman with a great sense of humour.

Staff Sergeant Philip Curass who had also been on the Pebble Island raid, was gone, along with Sid Davidson, Taff Jones, Lofty Arthy and Ian's sergeant major, Laurence Gallagher, who had restored the Union Jack to South Georgia.

Karen hesitated before breaking the news to me that Paul Bunker had been killed. I couldn't believe it. I started shaking from head to toe. I wanted to go to Vanda, but first I had to know if Ian was alive. The girls offered to make the call for me but I knew this was something I had to do myself. I also knew I had to see Pat Dawson face to face when he told me the news. I drove to the camp.

By the time I arrived I was strangely composed. As I parked the car and walked towards Pat's office, I was still trying to take it all in. All those friends killed, all those women widowed and children without fathers. Paul gone. It was too terrible to contemplate. Was Ian amongst the dead?

Pat was alone and sitting behind his desk. As I walked in, all I wanted in the world was for him to tell me that Ian was OK. A wonderful man whom all the wives adored, he must have seen the look of shock on my face because he stood up as soon as I entered.

'I have to know, Pat,' I said, my voice breaking. 'Is my husband dead?'

I stared intently at his kindly features in those few seconds with my mind screaming – tell me the truth but don't tell me the truth.

He took my hand across his desk and said, 'Jenny, I can assure you, Ian is alive and well.' My heart started beating again.

'Are you sure? How do you know? Can you prove it to me?'

'We have all the names now and he is fine. He is on HMS *Intrepid* and he is safe. You have to believe me. This isn't something they would get wrong.'

I could have kissed him there and then. I didn't know whether to laugh or cry. He did all he could to reassure me, he said the list had been checked and double-checked and that Ian had been ferried across to the *Intrepid* safely before the crash. He was kind, sympathetic and charming, and never once let on to me that his son Keith had been on the helicopter when it crashed and was one of the few survivors, about whom he was still waiting for news.

I left his office feeling suddenly very tired and very cold. I knew I had to accept what I had been told but I needed time for it to sink in. I wanted to go somewhere quiet and peaceful, to sit and think and pray. I have long been sustained in my darkest hours by a simple faith in God. I felt an overwhelming urge to sit quietly and talk to Him upstairs for a moment, to gather my thoughts and to thank Him for my husband's life. I wanted to pray too for the souls that had been lost. To pray for Paul and for Vanda, whose heart I knew would now be broken.

Ian and I had married at the Baptist Church in Hereford and I drove there, parking my car outside and hurrying up the little path, past the spent daffodils swaying in the breeze, only to find that the heavy double doors were locked. I leaned my head against them and wished they would miraculously open.

Feeling somehow cheated, I drove on to my parents' house, where I discovered my niece Lisa had gone for the day. As I walked in through the front door, my parents and Lisa took one look at my face and fell silent, their previously animated conversation abruptly interrupted by my arrival. I told them about the accident but assured them that Ian wasn't among the dead. He was, I said, one of the lucky ones but many of his friends and colleagues had died and it so easily could have been him.

As I heard myself say the words out loud, I started to cry. My father came to me and I held his hands and told him, 'When they come to tell me he is dead, you had better order two coffins, Dad, because I can't live without him and I can't let him go without me.'

My father, a pragmatic former coal miner from Durham, took me by the shoulders and looked me straight in the face. 'Shake yourself up, girl,' he said. 'You've got a lot more to get through yet. You think this is bad but it is going to get a lot worse. You've got to be strong. For both your sakes.'

I was a mess, and Lisa, bless her, took me by the arm and said, 'Come on Auntie Jenny, let's get you home and I'll make you a nice cup of tea and something to eat.' I did as I was told. I sat at home wanting so much to pick up the telephone and talk to Ian, to tell him that I loved him and that I was glad he was safe and to talk of our sadness and shock at what had happened to all our friends. I also wanted to know what had happened, why nineteen SAS men had to die like that, being flown between ships, not even on a mission. It was so frustrating not being able to speak to him or to find out more.

I wanted to go to Vanda that night and comfort her too, but I couldn't face her. It was just too hard. I spent the rest of the day with Lisa, who fussed around me, and between us we telephoned a few close friends and relatives to let them know what had happened before it hit the newspapers the following day. Tony and Linda, two good friends, came straight over to see me when they heard and offered to take me out for a drink. The four of us sat together in the pub that night, hardly able to speak. I left early to come home to bed, but couldn't sleep a wink until dawn.

With all that had happened, I completely forgot that I was having a new carpet laid the following morning until the doorbell woke me up from my deep late-morning slumber. I opened the front door in my dressing gown and the fitter took one look at me and laughed out loud.

'You look like you had a good night last night,' he said. When I told him that I had just lost nineteen friends in the Falklands, he was mortified. After that, I think I must have made him nervous because he accidentally drove a carpet tack through the telephone line and cut it off completely.

I became irrationally upset. What if Ian had somehow been able to get to a telephone to call me and couldn't get through? I went to a telephone box and phoned British Telecom to hear a young woman operator tell me it would take at least six days to repair. I burst into tears and told her my husband was in the Falklands and I needed the telephone mended immediately in case he called. To their credit, they came round in an hour and sorted it all out.

As soon as the phone was connected it started ringing and ringing with people who had heard the news and wanted to know if Ian was all right. The Regiment had taken the unprecedented step of publicly announcing that those who died had been in the SAS. They did it, they said, to fully honour those who had lost their lives. But they didn't release the names and everyone who heard and knew Ian was out there rang to check he was OK. I fielded all the calls and reassured all the worried friends and relatives then sat down with a cup of coffee and the newspapers. Tears streaming down my face, I read and reread the newspaper articles about the crash, feeling an uneasy combination of relief and guilt that Ian hadn't been involved.

It was later the following day that I plucked up the courage to go to see Vanda. I walked into her front room and she looked up, hollow-eyed and pale with sadness, from an armchair.

'Hello, fruit,' she said and we both dissolved. We hugged each other and wept. She was so brave, she kept asking how I was and told me not to worry about her. We talked and cried. I felt guilty that Ian had lived and Paul hadn't and I told her so.

That is when she told me that she knew from the day our men had left that Paul wouldn't be coming home. She said she had a premonition about it, and that when Paul was injured on Pebble Island, she was convinced he would die from his injuries but didn't say anything so as not to worry me. 'I knew he was going to die, Jenny,' she said. 'Don't ask me how. I just knew.'

I went home feeling drained and fell onto the bed. I tried to remember how I felt in that dreadful hour when I did not know if Ian was alive or dead. Would I have known, like Vanda, if he had not survived? Ian and I had only known each other for a short time. I had always told myself that I would have felt it in my heart and through our 'fluencing' if anything ever happened to him, but now I found myself dwelling on 'what if's and 'maybe's.

I spent an agonising night tossing and turning, dreaming about Paul and Ian and wondering whether I would ever see my husband again. I hugged myself, aching inside and crying for all I was worth, before eventually falling back to sleep. It was the first time since I had met Ian that I had been forced to consider that he might not always come home and the pain of the thought was almost physical.

I knew it would be weeks before I could speak to him so I wrote instead. My letters told him that I didn't know what to say that could offer comfort. The first letter I wrote was dated 30 May, nine days after I had been told the news. Normally I would write to him once a day or more, but that week I started a hundred letters and screwed them all up before I finished them. I prayed that of all the letters I sent him, this one would convey my message of love and sympathy across the miles.

His letters back revealed little, even though I later discovered that he had travelled in the very Sea King helicopter that crashed less than half an hour before the accident. He was standing on the deck of the *Intrepid* in the dusk waiting for his friends to be ferried across after him when he saw the lights of the helicopter suddenly disappear from view less than half a mile from the ship. Realising that something terrible had happened, his immediate impulse was to dive into the freezing water and swim out to rescue his friends and fellow soldiers. The frustration of waiting on the deck on that windy night as he watched the floodlights of the small search boats circling in the distance was unbearable.

Only two bodies were pulled out of the water by the *Intrepid* crews, one a dead helicopter crewman whom Ian watched being given last rites below deck by a priest, and the other a medic Ian knew called Dave who was blue with hypothermia and shock and whom Ian helped place fully clothed into a bath of hot water to try to warm him up. When Ian heard that Paul Bunker was among those who were missing, he went up onto the deck and stayed out there all night, looking out to sea, alone with his thoughts.

Even in the diary he kept throughout the Falklands, he couldn't bring himself to write more than a few lines about the crash. His entry for that day read:

> May 19: Left ship by Sea King helicopter for Falklands. Three-hour flight sea level. Aborted at the coastline due to bad weather. Three-hour flight back. Got off aircraft and found we were deaf for a while due to noise. Moving to HMS *Intrepid* to join 3 Para and 42 Commando.
>
> Moved in first heli and got a decent bed space. Sea King heli crashed transferring Sqdn from *Hermes* to *Intrepid*. Total on board of 30, only a few survivors. Paul Bunker missing, presumed dead. Apparently an albatross was found nearby and may have hit the aircraft. Tragic blow to the Sqdrn, and also G Sqdrn lost a number, including Bill Begley. Too stunned for words and can't sleep.

Later, when he had allowed himself more time to think, he wrote, 'The loss of the helicopter was fearsomely tragic to everyone. It affected us all very personally. The first couple of days after the loss it was terrible because we were just sitting around. Luckily after that, we were flat out almost all the time and had to put our own feelings of grief and loss to one side. There was work to be done. Nevertheless we had sustained a major loss. For months afterwards, I kept on getting images of some of my friends at the bottom of the sea. And it had the effect of making you take stock of your life. Every time we got onto a helicopter there would be a scramble for the seat by the door in case that chopper came down in the sea as well.'

After the crash, the Regiment CO Mike Rose visited the surviving members to give them a pep talk and to tell them to get on with the job in hand. Ian never forgave him for the words he uttered, 'The Regiment must be seen to be taking casualties.' Ian and the rest of the men were very hurt by that. They didn't need some rupert (officer) telling them that the senseless death of so many friends was somehow a legitimate casualty.

It took me weeks to shake myself up after the helicopter crash. My work and health suffered. The only way I felt able to sleep at night was by having a stiff drink before I went to bed. I felt permanently on edge, anxiously waiting for the next trauma, anticipating the next disaster. Every time there was another major incident in the Conflict, I shuddered at the thought that Ian could be amongst the dead. Despite all my best endeavours and my vow to Ian to be strong, I was feeling far from brave.

Ian's diary and letters continued to record the events of the war. He was not only suffering emotionally, he was also, by this time, in some considerable physical pain. He developed severe frostbite from lying for days and nights out on glaciers and mountainsides and then having to march through snow and ice carrying bergens weighing up to 100 pounds.

The Falklands Campaign was both wonderful and terrible for him. He was a soldier after all, and every soldier dreams of the chance for some real live action. I had seen how that made him feel those last few days before he set off. But war is not all action and heroics and his diary entries chronicled its frustrations and sorrows, from the long waits on board ship to the night-time missions, lying cold and hungry in the snow, waiting for the chance to strike.

I read his diary afterwards and it all seemed so distant to me, as if it had been written by someone I didn't even know. The only entries that made any real sense were the ones that spoke of his concern for me, and how much he missed me, lying in his cabin or on a mountainside thinking of me and singing our favourite songs in his head, like Anne Murray's 'Just to Feel This Love from You'.

Other accounts were of covert manoeuvres and attacks, like the time he took part in a running battle with a squad of Argentinian special forces, the equivalent of the SAS, whom Ian's squadron ambushed as they were doing a recce for a future attack on Mount Kent.

Ian and his men got there after a long march and dug themselves as best they could into eighteen-inch-deep camouflaged scrapes on the granite outcrop. They were freezing cold, suffering from hypothermia, permanently soaked to the skin and all suffered from frost nip and trench foot, conditions of the skin of the feet caused by constant dampness. They even had to be careful going to the toilet, in case the steam gave them away.

As they watched and waited, a Huey helicopter deposited about a dozen or so Argentinian paratroopers just below their position. The enemy troops made their way up the mountain-top as Ian and the rest of the troop – signalling silently to each other – spread out to create a linear ambush. Unfortunately the Argentinians spotted some of the troop before the ambush line was set and opened fire. All hell broke loose and two of Ian's troop were hit, one quite badly. The Argentinians fled and Ian and the others fully expected them to turn tail and run all the way back to Stanley, which some of them did. To their dismay, however, a small number of them decided to do or die the following night and came charging in at the troop with grenades, all of them dying in the attempt. Ian described them as either very brave or very stupid.

On another troop attack on an Argentinian position, the enemy all ran off as soon as they realised what they were up against, firing and manoeuvring as they did so. Ian charged down the hill after them, firing and running, zig-zagging across the rocky ground, when he suddenly realised he was alone.

He looked back to see that the rest of his troop had inexplicably stopped and dropped to the ground further back. Ian was now not only very vulnerable to enemy fire in front of him, he was in real danger of being hit from behind by his own side. The reason why he was alone dawned upon him. Carried away by the moment, he had inadvertently run straight into the middle of a minefield. He dropped to the ground and lay there for a moment, wondering how the hell to get out. Fortunately, the mines were all fairly visible and he managed to crawl back on his stomach without injury. The rest of the lads ribbed him mercilessly about that.

He wrote in his diary of the attack on Beagle Ridge, during which he once again came under heavy enemy fire, about the twenty-mile marches across rocky landscapes and sheep-filled pastures, and of how he repeatedly gave emergency medical attention to injured fellow soldiers. When they weren't on a mission the Squadron were practising being dropped from helicopters into the ocean to suddenly find themselves swimming alongside enormous humpback whales that rose to the surface beside them, blowing huge jets of water from their air holes. In the evenings on board ship, they drank beer and watched action-packed movies like *Apocalypse Now* and *The Boys from Brazil* to keep the adrenaline up.

I sat at home, watching movies on the television and playing our favourite songs on the stereo. Girl friends would take me out every so often and the people at work were largely supportive, as were our families and friends. The whole country seemed to be behind 'our boys' going and giving the Argentinians hell, and the newspapers were full of rallying propaganda against General Galtieri and his military junta. I was tremendously proud of Ian, it felt good to know that he was part of this amazing British fighting force, but that didn't mean that I wanted him to continue putting his neck on the line for very much longer or that I wasn't torn apart by his absence from me.

The problem of regular contact between the wives back home and the men all those thousands of miles away was eventually addressed by the Regiment. Realising the difficulties of getting the airmail letters back and forth so far across the oceans, they encouraged the wives to send Family Grams, the Army telegrams, which have to be read out to someone in the camp who sends them on for you via the electronic signalling system and which arrive in brown envelopes marked 'On Her Majesty's Service'.

One day in June, all of the wives were summoned to the camp to be told we could send special morale-boosting Family Grams to our men. The senior personnel called us all and told us to send any message we liked. I wondered what I would say and asked to go last. I watched and listened as most of the wives sent the same kind of message – 'Hello darling, Johnny and Jane are fine. We all miss you terribly. Come home soon.' When it was my turn, and despite my impulse to say something sloppy too, I decided to give Ian a laugh instead.

The scarlet face on the young man taking down my message was a picture. I read my message to him and asked him to read it back. 'Hi, baby, I have got black stockings and suspenders on and it's about time you got here to make use of them. I love you very much. Bye, Pig.' (My nickname because I used to collect pigs.)

None of the other wives could believe I had the cheek to send this telegram all the way to the Falklands. But one of the first messages to come back to the camp was from one very happy husband: 'Hi, Pig, you are sounding good to me, love Ian.'

As the weeks dragged on, the Regiment also suggested that it would be good for everyone if the wives met together regularly in a group to share their experiences and do something specific for their men, as a way of keeping us all in touch. We were asked to meet up with the colonel's wife in the camp on a Saturday afternoon, but I decided not to go. It wasn't really my scene, all that women's circle stuff. I felt I was doing much more good waiting at home, writing letters, making up parcels of sweets and cigars for Ian and sending him my love across the air waves.

When I didn't turn up, the colonel's wife telephoned me at home and said she thought I would like to know that all the women had decided it would be a great idea if we knitted socks to send out to our men. I laughed and told her, 'I am not doing that!' She seemed surprised and said, 'Why not? It would be good therapy.' Tired of her interference in what I regarded as my personal affairs, I finally snapped. 'My husband doesn't need a pair of socks, for God's sake, what he needs are my tits.' The line went dead and she never bothered me again.

Occasionally Ian would be able to telephone me from the ship on special ship-to-shore satellite links, and the calls would boost us both tremendously. It was wonderful to hear his voice again, albeit so far away and for such a short time, and I would be on a high for days. But we largely relied on the letters we wrote to each other each night, many of which were pretty slushy, but we were still young and it felt right somehow to spill our hearts out onto the blue airmail paper before sealing the letters with a kiss.

Ian got one batch of my letters while he waited to take part in the first successful attack on South Georgia which involved the first British naval bombardment since World War II. It was his colleagues from Mountain Troop, D Squadron, who raised the British flag. Vanda and I read the reports of the incident back home and, having been told by the camp who the 'Paras' credited with raising the flag really were, felt so proud of the men we knew.

Ian went on to Leith Harbour, a whaling station on South Georgia, and was all set to take part in an assault from the sea but the Argentinians surrendered minutes before the attack was due to start and warned them that the whole place had been booby-trapped with explosives. A group from the Special Boat Squadron went in and made it safe, simultaneously 'liberating' much of the kit and fine red wine from the captured Argentinian officers to take back to HMS *Endurance* for what Ian described as a 'fearsome piss up'. As well as the cases of wine and tins of corned beef, the SBS looted machine guns, hand grenades and all sorts of weapons but their pride and joy was a 3.5mm rocket launcher, which Ian then stole from them and hid in various cabins around the ship in a sequence of events that was like something out of an Ealing comedy. It was only when the SBS complained and the captain ordered a full search, that Ian and a colleague finally ditched the rocket launcher overboard as the net closed in, rather than admit defeat and return it.

In May, Ian and I were meant to have been going together to the wedding of our friends Tony and Linda, Ian as best man, returning the favour that the groom, who was ex-Guards, had done for us the previous year. Ian was on HMS *Hermes* at the time and he remembered the day in his diary, writing of his regret at not being there by my side. I braced myself for a wedding without him and travelled up to the bride's parents home in Longbridge, Shropshire. Linda had asked me to dress her long brown hair for the big day.

On the morning of the wedding, Linda's father insisted that we have the radio on in the bedroom, giving all the latest Falklands news. When the news came that the British had bombed Port Stanley, he was so elated, he thought it was marvellous. All I could think of was that there I was combing out my friend's hair and my husband was the other side of the world, in a situation of extreme danger. It was all I could do to stop myself from bursting into tears and running from the room. But I wouldn't spoil Linda's day for the world, so I held back the tears and joined in the champagne toast to British victory.

Later that week, on Tuesday 4 May, we heard that the *Sheffield* had been hit by an Argentinian Exocet missile. When the news came in that dozens of men were dead, I had no idea whether Ian had been on board the ship. He could have been anywhere and I had an anxious few minutes, waiting for confirmation from the camp that he was safe and well. They told me that he was on HMS *Hermes*, one of the ships close by and the one the burns casualties were transferred to after the attack. The idea of him being so close made me very nervous.

Seeing the casualties and giving medical help on deck as best he could, Ian was given a strong idea of what it would be like if a ship he was on got hit. He wrote in his diary the following day:

> I haven't felt so vulnerable in my life, sitting in a ship, below decks, unable to defend myself. How I long to get ashore soon. *Sheffield* now burning badly and is abandoned by crew who are now aboard. One Harrier lost, Lt Taylor, pilot attacking Goose Green airfield. *Sheffield's* dead may be as many as 30.

I did my best to keep his morale up by sending him letters and parcels but I had no idea if they were getting through or how much good they were doing. I could only imagine what he must be going through. If only I could hold him and tell him everything was all right.

It helped sometimes to talk to the other wives and to know that

I wasn't the only one feeling so helpless. Karen and I kept in close touch, particularly after the heli crash. I would visit her on my way back from seeing Vanda and we would have a drink and a laugh together. One night she ran out of cigarettes and all she had in the house was a pack of King Edward cigars, so she and I – drunk on gin – smoked the whole packet between us. We were both violently sick the next morning.

Ian continued to spend most of his time almost freezing to death on long cold nights in the snow amongst the sheep on the mountaintops. During a four-man patrol mission to West Falkland gathering information and reporting on enemy movements, he worked in the worst conditions he had ever been in. One of the troop went down with early symptoms of hypothermia and Ian lay alongside him to keep him warm so that he didn't die. After three days and nights of that, they were delighted to hear that they were to be extracted. They made their way to a helicopter landing point but the weather closed in and the chopper couldn't make it until the following night.

But when they did eventually get into the chopper they were thrown three days' worth of rations and told they were being dropped off at another point on West Falkland, along with just sixteen other men, to deal with the expected arrival of some 2,000 Argentinian reinforcements from the mainland. After three more days of bitterly cold weather, waiting for the Argentinian reinforcement drop which (fortunately) never happened, Ian was never so pleased to see the chopper which eventually arrived to get them out.

He worked right up until the end of the conflict and it was the night before the surrender that he was involved in his most dangerous mission, in which he was lucky to escape with his life.

On the night of Sunday 13 June, Ian and his fellow soldiers were sent down from Beagle Ridge, overlooking Port Stanley, where they had been laying up overnight to cover a combined SAS/Marine attack on an oil refinery across from Stanley Harbour.

They had been told that the refinery would be protected by less than a company of Argentinians, about fifty to a hundred men. But when they got into position and the attack began, they discovered a full battalion of defending Argentinians (about 600 men) as well as land mines, barbed wire fortifications and an armed observation post directly behind them.

Ian, who was the lead scout, described the whole operation as 'an unacceptable risk mission', and said afterwards that he believed the decision to undertake it was largely due to political pressure from above to make sure the SAS were the first troops into Port Stanley. He and about thirty of his men were taking fire from the front and behind. All he could hear was the 'crack and the thump' past his ear as the incoming fire from the ground-mounted anti-aircraft guns whistled over his head. At one point the rate of fire was so fierce that the wind the bullets displaced actually ruffled his hair.

They were saved only by the fact that they could crawl face down in the peat trenches cut out in the fields. They lay in these shallow ditches, unable to lift their heads even a few inches, and waited for the end to come, thinking it would be only a matter of time before the Argentinian troops were upon them. Ian tried to radio for help, but the rest of the assault team were equally badly off and no one could get to them. He was unable to defend the Boat Troop who were taking a lot of flak on the shore, and he said he thought wistfully of me on my way to work or pulling into the office car park as he waited for the 'voice from above' to tell him it was now his turn to die.

Ian claims there is no God, but at that point the Argentinians suddenly stopped firing. Ian knew he only had one chance and he and his men legged it as quickly as they could out of there and to relative safety. Afterwards, they realised that the Argentinians had only stopped shooting because they were low on ammunition. Boat Troop and 17 Troop were less lucky and Ian was later involved in patching up the four casualties.

Ian was sitting by a coal fire in a house in Fitzroy Settlement when he heard news of the Argentinian surrender. He had arrived at the settlement in the early hours with a soldier who had been shot in the chest the previous night. Once the casualty had been airlifted to the safety of the *Canberra*, Ian had to wait for a lift for himself to the *Lancelot*. A friendly islander invited him into her house for something to eat and drink and to warm his frost-bitten feet – now also afflicted with trench foot – by the fire.

It was just three weeks after the Sea King helicopter crash. As the warmth started to activate the blood vessels in his toes and with it the pain, the woman rushed in to tell him that she had just heard on her radio that the Argentinians had surrendered. The war was over. Ian was speechless. She watched the reaction on his face as he sat rubbing his feet and decided to leave him in peace. He stared into the fire, thinking of all the friends who had died and – for the first time since the helicopter crash – he wept.

That same morning, three hours behind Falklands time, I was sitting sweltering in the June heat at work when my boss, Barry, came running in and kissed me on the cheek. 'He's done it, he's done it,' he told me excitedly. 'Ian's won the war. It is all over. The Argentinians just announced a surrender. I heard it on the radio.'

I looked up at him with my mouth open.

'It's over?' I asked, my eyes filling with tears. 'So soon?' It suddenly felt like days, not weeks, since the helicopter crash and the start of hostilities. All those sleepless nights crying into my pillow were forgotten. It seemed like only yesterday that Paul had been lost and that I had thought Ian was too. I was thrilled by the prospect of Ian coming home, but I couldn't feel the relief I had expected to feel at the news that it was over. I was in shock. I wanted to go somewhere quiet and take it all in, the jumble of emotions fighting for supremacy in my head.

Barry hugged me and told me not to cry and promised me that Ian would be home soon. I sat stock still, feeling completely numb. What would Ian be thinking? And Vanda? I wondered. What had it all meant?

After the ceasefire was announced, Ian returned to his ship for much needed rest and treatment for his feet. He slept for ten hours without a break and then woke feeling incredibly hungry and devoured two breakfasts. The following day, 15 June, after the official surrender by General Menendez, he lay in his bunk and listened via the BBC World Service to Mrs Thatcher telling a jubilant House of Commons that the victory had been won by a British military operation which was 'boldly planned, bravely executed and brilliantly accomplished'.

I listened to the very same broadcast at work, my friends and colleagues huddled with me around the office radio. On opposite sides of the world, Ian and I heard our Prime Minister's words simultaneously and both fought back the tears as we counted how much the war had cost us in friends and loved ones.

# 2 | To Have and To Hold

IT WAS THE LAST WEEK in June before Ian could get a flight home from the Falkland Islands and I was waiting to meet him when he flew into RAF Brize Norton in Oxfordshire. I wanted to be there for that homecoming more than any other time. Paul wasn't coming home and neither were the other men who died on board the helicopter, but my husband was, thank God.

I had always welcomed him home, either at the airport or at Stirling Lines. The look on your husband's face when he sees you waiting there is worth a million airmail letters and telephone calls. Some of the other wives said they wanted to come to Brize Norton with me and meet their husbands too, but when it came to the big night, they all backed down. None of them felt up to the hour-long journey across country late at night and said they would wait at the camp for their men to be dropped back there. So in the end I made the journey alone.

I had been so nervous the day or so before his return. My stomach had been doing free-fall. What was I going to say to him? How would he look? Would he be affected mentally by all that he had seen and been through? I was relieved to find the airport virtually empty apart from a crowd of journalists who were waiting to give BBC reporter Brian Hanrahan a champagne welcome home.

As I sat in the arrivals hall, dressed up to the nines, my knees were knocking. I told myself that I mustn't cry when Ian came through the doors, that it would only make things worse. A young RAF lad asked me if I was OK and I couldn't even answer him, my jaws were so tightly clenched. Later an RAF personnel officer led me through to the customs area in case any of the journalists suddenly realised who I was waiting for. Older and wiser, he had the good sense to leave me alone.

It seemed to take ages for the plane to arrive and then to unload. I had given myself far too much time to get there and had been waiting for nearly two hours that warm June night by the time the men started walking through the arrivals gate just after ten p.m. I was the only wife there, looking and smelling like I don't know what, wearing black stockings and suspenders under my dress as I had promised Ian, a bottle of champagne in the car and a steak salad waiting for him at home.

Familiar faces emerged in the crowd that suddenly pushed through, all wind-tanned and dirty, smiling and laughing at me as I stood looking hopefully for Ian. There were so many missing faces too, I thought, as the men who had made it home filed past.

I knew Ian would be last through the arrivals gate, he always was, but this time he was even later because his feet were so sore that he could only walk slowly. All the other guys passing me laughed and said, 'He's coming, he's coming. Hang on, Jenny.' One man stopped right in front of me and inhaled very deeply, as if he was sniffing me. I thought he was very strange but I didn't say anything. I figured war affected people differently.

When I finally caught sight of Ian's face for the first time in three months, my heart quickened its pace. He looked older and thinner and his eyes showed how very tired he was, but it was definitely him; he was home safe and in one piece. I ran to his arms and nearly knocked him off his aching feet. Despite all my best intentions, I was quickly spilling tears and so was he. We kissed and hugged and held each other for what seemed like hours, neither of us able to speak.

When he eventually pulled me away from him and looked into my eyes, I could see the pain in his for the first time. 'Ian, I'm so sorry about Paul,' I started to say, tearfully.

'Shhh,' he hushed me. 'Let me just look at your big blue eyes and feel you and taste you.' He kissed me full on the mouth, his lips pressed hard against mine, his arms clamped around my shoulders. It felt so wonderful to be in his arms again. I wanted to make love

37

to him there and then. He felt and smelled so appealing, so right. I
had forgotten how good he made me feel.

By the time we had stopped kissing, the place was empty. I could
still taste the salt of our tears in my mouth, I could feel the roughness
of his unshaven face on my skin and my arms tingled from his grasp.
How could I have ever let him out of my sight?

On the long drive home he clung to me, stroking my neck and
hair, kissing my cheek. It was all I could do to keep on the road.
He cracked open the champagne, spraying bubbles all over the inside
of my car and we swigged from the bottle all the way up the A40.
I asked him what he had brought me home from his trip and he
told me how angry he was that his efforts to purloin some booty
had been thwarted.

It is traditional throughout the Army, but particularly in the SAS,
for the men to bring home trophies and 'prizes' they have picked
up from the battlefield. Ian is no better or worse than any of the
others and they are all dreadful thieves. I have some pretty peculiar-
looking ashtrays in my home that are actually mortar shells. I also
have the largest selection of men's jumpers, none of which I dare
wear around Hereford in case someone shouts out, 'Oi! That's
mine.'

As Ian and the boys came through Ascension Island on their way
home, the word went up that everyone was going to be searched
and that stolen weapons or any other booty would be confiscated.
Among dozens of items including clothes, food and Argentinian
spoils, Ian had a handgun which he picked up because he thought
I could do with it in the house. But when he heard about the searches
he threw most of his goodies out of the aircraft, literally, including
the gun. As they came through Brize Norton, however, a senior
Customs and Excise officer told his staff, 'Don't search this lot, they
are SAS.' Ian was not pleased.

By the time we got home, there was only one thing we were
interested in. We went straight to bed and spent the rest of the night
there. His steak salad was forgotten, but who cared? He slept for
hours afterwards, lying in my arms looking utterly exhausted. I lay
awake watching him, resisting the temptation to shake him awake

TO HAVE AND TO HOLD

and kiss him once more, and pinching myself into believing that he was back home with me, safe and sound.

Later the following night, after something to eat, we dropped in to a welcome-home party at the Paludrine Club, the camp social club named after an anti-malarial drug. The first person I was introduced to was Ian's troop boss and I recognised him immediately as the guy who had acted so strangely at the airport.

'Excuse me,' I said. 'But aren't you the one who sniffed me at Brize Norton?'

Ian's face was a picture of puzzlement.

'Yes, Mrs Simpson,' said the rupert, blushing. 'But I had a very good reason.'

I think Ian wanted to hear it even more than I did.

'You see, you were wearing the same perfume as my wife and I smelt it and thought of her.'

How sweet, we both thought, and the boss should have left it at that. Instead he added, 'All I've been smelling for the past few months is Falklands sheep and you certainly smell a whole lot better than them.'

Some compliment, but one I shall always treasure.

The days immediately after Ian's return were halcyon ones. We walked and chatted and slept and ate and spent a lot of time talking things through. At first sight, he appeared to be remarkably unaffected by Paul's death and the helicopter crash. The fire had dampened in his eyes, which looked duller somehow and wearier, but he seemed to be keeping himself together well and I was greatly relieved, although not altogether convinced that it would last.

He continued to keep his diary, as if writing in it every day would maintain the momentum, and I caught him flicking the pages back to 19 May on several occasions, counting down the weeks since Paul had been lost. Of his homecoming and the days immediately afterwards, he wrote:

June 28: Left Ascension early afternoon. Arrived Brize Norton 10.30 p.m. Jenny at the airport. It was a great reunion. Had a bottle of champagne in the car on the way home. Arrived Hereford and went to bed and my life improved 100 per cent. Great to be home and with Jenny again. We missed each other too much and have got a lot to catch up on. Finally got to sleep around 4 a.m.

July 1: (went to see family in Darlington) Arrived about 8pm and the drinking started. Had a good chat. Now I must forget about it and get back to normal. Don't want to be known as a waffler.

Four days after Ian's return from Darlington, I drove him round to see Vanda at her home. She had invited us over for a meal with Paul's older brother, Arthur. Ian was anxious about the meeting and not looking forward to it at all, but Vanda had been amazingly composed all the times I had gone to see her since Paul's death so I reassured him that the evening wouldn't be as difficult as he feared.

His jaws were clenched with tension as we walked up the garden path. I realised that this was going to be just as hard for him as it was for her, and when she opened the door and they stood staring at each other in a moment of mutual grief, I felt almost as if I was in the way. He hugged her and pulled her into his arms, grateful not to have to look into her eyes. She led us both into the lounge and we were introduced to Arthur. All four of us sat down, fighting back the emotions.

'I know all I need to know, old fruit,' Vanda told Ian straight away. 'You don't have to tell me and I can't talk about it right now anyway. Pat Dawson told me everything I need to know.'

Ian nodded and hung his head in sadness at the memory. He had been expecting her to ask him when he had last seen Paul and he had racked his brain to remember. 'It was on *Hermes* early that morning, we were all set for an op [operation or mission],' he had told me earlier in the day. 'I told him I'd meet him in the mess for a drink afterwards. He joked and told me it was my round.'

Vanda said she had to go and stir the chilli she had made for our supper and asked Arthur to pour us all a drink. Ian's expression was one of utter helplessness as she got up to leave the room.

'It's OK, Ian,' she said, looking down at him and trying to smile.

'It was destined to happen. I knew from that morning. I am just glad you are home and safe, for Jenny's sake.'

It was only much later on that night, when we had all drunk too much and were feeling sentimental, that Vanda started to show her pain. She asked Ian to have a slow dance with her on the patio, the way Paul used to do. I sat watching them dancing cheek to cheek through the patio windows, my heart breaking for them both.

The next big hurdle we had to get over was to go back to The Swan, the pub where we had all spent that last night together – Paul, Vanda, Ian and I. Normally we would have been straight down the pub on Ian's return, but this time we kept putting it off and finding excuses to go somewhere else. Neither of us spoke about it, but we knew it would be an emotional return. It would also be a difficult reunion with Mandy, the demonstrative landlady, and her husband Terry.

We had a couple of drinks at home to fortify us first before we went, and then set off. Pausing outside for a moment, I squeezed Ian's hand reassuringly before he pulled open the swing door and stepped inside. The bar was crowded and Mandy and Terry didn't notice us at first. Ian walked up to the bar, a fixed grin on his face and, finding a gap between customers, said, 'I'll have a pint of lager – on the house.'

Mandy looked up from the pint she was pulling, and her face crumpled. Putting down the glass, she reached out across the bar with both arms and pulled Ian's face towards hers. 'Ian, oh, Ian,' she said. I blinked back the tears. Terry came round from behind the bar to shake Ian's hand vigorously and pat him on the back. A few of the regulars did likewise.

Mandy followed Terry round from behind the bar and, bursting into tears, as expected, she fell into Ian's arms. He looked completely taken aback as he tried to comfort her.

'Oh Ian, it's so good to see you,' she said. 'When we heard about Paul, we couldn't believe it. It is so sad, so terribly sad. I can't believe he's gone.'

Ian stood uneasily, listening to her outburst and trying to fight the emotions raging within his own heart. He had never been

41

comfortable with other people's grief and he wasn't enjoying this now. Sensing his need for a rescue, I grabbed Mandy's hand and led her round behind the bar. Dabbing her eyes with a handkerchief and blowing her nose, she stood bewildered beside me.

'Right now,' I shouted across the pub, 'does anyone here want a drink, 'cos I know I bloody well do.' Ian smiled at me warmly across the room as the customers started talking again and moving back towards the bar. I poured him a pint and myself a large gin and tonic, and spent the rest of the evening doing a very good impersonation of Bet Lynch.

Once most of the regulars had gone home, Mandy and Terry decided to hold an after-hours party in our honour, and we drank far too much, stayed far too late and got far too emotional. I would probably have been all right if I had gone home early, but just before three a.m., when the gin and the sentimentality of the evening started to get to me, I suddenly found myself sobbing.

I was sitting on the bar stool, the same place I had sat the night that Paul and Vanda had last been with us, and my mind flashed back to that evening and how happy we had all been together. I recalled Mandy's tears, and how Paul and I had looked at each other across the bar. I missed his company, I missed his dry humour and his way of speaking and I wanted him with us. My face wet with tears, I buried my head in the shoulder of Ruth, an old friend, who put her arm around me and tried to comfort me. 'Let it all out, Jenny,' she told me. 'You are always so strong for everyone else, now it's your turn to cry.'

Ian spotted me across the bar and came over to where I was sitting.

'I'm sorry, babe, it is just this place, you know, and Paul . . .' I started to say.

'Shhh,' he whispered and held me tight. 'I know. You don't have to explain.'

He let me spill my tears and then he dried my eyes with a napkin, picked up my handbag and walked me home. The two of us strolled back to our house arm in arm in the early morning light, and fell into bed exhausted.

That night was a turning point for Ian. Having been upbeat for weeks, pretending that Paul's death was just another one of so many he had known, he seemed to lose some of his sparkle. His nights started to be interrupted by nightmares – vague, swirling visions of Argentinian soldiers, blizzards and helicopters – and his day were dogged by constant tiredness. Whenever I came home from work, I would find him slumped on the sofa, his tasks for the day untouched, his speech slurred from exhaustion, his mind anywhere but with me.

It took weeks of gentle coaxing on my part to get him to snap out of it. It was, I am sure, a manifestation of post-traumatic stress, post-Falklands depression and sheer grief at the loss of so many friends and colleagues. I would take him for long evening walks in the rolling hills around Hereford that he had always loved, and hope that the fresh air would wake him from his reverie. I would make him all his favourite meals to try to re-whet his appetite, I would curl up with him in my arms in bed at night, stroking his hair and talking gently to him, in the hope that it would soothe his nightmares.

Gradually – and it took much of that long, hot summer – the Ian that I had known and loved started to re-emerge from the emotionally battered man I had been living with since June. There was a spring in his step once more, he started to take more interest in the training exercises and lectures at the camp and was happier to socialise with friends and family.

I knew he was coming out of it finally when I was came upon his diary lying open in the lounge. There had been no entries for several weeks but suddenly on 15 August, he wrote, 'Jenny is my strength and I love her very much.'

Vanda really had the stuffing knocked out of her by Paul's death. What was so awful for her and all the widows was that there were no bodies to bury, no rite of passage with a coffin and all the words of grief and consolation of the funeral service. The Regiment did what it could. It held a special service for those who died and dedicated part of the Regimental cemetery at St Martin's church in Hereford as a memorial area for those who had died in the Falklands Conflict.

For each man lost there was a stone plaque set into a flint wall, above an urn in which to put flowers. As she later moved far away, I started to go up to the churchyard and place flowers there for her. I think I put flowers there for all of the men who died, and in thanks that Ian was spared.

Ian once told me that the helicopter crash would follow us wherever we went for the rest of our lives. He has never been able to bring himself to go to the graveyard and visit Paul's memorial stone. As far as he is concerned, that isn't where his friend is, even in spirit. He says he lost any religious faith he had in the Falklands, watching so many people die and that he never heard the voice of God, as he expected to, when he thought he might be on his way to meet his Maker. He no longer believes that those who die have souls that survive, he thinks we are all just flesh and blood and when we die that is it, there is nothing more. He won't even enter a church if he can avoid it.

I had always felt that I had a deal with God that if I carried on believing and persuaded Ian to too, then He would look after him for me when he was away and in danger. By announcing that he no longer believed in God, I was afraid Ian was not keeping his side of the bargain and I was terrified that he would no longer be protected. I would go to church or kneel by my bed at night and tell God that Ian didn't really mean it, that it wasn't really true that Ian had lost his faith and I sincerely hoped that I was telling the truth.

My hopes were partially restored when he bid for Paul Bunker's bergen in a squadron auction of his kit, which I saw as an act of faith, the only time he has ever bid in such an auction. It felt important to him that he, of all people, should have it. He said it almost felt spiritual. He paid more than £100 for the backpack, only to pack it away forever in the attic and not even let me see it.

But he then produced an Argentinian conscript's jacket for me to wear, the main spoil from the Falklands he had managed to hold on to after the customs scare. There was still blood on it and it bore the identification card of the young lad he had presumably killed to get it. He laughed and said the coat would keep me warm in winter. I knew then that he meant it when he said he had lost his faith and I was overwhelmingly sad.

Some years later, I thought he had he got his faith back again when he wrote to me from some faraway land, 'I think I had better speak to the Man in the sky because it is time we got on talking terms again.' I felt tremendous relief, but as far as I know they never did.

In the October after the Falklands War Ian went on a six-week parachute training exercise with Delta Force (the American equivalent of the SAS) in the United States. I was happy that he felt up to it and pleased for him because he loved free-fall training above all else. But I was also disappointed because it meant he would be away for that year's Remembrance Day service which was to be held at Hereford Cathedral and would specially commemorate those who had died in the Conflict.

Though he claimed to be an atheist, I had hoped he might attend the service. I had promised Vanda I would accompany her and had wanted Ian to be by my side, escorting Vanda into the cathedral with me. Maybe someone upstairs was listening to me because Ian injured his ankle on one of his first jumps and had to be flown home with his leg in plaster. It was the first time he had ever had such a bad fall, onto unusually rocky ground some way away from the Drop Zone, but once I knew he wasn't seriously hurt I couldn't help but smile.

The injury meant that he was home, in a suit and at Vanda's side during the memorial service, which was very moving for us all. The Last Post was played, the tributes were very emotional and Vanda and I sat side by side in tears while Ian fought to control his upper lip.

Vanda rarely let any of us see how much she was hurting inside and continued to play an important part in my life as a friend and confidante. Unlike some of the other wives who lost their husbands, she never made me feel that it was insensitive to talk about Ian, to tell her where he was and what he was doing, to talk of our plans for the future together.

One widow of the helicopter crash, who overheard me chatting to a friend about Ian, had piped up, 'Well, at least your husband is still alive,' before stalking off. I understood the bitterness and grief she was feeling, but the whole ethos of the Regiment is about life going on, about new horizons, and I didn't see why I should act as if Ian had died too just to show empathy with those who had lost their husbands.

Vanda, of all people, had every right to be bitter. She and Paul were very much in love, truly happy. He was taken from her so suddenly, so violently and so completely, and yet she always maintained a dignified stance in the face of such cruelty.

I only ever saw her break down once. It was a year or so after Paul's death and immediately after the sudden death of a friend of hers in the Regiment, who had been accidentally shot on a training exercise. She telephoned us tearfully the night of the funeral and asked us if we could go to see her. When we got to the front door, we could hear her crying inside. Ian braced himself as I hammered on the door and asked her to let us in. Once we were inside, she sat herself between us, holding our hands and sobbing inconsolably. 'What has happened to Paul?' she asked Ian. 'Where is his body? Have the fishes eaten him yet?' I thought my heart would break for her.

Ian was always the strong shoulder to cry on. He held her and told her to hush and asked me to pour her a drink. We spent the evening with her, talking to her, holding her, crying with her and calming her down, before putting her to bed.

I felt completely out of my depth in the presence of such grief. It utterly overwhelmed me. We drove home in shocked silence and that night was the first of many when I had a horribly vivid nightmare about Paul's body being washed up on an Argentinian beach. I awoke, sweating and panting, as if I had just run a mile, and shivering with fright. If I was having such a terrible dream, I thought, what must Vanda and Ian be going through?

Like so many of the guys in the Regiment, Ian kept his feelings locked deep inside. It was never part of the SAS training to open up about emotional matters, it was years before any form of professional counselling was introduced to the Regiment. Ian was doubly cursed because not only was it against the Regiment ethos, but it was also simply not in his nature to talk about such things. But I heard Paul's name murmured from his lips several times in the nights after the Falklands, and I knew from his eyes that, although outwardly he seemed to have returned to his old self, inside the pain had not yet gone away.

And, as was increasingly the way for me to find out how he was feeling, I noticed a couple of entries in his diaries, several months after Paul's death, which showed that it was still very much on his mind.

On 24 December 1982, he wrote:

> Christmas Eve and feeling really down at the moment. Must buck up. Took dogs for a walk and went downtown for some last-minute things. Got some flowers for Vanda.

After a New Year's Eve fancy dress party at the local pub, in which we dressed as Dorothy and the Straw Man from *The Wizard of Oz* and Ian won first prize, he wrote:

> Had quite a good night. Came home around 1 a.m.
> Jenny got quite drunk. Didn't see the New Year in too well.
> Can't stop thinking about Paul Bunker.

'Do you fancy a pint, girl?' were Ian's first words to me when I met him in the Booth Hall pub in Hereford in the spring of 1979. I was twenty-seven and he was twenty-three. I had lived in the Welsh borders cathedral town since I was fourteen when my family had moved there from Hetton-le-Hole, County Durham.

My father was a coal miner for most of his life, working down the Fasington Lane Colliery and coming home early in the mornings when he was on night shift, his face black with coal dust, to get us up and cook our breakfast.

I grew up on a council estate with my three brothers and two sisters and I was always the one who got into trouble. I used to punch other kids in the nose and then climb up a lamp post and jeer at their angry parents from the top. I was a proper little Geordie tomboy. My two sisters were my mother's children from a previous marriage and my father was quite hard on them, but that never stopped them loving me. My mother was a real beauty in her day, but like many of the women of her generation she had no confidence and resigned herself to a life of housework and drudgery, living only for her three sons.

My father enjoyed a drink and worked in the evenings as a singer in the working men's clubs. He had a wonderful voice but sadly he was never able to earn anything more than beer money from it. By fourteen I had calmed down, was doing well at the local grammar school and planning a career as a teacher. I was enjoying myself in Hetton-le-Hole with my friends and family but my parents' marriage went through a sudden crisis and before I knew it the whole family was uprooted and moved to Hereford, where the kids had posh accents and seemed to hate me.

All my plans to study hard to go to teacher training college disappeared, along with my confidence, when the teachers and pupils at the Bluecoat Secondary Modern School in Hereford began to ridicule the way I talked. During my first week one of my teachers asked me to stand up and read a passage from a book and when I did, she said in front of the whole class, 'We will have to get rid of that accent, won't we?'

I stood there, all four foot ten and a half inches of me, with my fists clenched and declared, 'I haven't got an accent'. The whole class erupted into laughter. I was mortified but despite the teacher's best endeavours, she never did succeed in ridding me of the Geordie tongue.

I felt like a complete outsider at that school and couldn't wait to get away. It was so different from all that I had known and loved at my old grammar school. I left as soon as I could and went to work one of the local firms when I was just sixteen. It wasn't what I had planned for my career at all, but anything was better than the misery of school life.

I started off in the computer department of the company, which was largely staffed by young women. Listening to them I quickly discovered that many of the women in Hereford seemed to have only one objective in mind, to go out with, and ultimately marry, men from the 22 Special Air Service, which was stationed in the town. Once they had their catches, those who stayed the distance swanned around the town as if they owned it. It is a small town and they liked to let everyone know exactly who they were married to.

But it meant little or nothing to me. Not having been raised in the area, I shared none of the reverence the rest of the town seemed to have for the SAS. The last thing I wanted was to be married to some glorified squaddie who thought he was a hero.

I had a couple of boyfriends in my late teens and early twenties, including one guy who was in the SAS, but the Regiment was never an issue for me. As far as I was concerned, I was very happy going out three times a week with my two best friends, Sue and Anne, who worked with me. I wasn't even sure I ever wanted to be married and the girls did nothing to persuade me that it was something worth doing.

Anne was one of the first people I got to know in my job. I was a self-conscious teenager in a purple coat when I walked into that computer department on my first day, she was tall, fair, pretty and self-confident. A few years older than me, she took me under her wing and has been looking after me ever since. We became firm friends and would drive around town together in her little Morris Minor, we even went on holiday to Weymouth together in it. She married into the Regiment as a young woman and had a daughter, but the marriage failed early and she never married again.

Sue, nicknamed Toot since childhood, was the spitting image of Alison Moyet. Tall and blonde with a dry sense of humour, she towered over me in every way. We have quite an adversarial relationship, sparking off each other, with Anne trying to keep the peace, but she is great fun. She ended up marrying a Yorkshire man, who was in the Army but later became a lorry driver, and they are very happy.

By the time I met Ian I had been working with the girls for over ten years. We were all single at that time and went out every Wednesday, Friday and Saturday night. We always had fun, no matter where we went or what we did. If we were skint we drank cider, if we were flush we'd upgrade to lager, but we almost always got legless and we had some riotous times together. We would start in one pub, move on to another, grab a curry or a Chinese somewhere and then try some of the clubs.

On one memorable occasion we broke a toilet seat in a pub when we all tried to get on it, drunkenly, at the same time. We were the Three Musketeers, horribly intimidating and ruthlessly cruel to any man who tried to break into our coterie. It would have taken someone pretty special to split the three of us up on a Saturday night.

Ian, who had only just joined the SAS and moved up from London, obviously didn't know what he was up against when he pushed his way through the crowd to where we were standing to ask me if I fancied a pint.

'If it is a pint of gin I might,' was my response to this good-looking young man with piercing green eyes, as the girls giggled behind me. We started talking and I thought he was all right but it was not love at first sight for me. He said I looked like Brigitte Bardot and I told him to give over and get the drinks in.

Sue and Anne were going barmy once they realised he was with the Regiment, telling me to keep him chatting because he could get us into the Paludrine Club, which was the place to go in Hereford on a Saturday night. I didn't know what they were talking about at first, I hadn't even realised Ian was a soldier. When he introduced himself and said he was a Green Jacket, I said, 'Is that American?' He was a Londoner but he sounded like an American to me, he was so full of himself. He had a big blue fleecy puffer jacket on and I remember laughing because he had ripped the jacket on the arm and had put an Elastoplast over it, stuck on the outside. I thought,'My God, pet, does someone need to look after you.'

Once I realised who he was, I told the girls not to worry and promised that I would get us all into the Paludrine Club. True to my word I succeeded, after flashing my big blue eyes at Ian a few times. As soon as we got through the door, we girls headed for the bar and, ignoring Ian, spent the rest of the night having a riotous time together. Ian couldn't believe I could be so rude as to forget him, so he kept manoeuvring himself in front of me to talk some more. But, spurred on by the girls and the high-spirited mood we were in, I ignored him right up until the end of the evening, when I suddenly realised I needed a lift home.

'Right, pet,' I told him. 'You can take me home now.' I started looking around for my jacket and handbag.

He was indignant. 'Cheeky bitch, you've ignored me all night,' he said petulantly, his bottom lip stuck out.

I told him to get my coat and stop complaining. We got talking in the car on the way home and one thing led to another, as it so often does. Before I knew it we ended up spending that first night together and, despite all my best intentions, I was smitten.

I really wanted to see him again and I thought about him intensely for weeks afterwards. I went back to the Booth Hall regularly to try to find him but he never seemed to be around. I began to think I must have been little more than a one-night stand to him and that he was obviously avoiding me. I was hurt and upset and told the girls I would have nothing more to do with the scruffy toe-rag, but when he walked into the pub five months later my heart soared and the girls raised their eyebrows to the heavens.

Ian grabbed my hand, took me into a corner and told me how pleased he was to see me. He said he been away to Northern Ireland and had been thinking about me as much as I had him. He had only just got back to camp and had come straight out to look for me. He kissed me and held me tight and I ignored the open-mouthed faces of my girlfriends as he led me out away from the pub and into the night.

We saw each other fairly regularly after that and we were both well and truly hooked. I learned a lot about this tall, dark stranger in those first few weeks. I was insatiable, I wanted to know everything about him. He told me he was a Londoner, raised on a council estate in Hayes, Middlesex, with his parents and four sisters and brothers.

His mother was a true Romany, a remarkable woman who grew up in the New Forest in Hampshire until the council moved them into permanent accommodation in Downton, Wiltshire. It was during World War II that she met his father, who was a flight engineer with the Lancaster Bombers. Ian's two uncles were Royal

Marine Commandos and from as early as he can remember, he was indoctrinated into becoming one too.

He joined the army cadets and even wore his uniform to school each day, so focused was he on what he was going to become. Later, during training exercises with the Territorial Army, he had his first contact with someone from the SAS. He was on night exercises on a Wiltshire moor and an SAS soldier suddenly turned up from nowhere, joining the TA camp fire for a few hours. Ian, who was an impressionable young teenager, watched this mysterious stranger light a cigarette and then carefully bury the spent matchstick in the dirt. From that moment on he was bewitched.

After a disastrous start to his army career in the junior Royal Marines, when he became so heartsick for his teenage sweetheart that he was sent home in disgrace, he signed up with the Royal Green Jackets, with whom he travelled to Northern Ireland and Gibraltar and where he first met his friend Andy McNab. Ian ended up being one of McNab's senior officers when McNab was doing Selection at Hereford a few years later.

Ian did very well in the Green Jackets, jumping to corporal from rifleman, skipping a rank which is almost unknown. When he passed Selection – the months of intensive training and assessment that has to be taken and passed before any soldier is allowed into the SAS – he had to go back to trooper and work his way up again, as they all do. He was made up to corporal within a couple of years.

During the arduous Selection process, which only ten or twenty or so of an original 150-plus candidates get through each year, physical and mental endurance is tested to the uppermost limits. Some have even died in the attempt, so tough is the nature of the exercises each year's new group of hopefuls is put through. They include 'The Fan Dance' a double trek up and down Pen-y-fan, a 3,000-foot mountain in the bleak Brecon Beacons on the borders of Wales and Herefordshire. Written above the basha (sleeping quarters) at the Hereford camp, are the words: Death is Nature's way of telling you that you've failed Selection.

Each candidate who applies undergoes a three-week build-up period followed by the much-feared Test Week, which includes a standard fitness test followed by a daily diet of endurance route marches across the Brecon Beacons. If they make it to the third week, they are sent out on their own with a few meagre provisions and a bergen increasingly weighted down until it reaches the maximum fifty-five pounds (just short of four stone). The route marches go on for up to three days and nights, with candidates having to cope with terrible weather conditions, blisters, fatigue. Many are RTU'd (Returned to Unit) within hours.

Those that get through then have to endure fourteen weeks of Continuation Training, learning basic survival skills, weapons training, sabotage, ambush and how to operate behind enemy lines. They are taught escape and evasion methods and how to cope under interrogation and mental torture.

Those who survive get sent to the Far East or Central America for their first six weeks of jungle training to put all they have learned into practice – an exercise they will continue to make throughout their time in the Regiment. They are given minimal rations and have to live on what they can find to eat around them, whether it is crocodile, snake, monkey or roots. At the end of the trip they take turns to play the hunters and hunted, learning how to evade detection and hide deep in the bush. When, and if, they get back from that unscathed or without malaria or seriously debilitating insect bites, their final test is an intensive four-week parachute course at Brize Norton.

If they get through all of that, the successful soldiers are badged – given the famous SAS beret with the winged dagger emblem. They then start their advance training and each have to learn a patrol skill – medicine, demolitions, communications or languages (although they all learn a little about each in case the expert amongst them is killed). Ian's chief patrol skill was medicine, learned on a course in the casualty department of a general hospital, giving him the skill to administer first aid and even perform emergency surgery on anyone who is injured in the field.

The Regiment has four sixteen-man troops in each squadron, each with its own area of expertise – Mountain Troop, Boat Troop, Mobility Troop and Air Troop. Each of the four main squadrons is differentiated by a letter and Ian was put in D Squadron Mobility Troop, which deals with transport. Not long after passing Selection he went on exercises in Florida and got very drunk one night and told everyone he secretly wanted to join Freefall or Air Troop (known in the Regiment as 'the ice cream boys' because they are always in the sunshine). The next morning, his sergeant woke him up, pointed up to the sky and said, 'Right, sonny, you are up there today.' He had been moved to Air Troop.

He had two hours' so-called 'training' – jumping off a six-foot table – and then they took him up for the real thing. He couldn't even remember his first jump because he was still drunk from the night before. A couple of jumps later he nearly died when, shortly after jumping out of a plane at 18,000 feet, he went into a spin that his instructor couldn't get him out of.

Because of the changes in air pressure, all the blood vessels burst in his eyes. When he finally landed safely he looked like Dracula. He showed me photographs of it later and it was horrific. His eyeballs were filled with blood.

I found out as much as I could about Ian's early life in the first few weeks of our courting, but I could tell there was something he was holding back. I joked with the girls that there might be some dreadful skeleton in his closet, a mad aunt locked in an attic, or maybe a Vietnam-style trauma he had experienced in Northern Ireland that he couldn't yet bring himself to tell me about. We laughed about it over lunch in the works canteen, wondering what his dark secret could be.

His way of breaking it to me was typical of Ian – blunt and to the point. We had been out to the pub one night and I was driving him home, which I had always assumed was back at the camp. I pulled up at the gates and stopped but he didn't attempt to move or get out of the car.

'This is where you live, isn't it?' I asked him, puzzled by his silence.

'No,' he said, studying his hands. 'I don't live at the camp.'

I wondered what on earth he meant. Of course he lived at the camp, I had been dropping him off there for weeks. What was he saying?

'I don't live in the camp because . . . I live in married quarters,' he said, looking sheepishly across at me.

I was dumbstruck. So that was it. He was married. That was what he had been holding back. That was why we hadn't always been able to spend the night together. All those little excuses and mysterious exits suddenly fell into place. It wasn't because of some terrible trauma or embarrassing secret, he was just a two-timing, adulterous son-of-a-bitch.

I was distraught. I screamed at him to get out of the car, to get out of my life and leave me alone forever. He didn't budge. He quietly waited for me to vent my fury, to finish spilling my tears. When my sobs had reduced to manageable proportions, we sat in the car for hours, talking it over.

He told me he was very unhappy in his marriage, that his wife – who had married him when he was still a Green Jacket – had never wanted him to join the Regiment in the first place and was vehemently opposed to becoming an SAS wife. Nobody knew very much about the Regiment in those days and she was understandably terrified by the little she had heard.

He had been forced to abandon his first attempt at Selection after his mother-in-law telephoned the camp half-way through it to tell him his wife was having a nervous breakdown. When he got home and realised that she wasn't, he told her that nothing would stop him the next time. He took and passed Selection the second time around, moved her to Hereford from her native Yorkshire against her will, and felt that she had been punishing him for it ever since.

I cried and cried and berated him for not telling me before. I was furious with myself for getting involved with a married man, for being so stupid, so naive. Imagine thinking that this could have been the one, allowing myself to fall in love and hope for a life together. With intuitive good timing, Ian decided that this was the moment to drop his second bombshell.

'I've got a son,' he said. 'He is just a few months old. His name is David.'

Try as I might, I couldn't stop loving Ian. No matter how much my head told me that this was not the way to start a long-term relationship, I couldn't bear to give him up. He knew he had won me over and he also knew that, with my love and support, he would now have the courage to do what he had been wanting to do for months. Within a few days he broke the news to his wife and left home. Not surprisingly, she and their baby moved back to Yorkshire in a state of considerable distress.

Ian and I both felt guilty about his wife and the baby, but I believed Ian when he told me the marriage had died long before I came on the scene and Ian was fully prepared to provide for them as best he could when she moved back to her family.

Ian wasn't over the worst yet. He still had to be officially approved by Sue and Anne, a process which he described as worse than Selection training. They clearly thought I was mad, but they also knew how crazy I was about him so, like the true friends that they were, they put aside their personal objections and told me to go for it.

Despite the stress of what then became a very difficult divorce, we were very happy. I had got the man of my dreams and he seemed to feel the same way about me. He was thoughtful, kind and caring. He was all that I ever wanted and I looked forward to our life together, whatever it would hold. I was staying at a friend's flat and he was in quarters, so we only had a few snatched evenings together, but we were truly in love.

It was an evening not long afterwards, as we were driving home from a party, that Ian suddenly asked me if I would marry him when his divorce came through. I thought, 'Yeah, right, pet,' and didn't give him an answer. But the following morning, on our way to a local pub for a Sunday lunchtime drink he asked me again. 'Do you remember what I asked you last night?' he said. I told him I thought he had only said it because he was drunk.

He insisted that he had meant it and he asked me again. I didn't answer immediately, so he drove around and around a roundabout until I said 'Yes' for fear of being sick. Unfortunately for me, he then drove around and around it some more, shouting out of the window to all the other drivers, 'She said "Yes", she said "Yes"'. I thought to myself, What am I doing with this lunatic?

That night, we slept together in the car, parked up on Dinedar

Hill above the camp. Ian borrowed two old sleeping bags from the stores and we cuddled up close and told each other all our hopes and dreams. We didn't have two ha'pennies to rub together, especially since Ian was paying maintenance for his ex-wife and child, but we had never been happier. When we woke up in the morning, I laughed and laughed until I cried. We looked like we had been tarred and feathered. The sleeping bags had split and we were covered in down. It was in our eyes, noses and mouths, but we were laughing so much, it didn't seem to matter. 'If this is how we are going to have to live, then so be it,' he said and I honestly didn't care.

Ian and I moved into my parents' house for a while, until we could save enough money to buy ourselves a home. He spent most of his days in and around the camp on training exercises, and his evenings with me. To my great pleasure there seemed to be little call for his services around the world at that time.

Ian has always had a knack for training others, he is an excellent teacher and people respond to his warm, friendly manner extremely well. Having taken several courses in Counter-Revolutionary Warfare – how to extricate people kidnapped or held hostage by terrorists or blackmailers – he was asked to help train another squadron in the specialist techniques he had learned.

By the beginning of May 1980, his training task was completed and he had also just finished being 'on team' at the camp – when one of the squadrons is on twenty-four-hour standby for a week or two, ready for any special operational mission which might come up. He had handed over to another squadron less than a week earlier and we were looking forward to a few days off together.

A friend of ours, Ron, had invited us over for lunch on Monday 5 May and later that evening he and Ian were watching the John Wayne film *True Grit* on the television, when their viewing was interrupted by a newsflash. The BBC reporter Kate Adie burst onto the screen and said she was at the scene of an ongoing siege in central London, which was being filmed by the world's media.

'Jenny, Jenny, come here, look at this,' Ian suddenly screamed at me from our friend's lounge. I rushed in from the kitchen to find him and Ron, who was also in the Regiment, staring at the screen with their mouths open. We all watched in silence as Miss Adie told the world that the Iranian Embassy siege in Prince's Gate, Knightsbridge, had just been ended spectacularly by the SAS.

As we watched with the rest of the world, we saw the familiar black-clad men in balaclavas lowering themselves on ropes from the roof and then jumping through the front windows from the balcony to save the day, shooting dead the Iranian gunmen and rescuing nineteen of the hostages. To the millions watching the action on live television, it was the first time they had seen the SAS at work and the public fascination with its members and *modus operandi* had begun. The whole operation was over in just eleven minutes, but in that short time, the Regiment's cover was blown. We felt instinctively that everyone would want to know everything about it from that day on.

When the newsflash was over, I switched off the television and we sat in stunned silence for several seconds.

'I trained those guys, I bloody trained them,' Ian said excitedly, grinning from ear to ear and swigging from his beer can. 'Well done lads,' he said, raising his can to the blank television screen. 'You did it for all of us.' Ron lifted his can too and made a similar toast.

I smiled affectionately at Ian. I knew he would have given his right arm to have been in on the siege personally but the fact that the lads had done it and that he had helped in the operation in some small way was good enough for him. We all realised its importance for the Regiment from the minute we saw the first images on the screen, and Ian was entitled to claim his share of the glory.

'I would have gone like a shot if they'd called,' he added, checking the radio pager clipped to his belt to make sure he hadn't missed anything.

'Don't be silly, you're not even on call,' I scolded him. 'And anyway, you're far too pissed to go climbing around on balconies.'

Ian looked up at me and over at Ron and swigged once more from his can. 'My darling Jenny, how right you are,' he said, grinning. 'And guess what? After such a momentous day for the Regiment, I am about to get blind, bloody legless.'

(Years later, at a military function, a young defence journalist assumed Ian had been among those on the balcony, and asked him, 'Were you frightened during the Iranian Embassy siege?'

Ian thought about it for a minute and replied, 'Yes.'

Great, thought the budding young hack who had never managed to get anyone else in the SAS to admit to their fear. 'Was it terrifying?' he asked, hoping for an exclusive quote.

'Well, I was certainly terrified,' Ian said as he watched the reporter scribble his words down excitedly. Before he could be asked another question my hero added, 'And I was only watching it on television.' He said he thought the reporter might burst into tears, he looked so disappointed.)

After several weeks of living with my parents, Ian and I finally scraped together enough money for a mortgage and bought ourselves a little Victorian house in the centre of Hereford. I had to choose the house, organise its purchase and arrange the move as Ian was too busy with training exercises, but I was so looking forward to the day we moved in that I didn't mind in the slightest.

I had a romantic image in my head of what it would be like – the two of us settling down between packing cases, tired and dirty at the end of the day with a fish-and-chip supper and two glasses of wine to welcome us in. There would be a single light-bulb overhead, a hastily laid mattress in one corner and a howling gale coming down the lovely old Victorian fireplace, but we would be together and happy and that would be all that mattered.

But when the day came, I was alone. It was late autumn 1980 and Ian had been sent to Italy for two weeks on exercises. Friends and family came round to help carry things and settle me in, but at the end of the day I sat alone but content eating my fish and chips under my single light-bulb, wondering where Ian was at that moment. Wrapping up the greasy paper holding my food, I threw it into a dustbin liner and told myself out loud, 'Well, Jenny, pet. This is what it is going to be like, so you had better just get on with it girl.'

By the time Ian came home, I had the place done up like a doll's house. I had pretty curtains at the windows and pictures on the walls and an open fire burning in the grate. It was a truly welcoming scene and he appreciated all my efforts. Right, I thought, I've got him home for a while and in a good mood, now where is that list of all the jobs that needed doing?

Within a few weeks I realised that this highly trained crack trooper of mine was utterly useless when it came to DIY. He might be able to shoot a moving target from fifty paces blindfolded but he hardly knew one end of a screwdriver from the other and as for wallpapering, well, blindfolded might have been better. I knew more than he did from watching 'Blue Peter'. I decided to take control of the situation and started learning all the techniques myself. With the help of a few books and much-needed advice from family and friends, I was soon mastering painting, plumbing and even wallpapering all by myself.

It was probably just as well because in October 1980, not long after we bought the house, Ian was sent to Northern Ireland for six months, only coming home for a couple of weekends during the entire period. We both knew the trip was on the cards as the tensions built up in the Province and there was more talk on the mainland for the need for Special Services to be deployed. Knowing it was likely to happen didn't make it any easier when the time came.

I stayed behind, I couldn't have gone if I had wanted to. In the regular Army, wives and girlfriends can accompany their men, but not in the SAS. It would be too dangerous for us both and anyway I had the back bedroom to strip.

I was very naive about Northern Ireland and never particularly interested in the politics of it all. I believed, I suppose as most English people did, that it was all bad news and because it didn't personally affect me, I didn't really think too much about it. The only time I saw stories from the Province was when I looked down from the top of my stepladder to read what was under the paint pot.

This was Ian's first big trip since we had started living together and our first long separation. I told myself not to worry too much about him and told him that it would give me time to do up that house as I wanted. I had always known that I would have to enjoy being with him when I could and I promised him we would keep in touch via our letters when we were apart.

The hardest part was not being able to pick up the phone and call him because he was undercover. He phoned when he could but our conversations were often quite strained or filled with discussions about mundane household matters. Our letters were our lifeline. We became pen pals, I suppose. It seemed that to sit down and think about what you were going to say concentrated the mind on what was truly important.

Ian summed it up in one of his first letters to me:

> 'As soon as I go away I think I've got to say the things I don't seem to be able to say at home. I don't know if it is pressure, lack of time or what. I know it isn't because I don't care.'

He would sit and write to me from his cramped little hovel somewhere deep inside some heavily armoured police station, and I would sit in bed each night at home, specks of paint in my hair, writing back to him and trying to imagine where he was.

Much of his work was in Londonderry in the early days and was extremely sensitive. Intelligence gathering was the name of the game along with personal protection of those who were on a hit-list or had received some specific threat from the IRA, whether they were members of the police force or judiciary, the Armed Forces or businessmen who were viewed as having some connection with them. Even builders who worked on Army or Government buildings were targeted and all had to be protected.

It was the Regiment's role to undertake all the long-term operations, watching some arms cache or remote farmhouse for weeks on end, taking notes of which suspected terrorist turned up with whom for which meeting or to collect which weapon. Noting down numberplates, routines, details and taking dozens and dozens of photographs using special cameras with long lenses. Individual weapons would then be traced and followed, using sophisticated tracing equipment, with a view to identifying their handlers. Watching and waiting for all of this to happen was tiresome, boring and often deeply frustrating. But the men knew it was vitally important so they put up with it.

Most of the time, Ian lived in deep hides and I knew from what he told me, and from the state his clothes were in when he came home, that he spent most of his time lying in cold, water-filled ditches, cammied up (camouflaged), shitting into plastic bags and pissing into special bottles to avoid leaving any trace of his presence, living on cold rations, not even able to brew up a cup of tea or cook anything hot to eat.

It rained almost the whole time he was there, and he seemed to have a permanent cold from never being out of the inclement weather. He would daydream about his favourite food and then have to chew on a dry biscuit in the rain to satisfy the appetite he had whetted in his mind. He wore the full camouflage and belt kit – which contained everything he needed, including water bottles and food rations to compass, maps and ammunition – with only a bobble hat to keep his head warm. His face would be thick with camouflage paint (which never really got out of his pores) and he would be dug into the ground, half-freezing to death.

Sometimes he would get a treat. A member of the Regiment, posing as a local farmer, would drop off a pack of fresh sandwiches for him and his fellow soldiers, hurling it from his moving Land Rover into the hedge where they were lying. Other times, when they knew their target was out of range, they could light a small fire and brew up some tea, filling their flasks with the hot liquid. It was all a very far cry from my centrally-heated works canteen and the huge tea urns from which we could take our fill.

This was his first time back across the water since he had passed Selection. His previous two tours had been as a Green Jacket, up front in uniform and very much in the firing line. His bedroom at Forkhill police station in South Armagh had been destroyed by a mortar attack in 1978. He had been on patrol and watched helplessly as the mortars came in, killing and wounding several men. Later, he had seen the SAS guys ferreting around, dealing with the terrorists on their own terms, not sitting around waiting to get hit. The secretive nature of what they were doing and how they were doing it increased his urge to join the Regiment.

Now that he found himself doing the same work, it was all very different. Sure, it was still 'sexy' work, with all the tools of the trade that attract young squaddies to the SAS in the first place, but it was also very much self-taught. There were no rule books, no one to tell you what to do, just general orders about protection or intelligence-gathering, where and when. Ian and his mates had to get on with it as best they could, never really knowing what they might come up against.

He was left to sort out his own kit and on one brief, unscheduled trip home to collect some equipment, he decided to try to set something up that would help him with his surveillance work.

'I've been thinking about the sort of thing I would need,' he told me distractedly, disappearing into the bedroom with a mysterious box of wires and tools. 'Now where's that old overcoat of mine?'

He spent an afternoon in the bedroom banging and cursing, crashing around and only emerging for more parts. Inside, he was rigging up a Heath Robinson-style monitoring kit with the lining of his overcoat taped up to the seams with wires, microphones and a huge battery pack.

His mission completed, Ian slipped the coat on and came into the lounge, walking with the ease of an astronaut with piles. He stood in front of me, lumps and bumps clearly visible under the herringbone coat and wires dangling by his feet. He looked like something out of 'Steptoe & Son'.

'Tell me honestly,' he asked me and Lisa, who was spending the afternoon with me. 'Does this look obvious?'

We were speechless. Finally Lisa erupted, 'He looks like Rolf Harris . . . as Jake the Peg.'

We both exploded, laughing so hard that we ended up falling off the sofa and knocking over a pot of paint, spilling it all over the floorboards. That only made us laugh even more, tears streaming down our cheeks. Looking truly hurt, Ian limped back to his bedroom to dismantle his home-made contraption, slamming the door behind him.

Ian told me very little about what he was doing in Northern Ireland, because he knew that I would only worry. My imagination is quite vivid enough without him adding fuel to the fire. If I knew that he was going to be lying in the foot well of a lorry that was about to have a car-bomb placed under it, or waiting with his gun in the bed of an RUC officer who was targeted to be shot in his sleep, I would never have let him take the helicopter across the water in the first place.

Sometimes he would tell me snippets of information that gave me a brief insight into his work. He spoke of his immense admiration for the security forces in the Province, he said he couldn't live like they do, with the constant threat of death for themselves and their families. His words made me feel humble about my own fears.

'They live with the IRA all around them, each knowing who the other one is and that one day they will come for them,' he wrote to me one night when he had drunk a little too much beer. 'And they say the SAS are the heroes.'

Ian lived with these people, sometimes for weeks on end, sleeping, eating and washing with them in their terraced council homes, as they watched and waited for the moment of attack; having to keep the guns away from little fingers of the children running around under their feet; moving out of kitchens and laundry rooms to allow the women to cook or clean. When I heard that he was doing that kind of work I felt momentarily jealous of the women in the house with Ian, envious of their contact with him, of his protection of them when I was home alone, cooking and cleaning just for myself.

Some of Ian's colleagues became emotionally involved with the families they were protecting. One lad, who had never had a very happy home life, became a sort of adoptive son to one RUC officer and his wife, taking to the man's children as if they were younger siblings. Long after his task was over, he would visit them for meals and take them presents. He was devastated when the officer and his eldest son were blown up by a car-bomb a few years later.

One protection job Ian did was in the home of a wealthy land-owner who had received a death threat. Ian and two colleagues lived in the pantry of his big country house, among tins of food and rounds of cheese, with pheasants and rabbits hanging above their heads and bottles of wine at their feet. The housekeeper was the only member of staff to know of their presence and she alone was allowed into the pantry to collect the food.

The poor woman would get terribly flustered each time she had to walk into the small enclosed space with three armed men blinking at her in the darkness. She would drop things and curse them, but she always left them delicious 'doorstep' ham sandwiches and a jug of fresh milk. At night, when the staff had gone home, the men could sneak out and take control of the house, returning to the pantry at dawn. Ian craved ham sandwiches for ages after that job, and complained when I didn't cut the bread thick enough at home.

Ian never lost anyone he was protecting, although he did once witness from afar a murder and arson attack on one family who had been protected by the SAS previously. The father was a judge and he and his family lived in a castle close to the Irish border. Ian and his troop were watching a house nearby that night, after receiving information that a wanted terrorist was going to be there. The terrorist never turned up but in the distance they heard some noise and saw a large fire.

Ian felt very frustrated, unable to abandon the operation he was on to move or offer assistance, uncertain if it was a serious incident or simply a diversionary tactic. He was devastated when he discovered the next day that the entire family had been taken out by an eight-man IRA assault team who blew the doors in with explosives, executed the judge and his family and then ambushed and wounded the police team which arrived to help.

I kept myself busy at work, carried on doing up the house, saw quite a lot of Lisa and her friends and went out a couple of times a week with Sue and Anne, just like the old days. I never once let any of the concern I was feeling about Ian register in my voice or in my letters to him. He didn't know that I had started to watch the television news and scan the papers for stories from Northern Ireland, cutting them out and pasting them into a scrapbook I kept hidden in the back bedroom.

He had no idea that I was pouring myself a few glasses of wine on the nights I sat alone at home, wondering what he was doing and when he would be back. I knew it wouldn't help either of us if he had an inkling of the fear and loneliness that I was starting to feel inside.

We spent Christmas together at home that year and I was thrilled to have Ian back with me. We ate our turkey dinner on the floor, drank a cheap bottle of sparkling wine and then telephoned all our friends and relatives to wish them well. It was all we could afford to do, with the mortgage and the maintenance payments to his wife and child, but we had never been happier. It was a strange, magical time.

I showed him all that I had done about the house and he looked around in amazement at my DIY successes. There were the wedding plans too and we drew up a list of possible guests, only to cross most of them out because we couldn't afford all the ones we wanted.

The joy of having him home with me made up for the pain I had been feeling at his absences, but I was still dreading him going back, dreading the loneliness that welled up from the pit of my stomach as I sat alone mending something or painting yet another door.

I confessed to him, rather reluctantly, that I had become occasionally fearful around the house on my own. Not normally prone to paranoia, I had even started to imagine there was a ghost who I called Charley who moved things around and made strange noises in the back bedroom. Ian was so concerned for me, that he even told his CO about it. The CO looked patronisingly at Ian and told him, 'She is just lonely. It happens. Get her a dog.'

On New Year's Eve that year he was away and I went out to celebrate with Sue and Anne at a local pub. The evening rushed by and before I knew it, it was ten to twelve. Suddenly feeling the need to speak to Ian in Belfast, I left my drink, grabbed my coat and ran home as fast as my little legs would carry me. I put the key in the door just as the clock struck midnight. A second later, the telephone rang.

'Hello, babe,' I heard him say. 'I'm so glad you're in. I suddenly had the urge to ring you and wish you Happy New Year.'

\*　　　\*　　　\*

By January 1981 he was undercover again and I was left alone with my paintbrushes and wallpaper books and Charley. Oh well, not long to go now, I thought, and started laying out the dust sheets.

On a Friday evening later that month, the telephone rang as I was painting the ceiling in the kitchen and I got down to pick it up and hear Ian's voice on the other end of the line.

'Hi, babe,' he said, breathlessly. 'Can't stop. Just rang you to tell you to watch the news tonight. It is important. Can't say too much but you'll understand when you see it.'

I unearthed the TV and watched anxiously, wondering what heroic thing he could have done that was going to be on the Nine O'Clock News. What I saw and heard I could hardly believe.

Bernadette McAliskey, formerly Bernadette Devlin, the MP who was the most outspoken critic of the British Army and who campaigned on behalf of convicted IRA terrorists in the Maze prison, had been shot by three men who, according to the news reports, had smashed their way into her remote farmhouse and fired seven bullets into her in front of her children. Her husband, Michael, was also shot. She was in a critical condition in hospital and he was stable.

My naive reaction was that Ian must have shot her, but I had got it all wrong – he was the one who had saved her life. He and two other SAS troopers were on an operation in Belfast and were told to go quickly to the McAliskey house in County Tyrone to cover her and to protect the scene, because the police had been given a tip-off that Loyalist paramilitaries might be planning to make a move on her. The three men had only just arrived on this freezing cold night and were trying to get their radio to work and report on the situation at the farm when a car pulled up outside more than 600 feet away.

They didn't think anything of it at first, but then they heard banging – the gunmen using a sledgehammer to break down the front door. Immediately after that they heard gunshots and realised that the attack was happening there and then and they weren't even ready for it. Ian grabbed his gun and ran towards the front door of the house, while the other two ran round the back. He suddenly came face to face with one of the gunmen, who was wearing a balaclava and was running out of the door.

For a split second both of them stared at each other, deciding if they should fire. Being a Loyalist, the gunman couldn't in all faith shoot someone he knew to be a British soldier and he surrendered. Had he been an IRA gunman, Ian would have undoubtedly been shot at.

The other gunmen came running out and also surrendered when they realised they had been caught red-handed by British troops. Ian, with his medical training, went inside to see what he could do while the others guarded the terrorists and tried unsuccessfully to radio for help. Ian found Mr McAliskey lying on the floor behind the kitchen door, severely injured. He didn't honestly think there was any hope for him and went to Mrs McAliskey, who was, after all, the one he had been told to protect.

She was lying naked on her children's bed, and they sat silently staring at her as she lay groaning, almost bleeding to death. Ian later said he had never seen such hard-faced kids.

Ian didn't think she would make it either but he grabbed whatever he could to stuff into her wounds to stem the bleeding. The house was filthy. The whole place stank and was full of whippets, with dead chicken carcasses strewn around for them outside. All he could find was newspapers, so he stuffed her chest wounds full of them, pulled a quilt over her and ran for help. He once said that he couldn't give up a life needlessly, no matter whose it was.

He made it to another farm and called for help and when he ran back – dressed for all the world like a terrorist – he nearly got shot by a nervous young RUC officer who was patrolling a hastily erected roadblock outside the McAliskey farm. When the Army arrived, the SAS men were thrown three red berets of the Parachute Regiment to wear to disguise their identity, which Ian always thought was funny because the Paras didn't even patrol that area and everyone knew that.

It was reported in all the newspapers the next day that the Paras and the Sutherland Highlanders had saved the day. Mrs McAliskey, who recovered along with her husband, said afterwards that she believed a Para had saved her life. She presented the surgeon who operated on her with a cut crystal drinks decanter. There were no commendations for Ian, although the Prince of Wales came up to Hereford several months later to meet the Ian and the other two men who had been involved and award Ian's troop sergeant David a medal.

Ian's long weekend home that spring was something of an anticlimax. I had been looking forward to it for so long and had planned and rehearsed in my mind what we would say to each other and how we would spend it, that when it came to it, I was pretty nervous.

I went to pick him up from the camp and I walked right past him, I didn't recognise this scruffy, bearded young man with wild dark hair and a Mexican-style moustache. He was wearing old flared jeans and a donkey jacket and looked like something from a television sit-com.

I took him straight home to bed. Unbeknown to him, I had attached a row of inverted bottles, complete with pub optics, to the window sill next to the bed, hidden by the new curtains I had made. After we had said our hellos, I asked him if he fancied a drink. 'Yes, great,' he said. Pulling back the curtain and reaching for a glass, I poured him a large Jack Daniels from the upturned bottle. He sat there, speechless, until finally he said, 'Is it any wonder why I can't wait to get home,' and pulled me towards him, laughing.

We spent the weekend quietly together, both appreciating the importance of the brief time we had. Yet Ian seemed distant, though he tried hard to overcome it, while I resisted the temptation to complain at the unfairness of not having him around. I didn't mention my unhappiness at being alone and too skint even to go out for a drink with the girls, nor that I wasn't sleeping at night.

For both our sakes, I wanted the weekend to be a memorable one, filled with love and laughter, but in what seemed like the blink of an eye, the time was over and he was gone again. I shut the door behind him and wondered, momentarily, what it would have been like if I had married someone like the lathe operator who had been my previous boyfriend.

In his first letter home after the weekend, Ian apologised for his mood. 'It is hard to chill out so quickly and pretend you are a normal human being again,' he wrote. 'The time seemed so short and I found it difficult to relax, knowing that I was coming back over here in a few days.'

As he got busier and busier, however, Ian's letters home became less and less frequent and he started to rely on the telephone. He usually called late at night, and often he was drunk. After a few nights' sleep interrupted by a slurred voice on the other end of the line telling me he loved me, I began wishing he would put pen to paper instead.

I, too, was drinking more than I should and that scared me a little. It seemed an easy solution to my boredom and loneliness. Sue and Anne would drop in to take me out to the pub. They knew I didn't have much money and were very understanding.

On the nights they didn't come, I found myself drinking alone, finishing off a bottle of wine or cider, curled up on the sofa in front of the television and wondering if I would always miss Ian so intensely. Finally, picking up my drink, I would turn off all the lights and head for the stairs.

'Come on then Charley,' I would call out. 'Time for bed.'

# 3 | With This Ring

'CIRCLE ROUND AGAIN, circle round again,' I urged the chauffeur as our coffee-coloured Rolls-Royce pulled up outside the church. It was 11.20 on a summer's morning in 1981, a few months after Ian's tour of duty in Northern Ireland had ended, and I was in the back of the Rolls with my father, nearly twenty minutes late for my own wedding.

'You've got to go through with it, Jenny, girl,' Dad told me in his broad Geordie accent, patting my hand. 'You can't leave all those people waiting any longer.' We had already circled the block three times.

'I know, I know,' I said, as much to myself as anyone else. 'It's just that I've been thinking, I'm twenty-nine years old and maybe I am too old to settle down now. I mean, a soldier in the SAS, what am I thinking of?'

The car turned the corner gracefully once more and this time, Tony, my younger brother and the chief usher, was standing impatiently on the kerbside. The car had barely pulled to a halt when he wrenched the passenger door open.

'What the hell's going on here?' he asked Dad.

'It's your sister,' he sighed. 'She's got cold feet.' I looked suitably coy.

Before I knew it, Tony had grabbed my hand and yanked me unceremoniously from the back of the Rolls. I stood on the pavement smoothing down the creases in my coffee and cream coloured dress and gripped my bouquet as if my life depended on it.

'Now listen, Sis, what are you playing at?' Tony asked me as he started to drag me towards the church door. 'We've got a church full of guests and your mum and all your friends are in there all looking gorgeous and you decide that now is the time to have second thoughts?'

'I just don't think I can go through with it,' I told him, through teeth clenched with nerves. 'I'm too old to be gettin' wed.' We got to the door and my waiting bridesmaid, a young cousin, who looked bewildered. Beyond the glass inner door, I could see Ian's back as he stood waiting at the top of the aisle with his best man. Butterflies did the fandango in my stomach.

'No way. There is no way I'm going down that aisle,' I said, heading back towards the car. Tony and Dad took an elbow each and frog-marched me back up the stairs.

'Now, don't be silly, Jenny,' said Dad. 'It's just nerves. You've got to pull yourself together. Come on now, girl. Everything will be all right.'

My mind was racing with all the terrible things that might happen if I walked through those doors. Ian and I were happy enough as we were, living together in our little house. Why did we have to go and spoil things? What about my mates, Sue and Anne? Weren't we the Three Musketeers, never to get hitched up or leave the pack? What would marriage to the SAS really be like? I had already experienced some of the loneliness and I knew how notoriously selfish and unfaithful the men in the Regiment were supposed to be. Hadn't Ian already left one wife? Would I be just another casualty?

The chauffeur was out of the car by now, leaning against it, smoking a cigarette and watching the farce unfolding before his eyes. He was thoroughly bemused by the whole event. First, he had picked up the groom, a man he was told was in the SAS, who had lain on the floor of the Rolls-Royce as he was driven through Hereford town centre in case any of his mates saw him. And now there was the demented bride who couldn't make up her mind if she wanted to marry the man or not. It was promising to be an interesting day.

I was back in the vestibule, staring at the back of Ian's head once again. My young bridesmaid was telling me how lovely I looked, and I was wondering if I could make my getaway by running past her, through the doors, down the aisle and out the back door before any of the guests saw me.

Just as I was contemplating that idea, Ian turned around and looked straight at me. A broad grin broke out across his tanned face, his gypsy eyes looked as if they were on fire and he winked at me. In that second my heart melted, my nerves vanished and I suddenly knew I was doing the right thing.

'Come on then, you lot,' I told the group fussing around me. 'Let's get down that aisle before someone else beats me to it.' They hardly had time to close their mouths before I had pushed on through the doors.

Despite my sudden confidence, it was still a nerve-wracking experience and I could hardly move or speak by the time I got up to the altar. Ian grabbed my arm and wedged his body against mine so that people wouldn't notice how much I was trembling. He was a real stalwart. The vicar had to prise the bouquet out of my hands to get me to take the Bible. He whispered, 'It'll be all right, don't be nervous, just follow me, like we did in the rehearsal,' but nobody in the church apart from him and Ian heard me whisper my vows.

Six months before the wedding, I had changed my name by deed poll to Simpson. It was Ian's idea. His first wife was being sticky about the divorce and he wanted me to take his name more than anything in the world, so he and I went to the registry office and I became Jenny Simpson, with or without her consent. When it came to the taking of the wedding vows it was, 'I, Jenny Simpson, take you, Ian Simpson, to be my lawfully wedded husband'. It may have seemed strange to outsiders, but to the two of us standing at the altar looking into each other's eyes while the first bars of 'Praise my Soul, the King of Heaven' struck up, nothing had ever felt so right.

The chauffeur looked almost disappointed when we emerged, arm in arm, smiling. 'Love will find a way,' he muttered sarcastically as he helped me into the car.

We had a reception for thirty-two friends and relatives at my firm's works social club. We couldn't afford any more guests and if Barry and Paula, the landlord and landlady, had not paid for the starter course in the buffet as our wedding present, our guests would have gone home hungry.

It is common practice in the Regiment for anyone getting married to put a note up on the camp notice board so that whoever is around can come along. We couldn't afford to do that in case the whole squadron was in town and cleaned us out, so we only invited two of Ian's friends from the Regiment, one a mate from the Mobility Troop and the other an Irish signaller who went on to become an officer.

Ian really is everything I have ever wanted and more, I thought as I sat next to him at the top table. Friends told me I looked like the cat who had got the cream from the minute the marriage certificate was signed. He was mine, I had got him and I was going to keep him. It was a wonderful day.

After the reception Ian and I drove to the Red Lion Hotel at Weobley, about fourteen miles north west of Hereford. My brothers had sabotaged the car with chicken skins and the hotel room and bed with all manner of surprises, but we didn't care. They had at least been decent enough to order a bottle of champagne for our room which we drank before going down to dinner.

Just as we were leaving the restaurant, the barman told me I had been voted 'Bride of the Month' and qualified for a free Pina Colada. I should never have drunk it, not after the drinks at lunch, the champagne and the wine at dinner. I had barely taken a sip when the combination of wedding-day nerves, excitement and alcohol hit me. I spent the rest of the night and much of the next day throwing up. Some wedding night, Ian complained, and my brothers had even taken the fuse out of the television set in the bedroom.

The next morning I couldn't face the cooked breakfast we had paid for and wouldn't allow Ian to eat his either in case the smell of it on him made me sick again. He drove me to my mother's house and, when I felt a little better, we set off for our week-long honeymoon at the Lizard in Cornwall. I was as sick as a dog all the way down and it took another two days for me to fully recover. Then, when I did feel well enough to go out, I got dreadful sunburn and had to wear a large floppy hat and sun block for the rest of the week. Ian must have been beginning to wish I had done a runner in the church after all.

*　　*　　*

Once the honeymoon was over, it was a question of getting on with the 'routine' of an SAS wife's life. There were weeks on end of having Ian around under my feet – getting in the way at home, picking me up from work, following me around, taking me out to lunch. He was like a fish out of water when he wasn't on an operation or training exercise; he didn't know what to do with himself when he only had tactical and operational matters to get on with at work, nothing that he could really get his teeth into.

Not that he wasn't taking an interest in everything that was going on in the world that might need his attention. Northern Ireland had always held a particular fascination for him and he watched all the news bulletins from the Province with a special interest. Never one for giving anything away, he would register the latest atrocity quite dispassionately, telling me of it over a pub lunch or slipping it into an otherwise mundane conversation. I would study his face to see if he was upset by the news, but it was always difficult to tell.

His diary entries show his attitude at the time:

> 25 Mar 1982: Jenny back at work. I got up at 10am and did the washing. 3 Jkts (2nd Bn) killed in Belfast. No news as yet. 1 injured. Met Jenny for lunch, came home. Sorted out bills etc, went to the bank, did some shopping, went for a run. Muscle pulled in my thigh so didn't do much. 25 minutes and some exercises. Met Jenny from work.

After weeks of having him hanging around, he would suddenly get a call and be off, I never knew for how long. I had to get used to being on my own again, writing him letters every day and going out occasionally with the girls. I had become quite a fitness fanatic and started jogging around Hereford regularly – even if sometimes it was just down to the local chippy for my supper. I joined a local gym and worked out in the evenings, doing weight training and aerobics to try to keep myself in trim. Those were happy nights for me, doing my own thing at the gym and afterwards drinking coffee in the canteen with fellow enthusiasts.

Many of my friends told me how much they envied me my free-dom, never having any set routines or knowing whether I was going to be the single Jenny Simpson or the married Jenny Simpson from one week to the next. I certainly enjoyed the challenge of it, but I was never promiscuous like some of the wives, who took advantage of every trip their husbands went on to sleep their way around Hereford. I had sown my wild oats long before I met Ian and didn't feel the need to do so again now.

Not that I hadn't always enjoyed the company of men and I certainly didn't mind being flirted with by some of the chaps at work or the lads at the gym, but I quickly made it clear to anyone who might have had any other ideas that I was a Regiment wife who wanted to stay that way and I didn't want the Hereford gossip-mongers to have any reason to mention my name in their bulletins.

Besides which, I always missed Ian so dreadfully. Secretly, I even envied some of the non-Regiment wives the normality they enjoyed in their lives – even when they complained that their husbands expected fish on Fridays, beef on Sundays and sex on Saturdays.

I knew the reputation of a lot of the SAS men and how they boasted of having a woman in every port, finding bravado in infidelity, but Ian had never been like that. He had gone through so much guilt about his first marriage breaking up that he was determined not to be like the rest, with three or four ex-wives and a string of unhappy children behind them.

I wasn't stupid. I knew he was always going to get chatted up – he is a charming, handsome man – and I knew he might occasionally be tempted, but my attitude was there was nothing I could do about it if he were, so why worry.

Like all SAS men Ian ran with the pack, going out with a gang of lads from his troop or squadron – generally to get drunk and talk over their most recent experiences – althought he did not do it as often as most. The wives had to accept that their husbands found it difficult to socialise outside the Regiment and found comfort in each other's company, where no questions had to be asked and no answers given. These were men who had faced death together, who had helped each other through times *in extremis.*

Some of his 'pack' experiences became familiar anecdotes at Sunday lunches with friends. One of his favourites was when he and a gang of three lads went to Denmark on exercises. They crossed to Copenhagen on a North Sea ferry, and all got very drunk in the bar en route. Quite quickly they were spotted by a group of middle-aged housewives from Liverpool on a shopping spree. Intrigued as to what this small band of handsome men were doing together, the women moved in on them.

'What's a nice bunch of lads like you doing in a place like this?' asked one of the over-sexed housewives in broad Scouse. The men just laughed and didn't give an answer. For operational security reasons, those in the SAS never tell anyone what they do if they can help it. The IRA and other terrorist groups would be only too happy to get one of them and secrecy has always been the name of the game.

'Well, what do you do?' she asked one of Ian's mates.

'I'm a brain surgeon,' he replied, swigging from his bottle.

'Yeah, right,' she said and moved on to the next victim.

'Come on now, luv, tell me what you all do,' she asked the second man in the group, sidling up to him.

'I'm an astronaut,' he replied with a smile as she raised her eyes to the heavens in disbelief.

She had no better luck with the third man.

'Me? I fly Concorde. Would you like to come for a ride?' he asked as the other blokes sniggered.

By the time she got to Ian, she was far from expecting the truth.

'And you?' she asked him suspiciously.

'Well, you might not believe me,' he said, a twinkle in his eye. 'But I'm in the Special Air Services, you know, the SAS.'

The woman thumped her wine glass down on the bar in anger. 'Jesus Christ!,' she said to them all. 'What do you take me for, some sort of bleedin' idiot?' and stalked off as they fell about laughing.

Ian carried a bleeper when he was on call and could be called up for anything from quick jobs in Northern Ireland to sudden visits to the camp by the Royal Family, or to advise or stand by for potential hostage situations like the Iranian Embassy siege. The idea was that fresh teams would be sent to wherever they were needed from

Hereford, men who were well-rested, ready for action and able to take what equipment they needed from the stores. The job could be a false alarm or genuine, home or abroad, for a few hours or a few weeks, they just didn't know, and neither did their wives.

I came to resent his bleeper. It used to go off at the most inconvenient times and in the strangest places – just as we were about to pay for the big weekly shop in the supermarket, just as we had settled down with a bucket of popcorn in the local cinema or once, just as we had paid to get into Chester Zoo for a day.

I lost count of the times our lovemaking was interrupted by an urgent call to Northern Ireland or to the camp. 'Oh God, not again,' Ian would say, rolling out of bed to fumble for his trousers in the darkness as I giggled under the covers.

'Tell the bastards this is doing nothing for our sex life,' I shouted after him as he ran out of the door once again.

One evening we had just settled down in the Paludrine Club with a litre bottle of wine for the evening, when his bleeper went off. I could hear the blades of the helicopter on the pad outside and I laughed. 'Piss off then,' I told him. 'The wine is all mine.' He asked me to nip home and get his warm weather kit while he found out what the job was, and I marked the bottle and warned everyone in the club to keep their hands off it. I came back and finished it off as the helicopter took him up and away.

Even when Ian was home between jobs, the demands of the Regiment still ruled our lives. Instead of lounging around at home at weekends together or going shopping in the high street like any normal married couple, we would rush around the county taking part in fetes and air displays as a way of honing up on Ian's parachute jumping, something he was still quite nervous about.

We spent almost every Saturday going to fun jumps with a group of friends. The SAS gigs always drew a big crowd and were generally in aid of charity, so it was all in a good cause. But there were times when I resented the relentless nature of his job's demands and wished we could have just curled up in front of the football instead.

Not that the Saturday outings didn't have their moments. One summer's day in the early eighties we were at Pontrilas, the Regiment parachute school for a fete, and I was waiting down on the ground as usual, looking upwards. Ian had only just come back from an exercise abroad and someone else had packed his parachute for him, which always made him anxious. My hands cupped over my eyes to shield them from the sun, I watched all the men falling from the sky, their brightly coloured parachutes billowing out behind them.

'Who's that, jumping on the white parachute?' I asked naively when I saw one skydiver coming down at speed and looking as if he was out of control.

Ian's parachute instructor, who was standing next to me in stunned silence, said, 'I don't want to worry you, Jenny, but that is the reserve parachute, and it's your husband.'

Ian's main parachute hadn't worked and at the last minute he was forced to rely on the reserve. He couldn't steer properly with a reserve and was coming down at an alarming angle. As he got closer and closer to the ground, it became apparent to everyone that he was going to miss the Drop Zone and was heading dangerously quickly towards the car park.

A young woman was sunbathing on the bonnet of her MG sports car and for a moment it seemed as if Ian was going to land right on top of her. I yelled to her to get out of the way and she scrambled from the car. Ian ended up in a tree, from which he had to be cut down in a rather undignified fashion. He was never very good at hitting the Drop Zone.

At a similar event at a college in Gloucester he missed the Drop Zone again, this time because of high winds. He ended up on a railway embankment half a mile away, just as a train was pulling into the station. He had just missed the five o'clock express to Cardiff. I was about the last one left in the college grounds by the time he limped into view, carrying his 'chute. After that a friend at work drew a cartoon of Ian in all his kit, his parachute trailing behind him, asking a British Rail inspector at a station ticket office, 'One adult and a parachute, please.' It hangs on the wall in Ian's study.

His worst experience in the air happened in Cyprus when he was there on a covert mission to investigate the possibilities of the SAS freeing the British hostages being held in Beirut. Ian had been on team at Hereford and was suddenly sent over to Cyprus with a number of Head Sheds (senior officers) who flew on from there to the Lebanon to speak to advisers at the British Embassy about the logistics of a possible strike. Ian was not alone in considering any such mission to be suicidal, but he had little choice but to obey orders and wait for the word.

Fortunately for him, his bosses also came to the same conclusion and called the whole thing off. Ian and the others were told to take a couple of days' R&R (rest and relaxation) which they did. Not content with the dangers he had just been about to face against the full force of the Hezbollah, Ian decided to take up a friend's offer to do some sports parachuting while he was waiting to hitch a ride home. He jumped out of a plane at 12,000 feet to find that he had packed himself a malfunctioning parachute. Angry at himself for packing it incorrectly – he realised half-way down, travelling at 150 miles per hour, that this must have been the case – he yanked and yanked at it for several seconds, losing thousands of feet in height.

It was only at the very last minute, as the people below watched aghast, that he looked down and saw the ground coming up at speed and realised that unless he wanted to die in about a minute, he had better pull on his reserve. It flew up behind him at just a few hundred feet and he landed violently and far too fast, nearly causing himself serious injury. He had come close to disaster.

He was so shaken by what happened that he went on a two-day bender, getting totally obliterated. Ian didn't tell me about his near-miss jump or the reason for that visit to Cyprus until years afterwards. He said he had thought it might distract me from my decorating.

After these experiences in the air Ian was always very careful when packing his parachute and took ages to make sure all the folds were overlapping each other correctly. A few months after his trip to Cyprus, before another charity fun jump, he painstakingly packed his parachute on the living room floor, taking ages to make sure that it was folded exactly the right way. He put it into its pack and then laid it carefully on the front door step with the rest of his kit.

I was packing up the car for the trip and, since it was a cold and windy day, was dashing from the car to the house to keep warm. I bent down and picked up the pack, lifting it up by what I thought was the handle but was in fact the rip cord that triggers the release of the parachute. It slipped from its pack and, as the wind caught it, started to open out into the street. Hanging on for dear life, I shouted for Ian to come and help me. He came running out of the house, cursing and swearing at me and desperately trying to grab hold of this huge flapping expanse of parachute silk before I ended up in mid-Wales with it.

It took ages to get it under control and we had to ask passers-by for help. We had virtually stopped the traffic in Hereford by the time we got it back in the bag. Grabbing the pack firmly under his arm and flashing me the blackest of looks, Ian headed back towards the house to carefully repack his parachute.

'So much for us telling the neighbours you're a tax inspector,' I quipped. Ian threw the pack in through the front door and gave chase. I was half-way to Leominster before he caught up with me.

Learning to live with someone in the SAS, and with the secrecy that comes with it, had already become a cause for much mirth between us. The tax inspector line was always a good one. No one ever asks any more questions – they just sort of go red, say, 'Oh, that's interesting', and sidle away as quickly as possible. In a social situation the only solution is to lie, only Ian isn't terribly good at that. He tells people he is a British Airways steward (which explains his permanent suntan) or that he fixes cars or is a greengrocer, whatever comes into his head first.

The only problem with that is that his face goes blank when some housewife pipes up, 'Can you explain why artichokes are so expensive?' or her husband asks Ian to go and look at his troublesome fan belt. Sometimes Ian jokes with people and says, 'If I tell you I will have to kill you,' but then they just think he is odd. Most people accept what he says, but there is always some nosy so-and-so who wants to know more.

Of course, both of us would love to say exactly what it is that he does. It would really score a few points socially. Everyone wants to be able to say that they know someone in the SAS. I would love to boast about my husband, the hero, and tell how he fought in the

Falklands and trained those who were involved in the Iranian Embassy siege. But you can't. You have to pretend that you are just an ordinary couple, leading ordinary lives.

Once Ian decided to wind up an old boy we met on holiday who was determined to find out how he could afford a holiday when he looked so scruffy. (Ian was still working undercover in Northern Ireland at the time and was unshaven and unkempt.) On the last day of our holiday, this man – who was the spitting image of Warren Mitchell as Alf Garnett – approached Ian.

'Come on, sonny Jim, tell me the truth. What's your job?' he said.

'What do you think I do?' asked Ian.

'Bugger all by the state you're in,' replied the old soldier.

'Well, actually, I am in the Army,' replied Ian.

'Army, my foot,' replied the veteran, indignantly. 'They would have you on the parade ground on the first day looking like that.'

Ian leaned over and whispered, 'Didn't you see me on the balcony, then?'

Quick as a flash and without the slightest appreciation of what Ian was trying to tell him, the old man said, 'Which one were you then? Romeo or Juliet?'

Ian never tried to outwit an old soldier again.

Settling into married life wasn't quite the same for us as it might have been for any other recently married young couple. Ian was only just back from Northern Ireland when we tied the knot and within weeks he was off again, this time to Kenya for three months, his first post-Selection experience in a jungle environment. He was to arrive back home from that trip only to go straight off to the Falklands.

Ian grew to love the jungle more than anywhere else on earth, for its peace and beauty. A restless soul by nature, he revelled in the tranquillity of the world's wildest places: even if he had to pick blood-sucking leeches off his private parts, the mosquitoes were a pain in the arse, and he came to loathe and detest scorpions and hornets, the nests of which he seemed to be forever stumbling into. When all the marching and the wading through rivers and the crawling on his belly was over and it was time for bed, he slept better

School photograph of me, aged five, which Ian plastered all over Hereford on my fortieth birthday

Ian, aged three, holding a toy gun and wearing a SAS-style beret. He has never looked back

Ian on his first trip
to Northern Ireland
with the SAS in 1979

The SAS storming of the Iranian Embassy in 1980.
Ian had trained those involved

ABOVE: The remote County Tyrone home of Bernadette McAliskey, attacked by Loyalist gunmen as Ian and two fellow soldiers arrived to help. He saved her life by stemming the bleeding from her gunshot wounds

LEFT: Bernadette McAliskey leaving hospital on crutches

ABOVE: Ian and me on
our wedding day, 1981

LEFT: Early days,
Christmas dinner, 1982

HMS *Intrepid*, the vessel on which Ian spent much of his time during the Falklands War and from which he watched the crash of the Sea King helicopter

BELOW:
The airfield at Pebble Island, in the Falklands, the morning after the successful dawn strike by the SAS on Argentine planes, 16 May 1982

A Sea King helicopter similar to the one in which nineteen men lost their lives during a routine hop across the water between ships, 19 May 1982

BELOW: The special memorial wall at St Martin's graveyard for those who died in the helicopter crash

INSET: The stone marking the start of the SAS section of the cemetery at St Martin's Church, Hereford

22 Special Air Service Regiment "God rest their souls."

LEFT:
Corporal Paul Bunker, a close friend, who died in the helicopter crash

BELOW:
Paul Bunker's memorial stone, St Martin's, where I still place flowers

24122095
CPL W. J. BEGLEY
15·4·50 – 19·5·82

24145047
CPL P. A. BUNKER
26·1·54 – 19·5·82

24369281
CPL R. A. BURNS
31·7·59 – 19·5·82

PAUL
APART BUT
ALWAYS TOGETHER
ALL MY LOVE
VANDA

there than anywhere else, eight or nine hours at a stretch, and it was under the green canopy of the rainforests that he felt most calm.

He had his most moving personal experience while on a jungle exercise. He was in Brunei acting as lead scout – going ahead of the other men to scout for possible camp sites and look for military personnel – when he came to a clearing in the middle of nowhere and found himself face to face with a wild orang-utan. He later described the encounter as almost mystical. There he was, camouflaged up to the eyeballs and weighed down by his kit, and just a few feet away was this huge orange-haired male ape staring back at him, a branch he was eating in his hand.

The pair of them stood stock still and watched each other for several minutes, Ian blinking through his sweat and camouflage paint, and the ape blinking back at him with his long brown eyelashes. Ian did not want the moment to end, but the ape suddenly stood up and lumbered off into the jungle. Ian sat alone in the clearing for over an hour afterwards, savouring the experience.

He had several close encounters with wildlife on his travels. In Kenya, where he went for free-fall and jungle training, he came face to face with everything from elephants to monkeys. He loved the animals and the scenery and wrote fulsomely about it all to me, promising to bring me back one day on a holiday, though he never did.

There was more to the jungle exercises than nature-watching, however, and Ian had some bad experiences. A friend of his nearly died in a mid-air parachute collision and Ian was called to the scene to administer emergency first aid and co-ordinate the transportation of this seriously injured man down the mountainside. It was the worst injury Ian had seen and he was almost out of his depth. For several moments he thought he had lost his friend.

On a jungle exercise in the Far East Ian contracted malaria for the first time, though he didn't realise he had it until after he got home. He was pleased to see me but he said he had a cold and felt a bit tired after all his travelling. Neither of us thought anything more about it, I was just glad to have him home again. On his first night back, we went to the Paludrine Club for a drink. We weren't planning on staying long, but Ian had promised one of the lads he'd join him for his wedding party.

He sat at a table while I went up to the bar to get us a couple of drinks. I looked round to see him stand up – and keel over. I rushed over to where he was lying, unconscious, across a table and a chair. A couple of the other lads helped me get him to his feet. At that moment one of the camp's most legendary drinkers walked into the club with a couple of mates. He took one look at Ian, being supported by me and two others and said, 'Bloody hell, lads, looks like I've got some serious competition tonight. We'd better try and catch up.'

We carried Ian home to bed. He was delirious and obviously very ill. The camp medic identified the symptoms of malaria straight away, and came three times during that first night. I sat by Ian's side, mopping his brow and keeping the bedcovers over his quivering body. I was desperately worried, I had never seen him so ill, he didn't even know I was there. The medic said if he wasn't better the following morning, he would have to go straight to hospital. I stayed up the whole night, wondering if he should go sooner. I had heard of men dying of malaria, full-grown SAS soldiers being felled like oak trees by the mosquito-carried fever.

I fell asleep in the early hours of the morning. When I awoke I was relieved to find that Ian's fever had broken. He was still seriously ill and had to stay in bed for several days, but the worst was over. He lost over a stone in weight and was quite weak for some time, but I nursed him through to a full recovery. By the end of it I was utterly exhausted.

On my first day back at work I was fetching a cup of coffee from the canteen when I bumped into a girlfriend from the computer department, someone who didn't know what Ian's job was.

'Hi, Jenny, how are you?' she said. 'I haven't seen you for a few days.'

'No,' I said, carefully. 'My husband's been ill.'

'Oh dear, I am sorry. Was it that flu?' she asked. 'My Bill's been down with that and he has been utterly miserable. You know what men are like when they get the slightest cold.'

I thought back to the previous week's vigil and the delirious, sweating, thrashing man that I had to pin down as I laid wet towels on his forehead and prayed that he would get through it.

'Yes,' I told her. 'It was the flu. See you.'

A month after he came back from the Falklands, Ian had a vasectomy. We had discussed having children, but I didn't think I ever wanted them, Ian had his son David from his first marriage and we both felt that we wanted the time we had together to be exclusively ours. That feeling was brought into even sharper focus by the Falklands War. Some of the blokes came home and said all they wanted was to start a family and know that they would leave a legacy, but Ian and I felt very differently.

The last thing we wanted to do was to bring a child into the world when neither of us felt that we could cope with the extra responsibility. Ian was more relieved than I was when we went ahead and made the commitment. In times of conflict, he had seen men with families worrying about what it would mean for them if their breadwinner were killed. He believed it took the edge off their fighting spirit. And when friends were killed and Ian went round to see the widows afterwards, it was always the faces of the little children he remembered the most.

As far as he was concerned, he only had me to worry about and he wanted to keep it that way. David was no longer a daily part of his life, although Ian has always hoped that they will be closer when he is old enough to make his own decisions in life.

As for me, I had sisters and brothers galore all with children to love, including Lisa, my niece, who came into my life when I was young and was special to me from the moment I set eyes on her little fat legs. Her mum Dotty, my eldest sister, has always been very close to me and she has been big-hearted enough to let me share Lisa and allow her to have a place in my life. Later, when Lisa had her own children, I had all the joys of surrogate motherhood once again when I became the regular baby-sitter and a proud great-aunt for her daughter Rhona and son Jack.

At the time of the vasectomy, my main priority was Ian. I had got him, I wanted to keep him and I didn't want anything else to get in the way. If it was what he wanted then that was fine by me. I didn't feel in any way pressurised by him. It was something I had discussed with my friend Sue years before and with Vanda more recently and none of us had ever wanted children.

We asked our GP to arrange the operation, but he was a Catholic and refused so we had to pay for it to be done privately at the Nuffield House private clinic in Hereford. I went with Ian and when they had him on the trolley, wheeling him down to theatre, he was laughing and joking with the nurses all the way.

'I'm not having my tonsils out,' he complained. 'Shouldn't I be up the other way?'

I will never forget the price, it cost £101 – which was a small fortune in those days. We always joked that the £1 was for the cup of tea afterwards.

To keep me company when he was away, Ian gave me a German Shepherd called Zorba, a massive shaggy dog whom we both adored. Zorba followed me everywhere, he was my knight in shining armour and Ian always included a 'kiss for the pup' in his letters. When Ian was away he carried a photograph of me and Zorba in a small frame that he put by his bedside – whether it was a hammock in the jungle or a mud-filled ditch. When I saw it, I said, 'That's nice, darling. What a lovely picture.' He replied, 'Yes, it's the best one we have of the pup, isn't it?'

Ian, Zorba and I were a family. We didn't need children and we didn't need anyone else, but on one of our early wedding anniversaries, Ian turned up at my office carrying a huge box with ribbons all around it. When he lifted the lid I was gobsmacked. There, sitting in the box, was a tiny German Shepherd puppy.

The girls who worked with me looked up and melted. They immediately christened her Annie for anniversary. I loved Zorba and didn't want another dog and I told Ian so, but the girls thought I was being terribly ungrateful and nudged me into submission. I picked Annie up and she licked my face and they knew then that she had won my heart. Before I had even got her home, I was in love with her, although I am not sure Zorba took to her so well.

Poor old Zorba, we lost him several years later and it nearly broke our hearts. He became ill very suddenly and the vet said he would have to be put down. Fortunately Ian was home or I would never have coped.

I had never seen Ian so upset. He locked himself away in his study for four days, only coming out now and again and always in his regulation-issue sunglasses to hide his red eyes. He wouldn't eat and he wouldn't talk about it. He grieved as if he had lost his best friend. He has always felt a great affinity with animals, something he believed was in his gypsy blood.

In early 1983, Ian was sent away to jungle camp in Belize. It was something he was really looking forward to – three months back in the jungle with a lot of mates who had been out in Northern Ireland and the South Atlantic with him. He was, by this time, slowly coming to terms with Paul Bunker's death.

The chief purpose of the trip was to train the resident battalions about survival and attack in the jungle. The Regiment effectively hired itself out to foreign countries for exercises like this. It was good for the men - it kept their training up and allowed them to travel the world at the times when there wasn't much for them to do at home, and it was great for the foreign troops because they got the best training in the world from the men who knew exactly what they were doing.

He packed his bergen for the journey, and, at the last minute, threw in the TACBE (tactical beacon) radio he had taken from Paul Bunker's kit which had been recovered from all the equipment carried across to the *Intrepid* before the helicopter crash.

It was a military-issue radio, not part of Paul's personal belongings – which had all been sent back to Vanda. Paul had been issued with the radio as troop commander but had already lent it to Ian on a previous mission and Ian had considered it a legitimate prize after his death. He knew Paul would have taken it from his kit if things had been the other way round and he also knew how useful it would be to his work. He didn't think twice about it. It was so unimportant to him, that he didn't even mention it to me.

The Belize trip started off well and Ian was glad to be back in the jungle. The training was successful and they even killed and ate a crocodile as part of their survival techniques. Ian was looking forward to meeting up with me in Florida afterwards for a two-week holiday. Just before he left for Miami, however, there was an incident at the camp which left something of a bad odour. Some cash, about £100, had gone missing from the troop fund, which was kept in the main office of the camp. The troop fund is something which all the lads chip into so that they can buy whatever they need by way of beer, cigarettes or food.

Everyone started blaming everyone else for the theft, although many suspected the native soldiers more than anyone else within the troop. It was an unfortunate incident but Ian's attitude was, Never mind, it is not important, let's all chip in a few quid each to replace it and forget about it. Against Ian's advice, the new young troop commander at the camp decided to make an issue of the theft, and – going strictly by the rule book – he threatened to call in the Special Investigations Branch, which everyone feared would open up a whole new can of worms, as almost everyone had something they should not have had.

Ian tried to calm everybody down about the missing money, but in the end he decided it wasn't worth getting involved and leaving them to it, flew to Miami to meet me for our holiday. I came through the arrivals gate at Miami airport to find him waiting, a rose between his teeth, singing, 'Welcome to America, señorita!' We had a wonderful two weeks and then we met up with his troop again in the States to hitch a ride home with a troop of the Royal Anglians in the belly of a VC10. Ian had left all his kit behind in Belize before the holiday and had asked the lads to bring it out with them, which they did.

We sat together in the VC10 on the way home, chatting and laughing. We were collected at Brize Norton by a driver from the

Regiment who took us back to Hereford. Nothing was said by anyone all the way to the camp.

The following morning Ian went to work and was summoned to the Squadron OC's office almost as soon as he arrived. Mystified, he went along, to see a stony-faced patrol commander waiting for him in the corridor outside the office.

'What's all this about?' he asked the patrol commander, with whom he had just spent six weeks in Belize.

'You'll find out soon enough,' came the frosty reply. Ian suddenly felt like a schoolboy waiting outside the headmaster's study for a caning. When the door was opened and he stepped inside to see a number of senior officers standing around, he knew it was serious. He stood to attention in front of his OC's desk.

'Corporal Ian Simpson,' said the OC, 'you have been summoned here today to face a charge of theft.'

Ian spun round to look at his troop commander. What was all this about? Surely they weren't charging him for the missing money? This was ludicrous. He hadn't taken it and there wasn't any proof to say he had.

'During a routine search of your kit at jungle training camp, Belize, this was found.' The OC pointed to Paul Bunker's green-painted TACBE radio with its distinctively long aerial. 'It is Regiment property and the serial number identifies it as belonging to Corporal Paul Bunker, killed in action in the Falklands.'

Ian couldn't believe it. He was devastated. He felt he had been betrayed by people he had considered his mates. After all they had been through in the Falklands together not one of them had stood up for him or made any attempt to protect his reputation. The Regiment was famous for pinching things from each other's kit, it was one of the perks. He couldn't think of a single fellow soldier who had a clean slate in that regard. He had even watched one man steal the kit of a seriously injured soldier Ian was trying to give medical aid to after a failed parachute jump. He felt as if he was really being charged with the theft of the money, not the radio, but they had picked on the radio to make their point.

He wanted to rant and rave, to ease the pain he felt in his chest, but he knew there was little point in even explaining the background to his possession of Paul's radio or trying to justify it. The matter had come this far now and he knew under Army regulations that there was no turning back. Strictly speaking, he was guilty, there was no room for mitigation, and there was nothing he could say that would do any good. He just had to bite his tongue and wait for the ordeal to end. He continued standing silently to attention.

'Whilst I appreciate that this radio was taken not for your own personal use or for resale but to help you in your professional capacity,' continued the OC, 'I cannot countenance theft of any kind and have to treat this in the strongest possible way. Do you plead guilty or not guilty?'

Ian looked across to one of the other officers standing in the room. He was wearing one of the Goretex jackets they had all been sent in the Falklands but had been ordered to hand back. Here was his senior officer telling him theft wasn't allowed while another officer was wearing Regiment-issue goods in front of his very eyes.

'Guilty as charged,' Ian replied, as the officer in the Goretex jacket blinked uncomfortably under his steady gaze.

The OC fined him £200 and the radio was confiscated but, much more seriously, a regimental entry of the theft was made on his record – to remain there throughout his career.

When I walked into the house from work that night, I could tell immediately that there was something wrong. His eyes registered pain, physical, tangible pain, and when he told me what had happened, fighting to control the pitch of his voice, my heart bled for him.

I felt helpless. I didn't know what I could do but give him all my love and support. Vanda was furious and far more vocal. She made an official complaint that Paul would have wanted Ian to have the radio, but to no avail. The theft charge stood and Ian felt as if all fingers were pointing at him for the missing money. I had never seen him so hurt.

I took him to a friend's caravan in Borth on the North Wales coast and we locked ourselves away for a weekend. He was hit with the sudden realisation that he was amongst people who did not seem to share his views about honour and he said he wanted to die. He lay in my arms that night and wept. 'How could they think that of me?' he asked. His overwhelming belief in honour sometimes seemed so naive and old fashioned to me. I didn't know what to say.

I tried to remind him what he had always told me about the Regiment. That when you have a group of highly competitive young men together in a restricted environment, people who have surpassed hundreds of others to get to where they are by being selfish, bloody-minded and completely focused, there are bound to be problems.

Everything about getting into the SAS is based on looking after Number One, and even though they have to work together in troops, they are awesomely independent and fearsomely competitive. It was that competitive streak that had stopped the others speaking up for him. None of them wanted to compromise his own position, even if it meant letting down a mate. They simply didn't understand about common bonds of friendship, or if they did, their ambition overruled it. It wasn't in their nature or, if it was, it had been drummed out of them.

I had been here with Ian before in a way. After the Falklands, when he was facing up to Paul's death, I had talked and talked to him, tried to draw him out, to get him to open up, grieve, and then accept what had happened. That time I had got him through the process relatively painlessly, this time it was even harder. I could see the pain behind his eyes. I knew he lay awake at night, his breathing rapid as his anger and distress increased the beating of his heart. I heard him pacing the kitchen floor in the middle of the night, like a trapped animal trying to find a way out.

I honestly thought he would walk out of the SAS. His heart was no longer in it. He kept himself away from the other guys and they from him. I hoped it would all calm down with time, instead it got worse. Within days of the news of his charge breaking around the camp, we discovered that we had been blackballed by his troop commander and friend, David, and his wife, Karen, the woman I had gone to after the helicopter crash. We were apparently considered social outcasts. As I had predicted, people didn't want to be associated with us in case their own promotion prospects were affected.

Vanda, who still saw Karen occasionally, tried to persuade her not to treat us like that, but Karen said that David had told her not to have anything to do with me and she had no choice but to obey him. I felt like going round to Karen's house and having it out with her. It was like being in the school playground all over again with everyone laughing at my accent. I was caught in the middle of something that was not of my making and I couldn't see a way out of it.

I persuaded Ian to let us attend a troop sergeant's dance we had bought tickets for long before the incident, in open defiance of the charge and the blackballing. It was an extremely uncomfortable night, we felt as if everyone was watching us, whispering about us behind our backs, but I was determined not to allow the buggers to think they had ground us down even if, in truth, they had. Ian didn't want to go, it took all my powers of persuasion to get him there, but once he walked in the door he put on a brave front and pretended to be enjoying himself.

Karen and David were there, and at first we ignored each other. Later Karen, who had drunk too much, followed me into the ladies' toilet and started to try to explain, rather tearfully, why she felt she had to obey David. I turned on her and snapped, 'Don't waste your breath'. She apologised again and again, but I told her if the shoe had been on the other foot and Ian had told me not to talk to her, I would have told him, 'On yer bike'.

I was angry and upset for Ian's sake, it bothered me immensely that this kind, sweet man who didn't have a dishonourable bone in his body should have his reputation so unfairly tarnished. I worried for the effect this would have on him, so soon after the trauma of the Falklands War, and prayed it was something we could overcome.

It shattered all our ideals about the Regiment being above petty internal politics and personal vendettas. It made us both realise that it was no better or worse than any other workplace, with just as many jealous and ambitious people all prepared to stab each other in the back to save their own necks. The daggers were well and truly out this time, only they weren't winged ones.

Ian thought he didn't have a friend in the world, and insisted that we lock ourselves away, avoiding the Paludrine Club and other venues where Regimental colleagues might have been. He felt he had been branded a thief in front of the whole town. They might as well have put him in the village stocks and thrown rotten tomatoes at him as far as he was concerned.

Just before he went away to Belize, he had been asked if he would like to go on Training Wing, being responsible for training up the new recruits for Selection. We talked about the offer in light of recent events and he decided that he might as well accept the job so as to get away from regular working contact with the men whom he felt had betrayed him. It was one of his most important career decisions and here he was being pushed into it by events largely beyond his control. I wished we had been given more time to consider what it would mean for us both.

But first there was Fiji to get through – a two-month jungle trip with the same men who had been to Belize – and Ian was dreading it. As the date loomed, he became more and more despondent and I couldn't find a way of getting through to him. He wasn't sleeping well, he had little appetite and his mood swings were getting me down.

'Why don't you just bloody well quit?' I finally exploded at him, two nights before he was due to leave for the airport. 'You can't go on like this, it isn't worth it.'

He looked up at me from the sofa in shock. Despite all that he was feeling and the pain of what had happened, I don't think it had occurred to him before that moment that he could quit the SAS.

'Well, what's stopping you?' I asked him defiantly, my hands on my hips.

I didn't know if I wanted him to leave or not but I knew that something was going to have to give, and soon, before he destroyed us both.

'We could go and live in America, like we always wanted to and you could be your own boss, doing security work,' I told him. His eyes flickered. 'Then you could kiss goodbye to this lot and never have to face them again.'

I knew that the thought of running away would not appeal and he clenched his jaw at my suggestion. 'Well, whatever you do, just do it soon before we both go bloody mad,' I said and stalked out of the room to make the supper.

Two days later, his bergen was in the hallway. I came out of the bedroom and looked down the stairs to see it there. Ian was standing by it, and he looked up at me helplessly. Without speaking, he slid down the wall and started sobbing. I ran down the stairs and put my arms around him as he held his head in his hands and wept aloud.

'Are you ill?' I asked. 'Should I call a doctor?' I had never seen him cry like this before. He was shaking so much, I thought he might have caught malaria again.

'I don't want to go,' he sobbed. 'I want to stay here with you.' He sounded like his big heart was breaking.

'You've got to go, Ian,' I said firmly. 'It's your job. Just go and do what you do best and then come back home to me, babe,' I whispered into his hair. 'I'll be waiting.' I felt his hot tears on my cheek and held his face in my hands. He looked like a little boy.

'I don't want to go,' he sobbed again. 'Please don't make me.'

I pushed him away from me and opened the front door before my own courage failed me. I knew that I had to get him back up onto the horse that had thrown him.

'The sooner you go, the sooner you'll be back, now get going,' I said.

He looked so vulnerable that I longed to lock and bolt the door and keep him with me forever. But I knew that wouldn't solve the problem.

'Go on,' I said, gently. 'You've got to face them one day.'

He grabbed his bergen and was gone. He didn't even kiss me goodbye. I felt terrible as I closed the door behind him and I prayed out loud to God to help him get through the next eight weeks without killing someone.

That trip to Fiji was Ian's Waterloo, and mine too in many ways. He felt as emotionally low there as he had ever felt in his life, and he struggled with his mind to stay in control. Much of his time was spent alone, lying in his A-frame, the makeshift hammock slung between an A-shaped frame of poles, which he erected on the far reaches of the camp, away from all the others. It was only by a supreme effort of will that he was able to work alongside his troop when he had to. He simply didn't trust them any more. At night he went back to his A-frame, to eat and drink alone, while the rest of the men all sat together around the main camp fire.

His letters spoke of his anguish and mental battles to decide whether to leave or stay. 'I have pretty much isolated myself here and the jungle is not the place to do that,' he wrote. 'But it is the only way I feel I can get through this. I have earned the right to be here amongst these people, and I don't have to prove myself to anyone. It isn't affecting me professionally, in many ways I am even doing better than usual in case anyone dare accuse me of not doing something right, but it is very tough.'

Reading these letters I felt as if I was there with him, living through his pain, his isolation and his fear. I wished him good thoughts with all my heart. I tossed and turned at night as much as he did, lying awake before the dawn, waiting for the birds to start singing.

The jungle environment was the worst he had ever been in, almost impenetrable in places, and the trip was not successful for a number of reasons. One of their local Fijian guides drowned when he slipped and fell into a fast-flowing river, the number and persistence of insects was almost unbearable even for hardened soldiers used to the jungle, and they had great difficulty getting enough good food and fresh water to eat and drink.

A soldier was bitten by a snake and then meningitis swept through the camp and Ian found himself nursing some of the very men he felt like killing. He had to arrange for three men to be casevac'd (casualty evacuated) out, one of them so ill from the meningitis that had spread into his brain that Ian feared he might die. Ian himself felt physically unwell, perhaps it was only his feelings of anger which stopped the fever overwhelming him.

His saving grace was the arrival of another troop, who camped a little way away from them in the jungle. Ian started to visit their camp in the evenings and became friendly with a man called Geoff who he had met before but hadn't really got to know. With Geoff's troop, Ian was able to practise some of the 'hearts and minds' techniques that the SAS are so famous for – infiltrating local communities and winning their hearts and minds – but which they rarely get a chance to put to practical use.

The troop travelled up country to a remote Fijian settlement and, communicating with hand signals and through the assistance of a friendly missionary nun, they were welcomed into the camp's long house (the equivalent of a straw-roofed town hall). There was a special ceremony laid on for them, in which they had to drink cava, a revolting concoction made of wood shavings and distilled alcohol. The villagers prepared a huge feast for them, and the menu included monkey brains and snake.

Using only hand signals, Ian managed to convey the story of the Falklands War to these people, explaining how the British chief Mrs Thatcher sent her bravest warriors to defend their islands thousands of miles away. The native Fijians thought this was wonderful and were in awe of the formidable woman tribal chief.

With the help of memorable events like those, and with the friendship of people like Geoff, Ian gradually started to face up to the disastrous consequences of the theft charge. The jungle was, as always, a tremendously calming influence on him and he felt himself relaxing and beginning to accept that what had happened wasn't, after all, the end of the world.

The clincher came when one of the most senior officers in the adjacent troop, one of those known in the Regiment as 'the old and the bold', gave Ian some advice that he never forgot. After hearing what had happened, he told him, 'You can either run away from it and live forever in the shadow of the shame, or you can stand and fight, face up to the enemy and all their weaponry, and prove the buggers wrong. I know what I would do.'

During the long, still nights lying in his A-frame under the jungle canopy, Ian chose the harder option. In what was undoubtedly the toughest decision of his career and probably the bravest, he decided to stay in the Regiment and prove his doubters wrong. He had fought his Waterloo and won.

\*        \*        \*

Sitting at home, waiting for his decision, was one of the hardest things I ever had to do as Ian's wife. All my instincts were screaming at me to beg him to leave. To take him away to a place of safety, where he couldn't be killed by enemy fire or tortured from within. To mould him into someone who expected fish on Friday, beef on Sunday and sex on Saturday.

When he wrote and told me he had chosen to stay, I wept, mainly from relief that the waiting was over, but partly from sadness at the knowledge that he had chosen the tougher of the two possible paths for us both.

I read and reread his letter and reminded myself that nobody had forced me to marry someone in the SAS. Standing in the vestibule of that church in Hereford only two years earlier, I had been given a choice and I too had chosen the tougher path. I knew then that I was going to have to stand by my decision, whether I liked it or not.

The stress of helping Ian cope and of waiting for his decision, finally came out in a physical manifestation of the pain I was feeling inside. After several weeks of sleepless nights and restless days and having hardly ever suffered from a headache before in my life, I started to get blinding migraines, pain that I had never experienced before, pain that I took to bed with me at night and woke up with in the morning, pain that no pill seemed able to cure.

I didn't write to tell Ian of the headaches. I didn't want to add to his burden, but as they became increasingly frequent and ferocious I started to worry that there might be something seriously wrong with me. I was taking more and more time off work, I was unable to concentrate and sometimes hardly able to see. I would lie in a darkened room at home, the curtains drawn, crying aloud for the pain to go away. I couldn't eat, I couldn't sleep. I found it hard even to write my nightly letters to Ian.

When he came home, he could see immediately that there was something wrong. I had lost over a stone, I looked pale and tired and had dark rings under my eyes.

'What's the matter, babe?' he asked me at the airport. 'Why didn't you tell me you were ill? What is it, what's wrong?'

I told him about the headaches and said I hadn't wanted to worry him. I assured him I would be fine now that he was home and through the worst of it, and I smiled gratefully when he said he had decided to take me on a fortnight's holiday to Greece as soon as he could book his leave.

But the headaches didn't stop. Even in Greece, they pounded my brain nightly. I spent several nights alone in the hotel room, a damp cloth over my face, while Ian was in a local bar, drinking with an English couple we had met. Nothing in his medical training had prepared him to deal with such overwhelming distress, pain that seemed to be untouchable by any medication in his kit.

We returned from Greece in pensive mood. Ian told me the night before we left that he was taking me to the doctor as soon as we got back.

'I don't want to worry you, babe,' he said, knowing full well that he would, 'but I think you should have a brain scan.'

He telephoned and made an appointment the following evening and took me to the surgery. 'Do you want me to come in with you or sit in the waiting room?' he asked. I told him I wanted to go in alone.

I sat nervously in front of the female doctor I had only ever met once before in all the years I had been registered at that surgery and told her I didn't like doctors. She smiled and asked me why I had come.

'I've been getting terrible headaches,' I said. 'They've been going on for four months now and they are driving me insane. My husband is a medic and, well, he thinks I should have a brain scan.' I looked up at her fearfully.

She put down her pen, leaned back in her chair and said gently, 'Tell me a little bit more about your husband.' I wondered what she wanted to know. 'Is he in the Regiment?' I nodded.

'Do you worry about him at all?' she continued. 'Have you lost anyone you both know?'

I don't know what it was she said that started me off, but the floodgates opened. Once I had started crying I didn't seem to be able to stop. She reached forward and patted my hand and remained silent as I wept and wept, waiting for me to catch my breath and answer her questions.

I told her that yes, Ian was away a lot, that yes, I did worry about him. I tried to explain to her what it had been like during his time in Northern Ireland and after the Falklands and then Belize, how much I had missed him and felt for him. I told her about the vasectomy and the decision not to have children, about Vanda and how much we all missed Paul, I told her how much I wished things could be different.

She was wonderful, a really good doctor. My ten-minute appointment lasted nearly an hour. She seemed to have forgotten all the other patients waiting outside. Gently, she coaxed information out of me, she asked me to tell her more, she listened carefully to my replies and jotted down a few notes. When my tears had all but dried up and I had used up her supply of tissues, she held my hand and told me not to worry any more.

'There is really no point in me sending you for a brain scan, you know,' she said. 'We wouldn't find a thing. All you needed was a really good cry and now all you need is some special care and attention. Now where is that husband of yours?'

She led me out, red-eyed and sniffing, into the waiting room and handed me over to Ian, who jumped up from his seat the minute the door opened. He was frantic when he saw my face, he reached out and pulled me to him as he asked what was wrong.

'Your wife isn't physically ill, Mr Simpson,' the doctor told him rather stiffly. 'But I think she may be on the brink of a nervous breakdown. I am afraid you are going to have to start taking a lot better care of her from now on. I have a lot of Regiment wives in here and a lot of them suffer from extreme anxiety. Jenny is in dire need of your help. It is up to you now to help her get better.'

She handed him a prescription for diazepam tranquillisers she had written out for me in her room and told him to make sure I took them for a month before bringing me back to see her. I thanked her and allowed Ian to lead me out to the car.

I felt completely drained, as if my outpourings had somehow cleansed me of all pain, all emotion. I went straight home to bed, unable to answer Ian's questions or to respond to his caresses, unable to care whether or not he understood what it was the doctor had told him. I took one of the tranquillisers he had collected for me from the chemist and slept better that night than I had done in months.

But we both knew what was coming and that it couldn't be avoided. Ian was due to go away the following morning for six weeks free-fall training in America, leaving me to fend for myself. He was wracked with guilt about it, but there was nothing he could do. He was on Training Wing now and this was one of his first trips in his new job. It was up to him to take the trainees out to America, there was no one who could take his place, and – particularly with his recent troubles – no way he could get out of it.

'I don't know what to do for the best, Jen,' he said, looking at me with a pained expression. 'I want to stay and look after you, but I can't.' I still felt too tired to talk or even answer him. I offered no resistance when he packed me a suitcase and drove me to my parents' house.

'Look after her for me while I am away,' he told my mum, as he stood at the doorway ready to leave. 'She needs us all right now and I'll take over just as soon as I get back.' He blew me a kiss and paused on the doorstep as if he was about to change his mind. Then he ran out into the pouring rain and got into the car. I smeared away the condensation on the lounge window to watch as his car pulled away. So much for all that special care the doctor had asked him to give me.

I took the Diazepam for a total of five days. They made me feel horribly strange, in limbo somehow, as if I was floating outside my body. I felt slightly sick and still had a headache so I threw the rest away. I moved back home the same day and decided it was time to get myself back into shape. I wasn't dying after all. The pain in my head was something I must be able to control. I was just stressed out and I had far too much on my plate to have any time for that.

The headaches gradually tailed off and although I felt physically exhausted for a weeks afterwards, by the time Ian came home I was very much my old self again. I could see the relief on his face when I opened the door to him.

We talked about it all that night. He said he had been thinking about me intensely on his trip and wanted to start being a better husband.

'I've been thinking,' he said. 'Your headaches must have been some sort of cry for help, babe,' he said. 'I was just too busy crying myself over that theft business to hear you. It will be better from now on, I promise you it will.'

# 4 | For Richer for Poorer

'JENNY, SOMETHING AMAZING HAS HAPPENED,' Ian said as he walked in the front door one night during the winter of 1984. 'They have decided to let some of the wives go into the Killing House.'

'What, on a guided tour?' I asked, putting down the wooden spoon with which I was stirring the soup I had made for our supper.

'No, stupid,' he said putting his briefcase on the kitchen table. 'To go in on a course and learn how to use a gun.'

I let his words sink in. His face was animated, he obviously thought it was a wonderful idea and I wasn't quite sure how to react.

'Why would I want to learn how to use a gun, Ian?' I asked, carefully.

His face fell. 'Well, I just thought it would a fantastic opportunity,' he said. 'I mean, wouldn't you like to learn how to handle a gun? And the Killing House? Wouldn't you at least like to see inside it?'

The words 'Killing House' had always conjured up all sorts of horrors to me. Few people outside the SAS were supposed to know what it was, where it was or what it was for. For those who did know, it was the Close Quarter Battle or CQB House where the men trained with live ammunition. Its nickname had acquired added potency because several people really did get killed there. It had happened to Vanda's friend the previous year, and another man we knew was lucky to be alive after being shot in the back and buttocks at close range with a shotgun. Ian was there when it happened. He heard the shot and the sudden shouts of panic, but he was in the middle of a search and rescue exercise nearby and could do nothing to help.

I wondered what it would be like to see inside, to taste a little of the life that Ian led there, to feel some of the fear and excitement of that place. The course was, he said, the idea of the new small arms corps instructor who thought it would help the wives understand a little of what their husbands did at work. He was young and keen, not badged but freshly imported from the Army, and Ian couldn't believe he had persuaded the Head Shed to agree to it.

Spurred on by Ian's enthusiasm and my own natural curiosity, I wondered what I had to lose. He signed me up the following day, still convinced that the Regiment would change its mind or that the course would be heavily oversubscribed. I got a call from the corps instructor the next morning, telling me to come to the camp for two hours the following Monday night, and every Monday thereafter. We would start in a mess hall, he said, and then go to the CQB House as the programme developed.

It was bitterly cold that first Monday night and as I headed towards the mess hall, my coat buttoned up to my nose and my hat pulled down over my ears, I wondered what the hell I was thinking of. I pushed open the door and stepped inside, to find just five other wives already there and one more following me in. So much for Ian thinking I would be trampled to death in the rush.

Sergeant Major Taylor was standing impatiently at a desk at one end of the hall. We peeled off our coats and scarves and walked nervously towards him, giggling and chatting. Two weapons instructors stood either side of him. The corps instructor sat smiling at the back.

'Good evening, ladies,' the sergeant major barked through his bushy moustache. 'If you would like to take your seats now, we can begin.' We all sat at a table in the first row and wondered what would happen next.

'This evening we are going to learn the ins and outs of this little beauty,' he said, holding up a large, ugly-looking gun in his right hand. 'The nine-millimetre Browning self-loading pistol. It is a weapon your husbands are very familiar with and something that you may have seen at home.'

'I must say I've never seen one that big, girls,' I whispered. The sergeant major was not amused and shot me a glare.

'Come now, ladies, let's all pay attention. This is serious,' he said. I buttoned my lip. 'We're now going to give each of you one of these pistols and train you in the art of stripping, cleaning and reassembling the weapon.

'This will involve learning the importance of being magazine-safe, removing the magazine from the handle, dismantling the release control, cleaning the springs and the barrel and putting it all back together again. We shall repeat this exercise until we get it right and can do it in double quick time.'

One by one the shiny black guns were placed in front of us. I had to use both hands to lift mine off the table. The schoolgirl laughing and joking stopped the second we touched the weapons. The gun felt cold, heavy and sinister in my hands. I could tell from the looks on the faces of the other women that theirs felt the same way. We all eyed our guns suspiciously and then looked up at the sergeant major, who was standing before us with a self-satisfied expression on his face.

'Right then, ladies,' he said. 'Shall we begin?'

For the next two hours, instead of learning how to ice cakes or arrange flowers like most Army wives on courses, we seven SAS wives found ourselves stripping nine-millimetre Browning pistols, laying out the five pieces on the table in front of us, and trying to slot them all back together in the right order and the right place. It was like a jigsaw puzzle and I'd always been good at jigsaws.

Some of the other wives didn't have a clue and were trying to jam bits of metal into places that couldn't possibly fit. Several of them cried aloud as the gas-propelled automatic mechanism shot back and trapped their fingers. Their hands, not yet thawed from the cold night air, were badly bruised.

'No, no, no,' shouted the instructors impatiently. 'Not like that, try again. Come on now, quickly. We haven't got all night.' These officers knew how to discipline, and discipline us they did. They stood in front of us and shouted, 'It is either your life or theirs. Do it again and do it right. Move your thumb out of the way this time.'

'Hang on a minute, mate,' I thought, 'this is only meant to be a hobby, we're not actually going to shoot anybody,' but I guess they had to make us realise that we could.

Not surprisingly, some of the wives dropped out after the first lesson. I couldn't blame them but I was hooked. From the minute I first picked up the gun, I knew that this was something I wanted to do. I had seen Ian's bergen packed up to the hilt with all sorts of strange weaponry before and it had never really tempted me. But there I was, holding this big steel gun and I liked the way it felt, cool and menacing in my hands. I couldn't wait to get into the Killing House and see for myself what the gun did when it was loaded.

My patience was sorely tested. By the time we got to the third week, I had my gun stripped, cleaned and reassembled in minutes. I looked like Annie Oakley compared to some of the others. The instructors were impressed. What they didn't know is that after the first week I made Ian bring his gun home each night so that I could practise repeatedly on the kitchen table. I really got on a high about it.

'You only love me for my weapon,' he complained bitterly one night, when I was sitting poring over his gun once more. He had just come in from work and I had hardly even greeted him before reaching into his briefcase for the gun, in its distinctive leather case.

'Stop complaining. It was your idea that I do this course,' I told him, as he skulked around the kitchen, looking hopefully for some supper.

'Chinese take-away all right again tonight?' I asked, as I fumbled with the loading mechanism. 'You choose.' I had emptied the magazine by the time he slammed the front door behind him.

On the fourth Monday of the course I turned up at the mess hall as usual, only to find the sergeant major standing waiting for me and the rest of the wives in the doorway. 'Tonight,' he said, meaningfully, 'we are going to the Close Quarter Battle House.'

We looked at each other in anticipation and said nothing. He led us silently across the camp past some Nissen huts and other areas we had not known existed until we rounded a corner and came to a bleak building that looked like a huge concrete cow barn standing in a pool of light.

My heart was racing as we prepared to step inside. The instructors were already in an anteroom in their overcoats, waiting for us. The sergeant major had never looked so serious. He waited for us all to line up in front of him before telling us, 'We are about to go through to the firing range. I want each of you to remember all that you have been taught, particularly about magazine safety, when you are inside.

'You will each be shown your positions and given your weapons and ammunition and will be allowed to fire in turn at the targets. Once you have fired, you must strip your weapon, reassemble it and reload. The ammunition will be provided for you at your station. Good luck.'

We walked in single-file through a heavy steel door held open for us by a stony-faced corporal. The room opened out into a large chamber, sectioned off into long corridors, each with a firing station at one end and a target at the other. There were five stations lit up, one for each of us, each one six foot away from the other and about thirty feet away from the targets at the end of the range.

I was shown to my position. My gun had been laid ready on a small metal stand with, for the first time, eight live bullets laid neatly alongside it instead of the usual dummies.

I swallowed hard. I knew what I had to do, although acknowledging that the bullets I was about to insert into the spring-loaded magazine were live this time made the palms of my hands suddenly sticky. I picked the gun up carefully with both hands and stripped it down, pulling the magazine from the handle and releasing the automatic mechanism.

Holding the magazine firmly in my hand to stop me from trembling, I picked up a live bullet and dropped it in, my forefinger poised to prevent it from springing out again.

I loaded each new bullet on top of the other, the pressure building up with every addition. The magazine could take up to twenty bullets, but the fewer there were the less the pressure and the training lessons had made the instructors realise that a woman's smaller hands found it difficult to load many more than eight.

We loaded our weapons in silence, each woman respectful of the moment and the tense atmosphere within the Killing House. I was ready first and stood to attention, waiting for the others to finish.

Looking straight ahead of me, I stared at my target for the first time. A black silhouetted figure of a Russian storm trooper running towards me, a rifle in his hand, he looked sinister and menacing, despite being stuck to an oblong sheet of brown paper. I tried to focus on his face, his eyes, but the features were too dark to make out. My instructor handed me my headphones and I put them on, after removing my gold clip-on earrings and smoothing back my hair.

'Can you hear me?' he shouted into my left ear and I nodded and gave him the thumbs up. 'When you are ready, take aim and fire,' he said. 'Remember, this is not a race or a test. Take your time. One round at a time. Keep it steady.'

I lifted the gun with both my hands and held it stretched out in front of me. The weight made me want to drop my arms to my side, and I could feel the strain in my shoulders. Closing my left eye, I married up the silhouette at the end of the range with the small raised sight fixed to the top of the gun.

I lined it up with the storm trooper's face, remembering what Ian had told me, 'You might only have one chance so you don't want to lose it. Blow his head off.' The silhouette seemed to develop a mocking smile the longer I hesitated and stared at his face. I could feel the strength draining from my arms as gravity pulled on the weapon in my hand.

Repositioning my finger on the trigger, and closing my eye again to better focus on the target, I levelled the gun once more and pulled the trigger slowly towards me.

Bang! Even with my headphones on the noise was incredible. The automatic mechanism flew back and a millisecond later the bullet blasted a neat hole into the blackness that was the silhouette's left shoulder. I was thrown back with the force of it, not just the recoil which jerked my arms upwards, but by the bright yellow flash, the sudden smell of cordite and the shock.

I quickly regained my balance and looked down the range. 'My God, did I do that?' I thought as I stepped forward to the line, peering at the menacing silhouette and the gaping hole I had just made.

'Well done,' shouted my instructor through the exploding noise that was still ricocheting around inside my head. 'Couple of inches lower and you would have got his heart.' I didn't tell him I was aiming for his head.

My whole body was trembling. Nothing had prepared me for the feeling of shock at what I could do with the gun. My heart was pounding and I felt clammy and slightly sick. What if the silhouette had been real? He would be mortally wounded by now, spurting blood, his flesh torn open by the impact of my bullet. I remembered what Ian had told me about Bernadette McAliskey and her gaping stomach wounds.

What if Ian had been on the receiving end? I couldn't take my eyes off the bullet-hole or my mind off the horror of what it could do. I looked down at the gun in my hand, its barrel still smoking, and wanted to drop it and run from that place. It didn't feel cold any more, it felt hot, burning hot in my hand. My heart was beating like a drum and the blood was rushing around my head, colouring my face scarlet. I thought I might have to sit down.

What had I been thinking of, going on this course in the first place? Why did I imagine that I could cross briefly into Ian's world and be as unaffected by it as he seemed to be? This was frightening stuff and I didn't like the way it scared me. I felt suddenly weak, as if the energy expended to propel the bullet down the range at speed had come from within my body. My knees felt like jelly, I had a sudden urge to go to the toilet, and the adrenaline still coursing through my veins was making me light-headed.

Bang! I was startled by the sudden noise. The woman next to me, a rupert's wife called Mary, had let off her round. I watched the same flood of emotions rush over her and in doing so, I felt suddenly calm. I wasn't alone in feeling this, then. Her face flushed and her eyes glassy, she looked over at me in utter shock. I regained my composure and straightened myself up. The instructor patted me on the back and asked me if I was all right.

'Fine,' I lied, taking deep breaths to steady myself from within. I walked back to the stand and prepared for the moment when I would have to level my gun once again.

Bang! There it was again, the noise, the flash, the smell of lead, that sudden rush of heat and smoke and fear. I lowered the weapon and looked down the range. My bullet had missed this time. The neat hole it had punctured in the brown paper was three inches from the storm trooper's left ear. I felt angry with myself for misjudging it and stepped back to the line once more.

Bang! . . . Bang! . . . Bang! Each time I hit the target, the fear of it lessened slightly until it became almost manageable. I couldn't help but quiver each time and think, My God!, but it now felt terrible and wonderful at the same time. It seemed to release so much pent-up emotion in me, some of which I had never even known existed.

It was as if there were nobody else in the room, just my Russian storm trooper and me. The more I studied his face, the more he seemed to mock me, my ineptitude, my inexperience, my weakness. I wanted to blast his head off, to prove that I was capable of doing so, to fight back for all the Regiment wives who had been too frightened to sign up for the course in the first place. This felt personal.

It was meant to be a passing phase, a one-off course, but I became completely addicted. Once I got over the initial shock, I was intoxicated. I couldn't wait until it was my turn to fire. It was undoubtedly the most exciting thing I had ever experienced in my life. I felt slightly drunk with the heady buzz of firing a gun.

By the time I got home that night, Ian could see the fire burning in my eyes. He grinned in recognition of it when he opened the front door.

'It was fantastic!' I told him, as I walked in and pulled my hat and scarf off. 'Absolutely bloody amazing, in fact! I had no idea I would feel like that. I hated it at first but then I grew to control it, and it felt so good.'

He nodded and smiled knowingly. I realised that for the first time in our relationship I was experiencing something he experienced in his work almost every day. He had tried to explain it to me once, to tell me how it felt to fire a weapon, but I hadn't really been listening and I had certainly never fully understood. Until now.

I hadn't really thought about guns before, or about killing people. But here I was, venturing into Ian's sphere for the briefest of moments, and I felt as if I was beginning to understand. Not that I could ever imagine what it felt like to be facing a real flesh-and-blood target, an armed Loyalist terrorist or a twitchy Argentinian conscript, instead of a paper cut-out stuck onto a wooden board.

I realised that I no longer had to worry about Ian taking a sadistic pleasure in firing a gun, as had crossed my mind briefly when he spoke with enthusiasm for guns before. Now I knew that there was so much more to it than I had previously thought. That the sense of power and strength could be intoxicating.

I suddenly understood how for some of the people Ian came up against, people with perhaps less than his sense of morality and justice, playing with guns could be a very exciting and very perilous game. I also now realised how dangerous that would make them.

Before that first pulling of the trigger I had known in my heart that Ian must have killed people but I had not liked to think about it. I had this rather simplistic theory that when you added up the numbers of people who were killed in conflict and compared it to how many were supposed to be killing them, then there were just not enough to go around. Maybe he had never killed anyone, I used to think, and I certainly never asked.

The first time I was really confronted with the probability was when he brought home that Argentinian conscript's jacket from the Falklands. When I found the owner's identity card in the pocket and stared at the young man's face, I was quite shaken by the thought. But I came to convince myself that if Ian had killed him then he must have done it for a good reason. Maybe this fresh-faced young boy would have killed him, or one of his troop. Maybe he hadn't looked quite so innocent in the heat of a battlefield when he was playing the dangerous game of war and had been foolhardy enough to confront Ian with a loaded weapon.

There is an SAS saying that I had never previously understood as I understand it now, 'Let the enemy die for his country, not you for yours'. It was a case of the target or you. It was as simple and clear-cut as that. Anyone who had willingly put themselves in the sights of Ian's gun over the years became like the storm trooper in my mind, not flesh and blood, just the enemy.

I never thought about who they might be, the men Ian had killed, or how their families were affected. There was no point. These men would have killed Ian just easily as he would have killed them and never given me a second thought. As far as I was concerned, they were all big boys out there, fighting each other under big boys' rules. Now that I had experienced for myself some of the myriad emotions of firing a gun, I understood that even better.

Ian had always wanted me to have a gun, but the Regiment wouldn't allow it. He was worried that because I was alone in the house so much I would be easy prey for a burglar or worse. He always said the best thing I could do if someone came into our home was to get them first and by the time I had been on the Killing House course for a few weeks, I knew that I could. I was all for it. I wanted a licence, I wanted to keep a gun by my bedside, I wanted to go on other courses, even join a gun club and become a better shot. The other wives thought I was stark staring mad. The whole thing had scared them witless. Two of the seven had already dropped out of the course, the rest were seeing it through, but chiefly not to lose face.

Each time I left the Killing House, I was already planning my next visit. I would practise stripping Ian's gun down again and again so that I got the maximum time on the range. After a few weeks I was way ahead of the other wives and I think the instructors started to get a bit suspicious.

Ian and I couldn't believe that the Regiment had sanctioned the course in the first place, but neither of us was going to say anything that might jeopardise my training. I think he was surprised at how much I enjoyed the whole thing, even though he had always been a gun fanatic, and how I couldn't stop talking about it to friends and family. He even talked about us joining a club together and entering competitions. Hereford's answer to Bonnie and Clyde, he said, but he told friends he would draw the line at lending me his black overalls and balaclava.

I was looking forward to being shown the rest of the Killing House, the part that had been built in the seventies after the Munich Olympics tragedy, when eleven Israeli athletes were taken hostage and killed by the Black September terrorist group. Lessons had been learned from the failure of that rescue by the German police and the Regiment wasn't alone in preparing itself thereafter for counter-terrorism, hostage situations and kidnappings.

That part of the building lay behind the ranges I was on and was compartmentalised into six or seven separate bullet-proofed rooms resembling an office, an aeroplane cabin or a cellar, each with a layout that could be altered into different configurations. Members of the Royal Family and the Government visited these rooms for familiarisation training – to learn how to react if ever they were taken hostage and had to be rescued by the SAS. Ian was there when the Queen and Prince Philip visited. He was one of those who demonstrated hostage rescue techniques and was introduced to them briefly afterwards.

It was there that Mrs Thatcher once hugely impressed everyone from the Regiment by not even flinching when the guns started firing (when all her aides had hit the deck) and not far from where the Princess of Wales had her hair accidentally set alight by a dummy grenade.

When there are no visiting dignitaries, soldiers take it in turns to be hostages or rescuers. They play out different scenarios, with lights being suddenly switched off so that they have to use night vision goggles, the layouts being changed to fool them and flash-bangs (fake maroons that make a big flash and a bang) being set off to disorientate them. They have less than four seconds to get the hostages out and slot (kill) the terrorists, and it is then that the initials of the Regiment are said to stand for 'Speed Aggression and Surprise'.

They use live ammunition to give that extra sense of danger and the soldiers who come flying in through the windows have to be very careful not to shoot their mates. I couldn't wait to get inside those doors and see it all for myself.

To my very great disappointment, just as the course was getting really interesting, some Head Shed decided to cancel it. I think the powers-that-be got wind of it and wondered what the hell the corps instructor was thinking of. Some said that, because of the high percentage of marital break-up in the Regiment, there was concern that one or two disgruntled wives might go home and shoot their husbands once they had learned how to handle a gun.

I was gutted but there was nothing I could do about it. I had to be grateful for the time I had there. What was really galling is that by the time the course ended I had become really good on the ranges, I was spot on every time.

Ian and I had been married about five years and were still remarkably happy. I had got over my headaches and was coping better with the lonely times and he had come to accept the events in the Falklands and Belize. He was on the Training Wing, away from those he felt had betrayed him, and he had already made many new friends.

The experience had taught us both, however, not to place too much emphasis on friendships within the Regiment. Paul and others had been lost to us, Vanda had moved away and remarried, and some of those whom we had previously considered friends had, we felt, let us down.

With my contacts in Hereford and at work, we began to form a small but close circle of friends outside the SAS who meant more and more to us as the years rolled by. People like Ruth and Jerry, our friendly local policeman and his wife with whom Ian entrusted my life when he was away; our neighbours Tim and Helen who were a great support to me in all practical matters when I was alone; Mandy and Terry at The Swan who were always so kind; Audrey and Paul – a local antiques dealer and her car salesman husband who went out of their way to invite us over regularly – and, of course, Sue and Anne, my mates from years back who still kept me sane and took me out drinking when Ian was away.

All of these people knew what Ian did for a living and they all revered him in their own special way. It is a fact of life that everyone loves to be able to say they have a mate in the SAS and neither of us minded that. But these friends also made me feel special and loved, and tried hard to maintain an interest in what was happening in my life – however trivial it might have seemed compared to what was happening in Ian's – so that I didn't feel left out.

Sue and Anne were always particularly good at that, mainly because they had known me for so long before I even met Ian and had not been that impressed by him, from the start. They had had their own experiences of life with people in the Regiment and they fully understood its very special difficulties.

To outsiders it might seem that there is nothing too unusual to have to cope with, in being an SAS wife. For the most part, in this peace-loving country of ours, there are thankfully few wars for our men to fight, only a steady stream of exercises and parachute missions to go on.

How different can it be to being married to a long-distance lorry driver who is away for weeks on end and is probably more likely to be killed on the roads than Ian was to be killed in action? Or to being a regular squaddie's wife, living on a camp in Germany or in Northern Ireland? Or to spending your life with a paramedic, someone who sees people dying every day? Probably not that different in some ways, but so very, very different in many others.

Does a truck driver always insist on sitting with his back to the wall when he is out with his wife in a restaurant or pub, his eyes constantly darting around the room, watching for a possible threat?

Will a paramedic be suspicious of every single person he meets, wondering what their motives are and who they know? Is he someone who can only sleep for a few hours at a time at night, spending the rest of the time lying on the floor because it seems more comfortable after weeks in ditches, or pacing up and down, or crouching downstairs, back against the wall in the half-light, biting his nails to the quick and remembering friends lost?

Can a squaddie come home after regular guard duty and eat, wash and go to the toilet normally? Does he know what it is like to experience days on end of lying in a water-filled ditch or jungle floor, shitting into a plastic bag, unable and eventually unwilling to wash, eating half-rations so that his stomach shrinks, controlling his bowel movements to the point that he hardly has to go at all and then can't when there are no constraints?

What type of wife would then complain when her man returns home and forgets to put the loo seat down, or fails to use deodorant regularly, or finds himself tossing and turning all night in a soft double bed? How can she complain that he is tired all the time, simply because his body-clock has become so confused that it takes him a while to get back into some sort of normal sleeping pattern?

Many of the wives do complain, and that is why their marriages often do not survive. They expect their husbands to click automatic-ally into the role of suburban man, picking up the kids from school, hosting jolly barbecues for the neighbours, doing the DIY around the house and going out to dinner or a movie on their first night back when all they want to do is sleep for twenty-four hours. They completely fail to understand that these men find it hard to return home to a 'normal' life after such concentrated effort. That, although they may be experts with weapons and tactical counter-terrorism techniques, they are often utterly useless when it comes to small talk or wallpapering, changing a plug or fixing the boiler – mainly through lack of experience.

SAS men often have no idea how to manage money or run the everyday finances of a home, they have a tendency to rush out and splurge on something extravagant the minute they get back home and often get into serious debt. How many wives dread the duty free shops at airports as much as an SAS wife?

I have always said that Ian is about as useful as an ashtray on the back of a motorbike when it comes to home finance and DIY, and I learned very early on in my marriage that if I wanted anything done around the house, I was going to have to get on and do it myself. From that day on, I have paid all the bills, organised the maintenance of our home and car, done all the decorating and gardening, and sorted out everything from pensions to insurance.

Pensions and insurance are in themselves a difficult issue for an SAS man and his wife. How do you begin to estimate a viable pension for someone who will be forced into retirement at the relatively young age of forty, after a maximum twenty-two years' service, with no comprehension of how he will survive psychologically, never mind what he will do to earn an income after that?

What company is going to insure the life and health of someone who runs around the Killing House firing off rounds of live ammunition, who jumps from aeroplanes five times a day, who deliberately tries to infiltrate the ranks of the IRA or lies in a mosquito-infested swamp for weeks on end with malaria already in his bloodstream?

The insurance question became such a problem for the men during the Falklands War that the Regiment introduced its own scheme to help out the widows and dependants of those killed or wounded in action. Underwritten by Army assurances, several companies then stepped into the breach and offered private life insurance schemes for members of the SAS, albeit at a considerably greater cost than the premiums for a lorry driver, paramedic or squaddie.

Insurance payouts caused great bitterness and rivalry between the wives and widows. Those who opted for the Army scheme found themselves receiving far less than those who had made their own private arrangements. Unable to place the blame on their dead husbands at a time when they were still mourning them, these widows blamed the Regiment, the other wives, anyone but the man who should have sorted it all out long before his death.

Ian was one of many who had refused to take out the Army insurance on the grounds that to do so would be unlucky. He felt that if he signed the forms, he would somehow be accepting the possibility that he might die. In his typically ebullient way, he refused to sign it in defiance of Death.

Paul Bunker had sorted out his life insurance while he was on one of the ships taking him down to the Falklands that April in 1982. He had taken out the full amount of units available under the Army Dependants (ADAT) scheme so that Vanda would be all right if anything happened to him. It seemed to us afterwards that she may not have been the only one with a premonition of disaster.

When it came to payment of the policy on his death, Vanda was one of the lucky ones. Paul, a mere corporal, had been very generous and had provided for his widow extremely well. But Vanda got some terrible flak from some of the widows of more senior officers, who received far less than she did under the Army scheme their husbands had signed up with, since they had not taken the full option. It provoked unnecessary rivalry and bitterness.

These women were all in the same boat. They had all lost their husbands and their breadwinners. The men who died were all irreplaceable to the women who loved them but suddenly the men's ranks and positions were being cited as an indicator of how much they should each have been worth.

Vanda left Hereford for good not long after that. She was disgusted by the response of some of the other widows when they found out how much Paul had left her.

Faced with such myriad problems, it is not surprising that so many women do not survive the white-knuckle ride that is marriage to the SAS. Or that those who do bear the scars of the years of loneliness and worry. I had had my moments, and there were many more to come, but I knew that with friends like Sue and Anne, and the companionship and support of people outside the Regiment – good, decent, ordinary people whose normality kept me in touch with reality – I could bear anything as long as I still had the man I loved by my side.

I am sure I would have loved Ian just as much if he had been a truck driver or a squaddie or a paramedic, and I am certain it would also have been a lot easier in many ways, but the thrill of the ride was part of it too, the constant living on the edge that kept me from becoming a bored suburban housewife. Ian was not the only one who had become addicted to the danger. It was becoming an antidote to the rest of my life.

My time at work hardly varied during all the years I was there. I didn't particularly enjoy my job but I had my two best friends there and it was my anchor, and Ian's too in a way. Whatever weird and wonderful things were going on in his life, we both knew that I would be at my desk morning and afternoon, from nine a.m. on Monday until five p.m. on Friday. Ian liked to imagine me sitting at work, safe and sound, surrounded by friends and colleagues and going home to Annie in the evening. He thought about me a lot while he was away and that is where he always pictured me, even though he jokingly referred to it as Colditz.

The company was always very understanding about the special needs of my marriage. If I suddenly needed time off to see Ian after a trip or wanted to go home early on a night he was coming home, they made sure it could be arranged.

At the end of the Falklands War, when I needed to take some time off to spend with Ian immediately, I got myself worked up into a terrible state because I had used up all my holiday entitlement for that year. My wonderful boss, Barry, called up personnel while I was in his office and told them why I needed extra time off.

'Her husband is in the SAS and he was nearly killed in the Falklands,' I heard him say into the telephone. 'She needs at least five days' compassionate leave for when he comes home.' He nodded, smiled and put the phone down triumphantly. 'Ten days,' he told me. 'I don't want to see you for ten days. Give my love to Ian.' He was marvellous.

There were plenty of company social functions – dinner dances, leaving parties and Christmas dos – which the staff were expected to attend. At one of the many such functions, a departmental party, I went alone because Ian was away. I was quite accustomed to braving these affairs alone, but on this particular night – at a time when Ian had been away on a mission for several weeks – I felt unusually miserable and lonely and stood in the corner while my friends and colleagues partied all around me.

Roger, one of the men I worked with and a good friend, sensed my unease and decided to cheer me up.

'Hey everybody,' he suddenly said, tapping the side of his glass with a pen to get everyone's attention. People started to gather around. I thought the raffle was about to begin.

'Listen up,' he said. 'I think we should all make a special effort to cheer up Jenny Simpson tonight.' My face flushed scarlet and I cringed visibly. I whispered to Roger to shut up, but he had the attention of the whole room by now.

'Yes,' he said. 'Poor Jenny, standing over here in the corner. Such a shrinking violet. And is it any wonder? Her husband has been away for months.'

My colleagues sensed his mood and all cried, 'Aaah!' in sympathy. I buried my face in my hands with embarrassment.

'Ian's been away on some foreign mission,' Roger added. 'But even when he is home, you know, they have a terrible problem.' I wanted the ground to swallow me up.

'Yes, poor Jenny. We see her in wages every day and we know the real anguish she suffers.' What is he on about? I was thinking.

'You see, ladies and gentleman, most of you know that Ian is in the SAS.' My face creased in pain and I looked to Sue and Anne for help.

'And this really affects her sex life,' Roger went on. By this time I wanted to die. 'The problem is,' he added, smiling, 'Ian can get in and out without anybody – not even Jenny – knowing.'

Everybody collapsed into laughter and Roger came over and planted a huge kiss on my forehead as they cheered. 'You bastard,' I muttered under my breath, smiling. 'I'll get you for that.' But he had succeeded in cheering me up and we all had a brilliant evening.

Roger, a big, jolly man, had a special place in my heart. He and I had worked together for over twenty years and had been friends from the start. He and his wife Madeleine had a son, Simeon, and I watched the pale, elfin-faced boy grow up. Roger would bring him into the office and he was just like his father, a practical joker and a real treasure.

While he was still a youngster, Simeon developed leukaemia. When Roger first told me I was devastated. We would all huddle together at work, praying for him, wishing him well. Ian, who had never met Simeon before but who knew how much I cared for him, gave him his helmet and his belt kit from the Falklands. He also had a special plaque made up for him at the camp, bearing the winged dagger and the inscription, 'To Simeon from D Squadron'.

Simeon was absolutely made up and he told all his friends at school that he had a friend in the SAS. His class did a special project on the Regiment and their involvement in the Falklands, using Ian's kit.

Tragically, his health slowly deteriorated until finally, aged seven, he lost his long struggle against cancer. I was shattered for Roger and Madeleine. He was their only son and had been the light of their life. For a little while, he had also been the light of mine. Ian was away when he died and I had to deal with the distress of it all on my own. I spent much of the first week after his death in a stupor. It was difficult to explain to anyone else how much this little boy had come to mean to me. I didn't really understand it myself. But my grief was palpable, it was something that ripped me up inside.

I broke the news to Ian later that month when I flew to join him in America after a job. He was as upset for me as he was for himself. Although Simeon had only touched our lives briefly, his impact was unforgettable and his smile will remain in my heart forever.

A few years ago, we also lost Roger. He complained of a severe headache late one night and when it got so bad that he was in distress, Madeleine called an ambulance. By the time the paramedics arrived, they told her there was nothing they could do for him. He had died of a brain haemorrhage. He was in his early forties. The little village church where his funeral was held wasn't big enough to hold all the people who attended the service, including Ian, who put on a suit and overcoat and travelled up from London for the service, despite his dislike of churches. Scores of people stood outside.

Ian continued to travel extensively throughout the mid-eighties spending an average of six months a year away on training exercises. As soon as he came back from one trip he started preparing for the next. Friends and colleagues joked that he only ever came back to Hereford to change his clothes, bed his wife and put in his expenses claims.

Training Wing was a delight for him because he spent so much time in the jungle conditions he loved, going to jungle camps for eight weeks at a time at least twice a year. Sitting by a little stub of a spluttering candle in the early hours of the morning, he would write me letters describing the way the mists clung to the camp, and how at peace he felt.

The rest of his time was spent up in the Brecon Beacons supervising the infamous Endurance test on the Selection training course, a particularly gruelling exercise in which even experienced SAS men have died of exposure and exhaustion. He also spent time in Muscat, Oman, and in America with Delta Force.

It was hard going, teaching young soldiers how to survive in extreme conditions, how to cope with being constantly wet from humidity, sweat and wading through swamps and chest-deep rivers. They had to learn how to keep their weapons and at least one set of clothing dry, so that they could change into it at night. Ian dealt with their sores, bites, blisters and complaints and enjoyed watching them rally together under pressure.

He thoroughly enjoyed the challenge of his role as instructor and mentor to the new recruits and took the position very seriously. He found it fascinating to watch the young survivors coming through, often against all the odds, and even enjoyed 'binning' (the expression the SAS use for failing a candidate, or later for expelling a soldier from the Regiment) some of the cocky mouths on sticks who would go home to their Army camps with their tails between their legs, their photographs back at Training Wing treated to the special SAS plastic surgery – scored across with a big red marker pen.

Ian kept an exercise book into which he stuck small photographs of all the young men under his charge. Under each name and photo he would detail his personal thoughts and opinions on their progress and assess whether or not he thought they would pass Selection. Some of them registered an 'Oh dear!' or 'Bloody useless' and these would never make the grade. Others, like the young Andy McNab, were said by Ian to 'show some promise'. He was invariably right in his assessments and McNab was one of several of those who passed Selection under his tutelage that went on to be legends within the Regiment.

It was very hard work for him, and even when he was home I didn't see very much of him because he was up and out at dawn, returning home late at night to fall into bed and get some rest before the next day's onslaught. I still missed him dreadfully on his short trips away, but he was happy in his work and I was relieved that he had found peace of mind.

At least he wasn't at war or in Northern Ireland for months on end, I consoled myself. I might only see him fleetingly, but I did see him, and we could even make a few plans. Among those plans was the sale of our house. I had only just finished decorating the last room in our little home when Ian announced that it was time for us to cash in on the housing boom and sell while the prices were high. I wept buckets when we left. I even missed Charley, the ghost. It had been our first proper home, the place where we had eaten Christmas dinner on the floor and celebrated all Ian's homecomings. It had so many happy memories, it broke my heart to leave.

We arranged to move into Army married quarters for nine months to save some money for a better house. It was very different having an Army house after one of our own, but we always knew it was only for a short while – living on subsidised rent – so that we could consolidate our finances, which needed a boost.

Yet again, I had to organise the sale and the move. Once again, I was in charge of all the paperwork and removal men and the fine details. Ian had an annoying knack of walking in through the front door a day or two after all the hard work had been done. If I didn't love him so much I could easily have grown to hate him.

A few weeks after moving into Army quarters, I decided to rearrange the bedroom. Trying to shift a wardrobe from one side of the room to the other, I slipped a disc in my back. The pain was excruciating and as Ian was out, I had to slide down the stairs on my bottom to reach the telephone and call for help. The doctor said I would have to rest for days, if not weeks.

The next morning, Ian got up and started pottering around the kitchen. How sweet, I thought, and smiled warmly when he produced an enormous lasagne, even though it was made – it seemed – with the help of every pot and pan I owned and several of my recipe books. I was less than happy with the words that accompanied it, however – 'Right, I'm off'. When I asked him what he meant, he told me not to get upset but he had been informed the day before that he was to go on a hastily arranged mission to the Far East for five weeks.

He looked at the dismay on my face and pointed weakly at the lasagne. 'Don't worry, babe. This will see you through while I am away.' If my back didn't hurt so much, I would have chased after him with the lasagne and thrown it at him.

I was so incapacitated that Vanda and other friends had to take it in turns to come in each day and feed me while he was away. He was right, the lasagne did last well, if not quite for five weeks, but by the end of it I never wanted to see another lasagne again.

At the doctor's recommendation I went to see an osteopath, who happened to be blind. He started to feel his way along my back and, within a few minutes, he said to me, 'You are married to someone in the Regiment, aren't you?' I asked him how he knew.

'Your back is full of stress knots,' he said. 'In Hereford that is a pretty sure sign.'


When Ian came back we were able to book a proper holiday in advance in the knowledge that for the first time in our married lives there was no danger of the holiday being cancelled. Normally we would dash down to the local travel agent when Ian was home between exercises and see what we could grab on special offer. Cancellation insurance was for us as important a part of booking the holiday as medical insurance is for anyone else.

Doing something as normal as flicking through holiday brochures months ahead and booking it all up in advance was a real change for us. So this is what it felt like to lead a regular life.

We booked a holiday to Spain and had a great time, getting tanned and drinking jug after jug of sangria by the pool. It was just what we wanted for a quick break away from it all in the sun. We were planning on moving to a bigger and better house, Ian seemed to be completely over his previous setbacks and things felt good between us.

One afternoon towards the end of the holiday, after a particularly heavy lunchtime drinking session, we were sitting at the bar and started to talk about what we both wanted from life. As far as I was concerned, I told him, all I wanted was to spend the rest of my life with him and to see a bit more of him.

When I asked him what he wanted, he replied rather drunkenly, 'I want to be free of the Army one day and for us to have kids.' I was stunned into silence.

Choosing my words very carefully, I said, 'But, Ian, you have had the snip. I thought we had both agreed that was what we wanted? I thought we made that decision together, for your career and so that we could always be together on our own when we had the time.'

He swirled the drink around in his glass and said, 'I know, Jen, but maybe you should have put your foot down, babe. Maybe you should have told me that it wasn't what you really wanted.'

Tears welled in my eyes as his words sliced through me. Yes, I hadn't completely ruled out the possibility of children until I met him. That was true. But I had been happy with our decision until then because I wholeheartedly believed it was a joint decision, something we had set our minds on for the sake of his job and our marriage. Now suddenly he was telling me he wanted it to be different and that he suspected I did too.

I looked across at him angrily. I wanted to tell him how much his words had hurt me. He was drunk and I had been too, but now I was suddenly stone-cold sober. It was too late for us to start a family. I was in my mid-thirties and we were too set in our ways. I knew in my heart that I couldn't be the little woman waiting at home with the kids. I just wasn't cut out for it. For me, it was always Ian. He came first and he always would. But that didn't make his comments any easier to bear. I felt physically sick, and left him alone in the bar while I went up to our room to lie down and think about what he had said.

We said no more about it for the rest of the holiday, but it remained a nagging question in the back of my mind for some time. They say people tell the truth when they are drunk. Was this something Ian really wanted, really hoped for, and had been keeping from me? Ian was a natural with kids. They loved him and he seemed to have limitless patience with them, something I did not possess.

Or were his words just the ramblings of a drunk, overly-sentimental after too much sangria and hypothesising about something he had no intention of pursuing. Either way, the shadow he had cast on my heart was not something that could be easily erased.

After two years on Training Wing, Ian rejoined his Squadron in 1985, which meant a return to the more unpredictable nature of squadron training and never being able to plan a holiday again. I gritted my teeth and told myself that at least the money would be better.

Our eight months in married quarters was up and so I concentrated my mind on the latest house move, which – once again – I had to organise alone. I found the house we wanted on the outskirts of Hereford, made the offer, organised the legal and financial matters and moved in by myself, with the help of friends and relatives. Although Ian knew the area and the road in which his new home was situated, he didn't see the house until he walked in the door one day between trips. There were times when I toyed mischievously with the idea of not giving him the new address.

He was happy with the place – a three bedroom semi-detached property built twenty years earlier – though it seemed to me that his gypsy blood prevented him from ever becoming too attached to a building or belongings. He spent so much time on the move in his job, with only what he could carry on his back, that it never seemed to matter much to him whether we had a south-facing garden or a nice bedroom or a pine kitchen.

For me it was different. I was normal, I suppose. My home was a beacon, the thing that guided me to safety, away from the rest of the world and the demands of my work or his Regiment. I made the house as homely as we could afford it to be and made a real effort with the garden and the neighbours. Having left my beloved little house in the town centre, I was determined to make this one just as special.

I think Ian hardly noticed. He was away almost all the time. One minute he was ski training in Norway and then he was off to America with Delta Force and its aeronautical boffins, developing parachutes for special services. He also did another few stints with what had by then become known as the SP or Special Projects team, which was being back on call again, carrying a bleeper, ready to deal with any counter-terrorism or sudden team jobs that required his special skills.

In 1986 he flew to Jordan for eight weeks' training, which he loved. The idea was much the same as jungle training, a few days' acclimatisation to the hot and arid conditions, then a week or so of learning how to collect water from the ground and air using special traps, how to map read when there was nothing but rock and sand for miles, how to survive in the deadly heat of the day and the freezing cold of the night.

They were shown how to scrape themselves out a shallow hide in the bedrock of a wadi or dried-up river bed and cover themselves with camouflage nets, rocks and any dried bush they could find. That is where they would lie up all day, hiding from Bedouins, goat herders and any passing camels or wild animals. All this prepared them for the final search and evade exercise.

Ian loved lying out under the stars in Wadi Rum, the remote desert place where *Lawrence of Arabia* was filmed. His father had taken him to see the film when he was a child and it had impressed him enormously. Now he was living the dream and he was in his element. When he got home, he insisted we sleep out under the stars for a couple of nights in the garden – he wanted me to share the experience of looking up at the night sky and waking up with the dawn. I gave in and let him drag me and the dogs and the sleeping bags out for a couple of nights, until we woke up one morning to a sudden thunderstorm.

Ian never lost his love for the desert and was particularly taken with Jordan. It gave him an opportunity to practise the Arabic he had learned with Paul Bunker all those years before and to top up his suntan which was in danger of falling below the Factor One level.

We used to get some funny looks walking down the street together, he the ice cream boy, all sun kissed and bronzed and I, all pale and pasty. No wonder people believed him when he told them he was a British Airways steward. He had certainly notched up enough air miles to be one.

Apart from nearly being bitten by a scorpion in the Jordanian desert and treading on a rattlesnake in Florida, his only really hairy moments during the late eighties were the sudden reinforcement calls to jobs in Northern Ireland throughout 1986 and 1987. His bleeper would go off and he would get as little as thirty minutes' notice before he had to be at camp and off in a helicopter across the water as reinforcements for a particular job.

I never knew whether he would be gone for hours or weeks, or if it was the type of job where he might not come back at all. Once the door had slammed and he was gone, I was left to ponder that thought alone while I cleared up the whirlwind that had just raged through my house, as he grabbed his kit, emptied drawers and cupboards, and just had time to kiss me goodbye.

Ian loved those quick response jobs. It really gave him a taste for the Province again and reminded him why he had joined the SAS in the first place. He was not having to do any of the intense covert surveillance, just the high-profile flying in and out, here-comes-the-cavalry stuff, saving the day.

One of the jobs he did in the winter of 1986 was an operation he was particularly proud of, because it was at a time when the so-called 'shoot to kill' policy was becoming so controversial and it went to show that the SAS arrested people more often than they shot them.

Information had come through that an IRA team near Lough May in East Tyrone had a plan to shoot dead an off-duty member of the Ulster Defence Regiment. Ian and his team were flown in to help when they heard an attack was about to take place. Using a series of cars, they traced and followed the four-man IRA team who were in two cars, and watched them collect the rifles they were to use from a quartermaster at the back of a local shop.

Ian and his men moved in to intercept the second car on the main road, and he saw the gunmen throw their rifles out of the window. The weapons were recovered and the gang arrested without incident. It was a textbook operation. The two men, who never even got near their victim, were each sentenced to fifteen years in prison.

Ian was on such a high after that job. His elation was clearly evident. He felt that he was fully back on track with the Regiment, being given the responsibility and recognition he deserved and achieving the job satisfaction he had temporarily lost.

If he was happy, I was happy, and it seemed to me that life was generally pretty sweet. I was feeling a lot better physically and mentally, we both seemed stronger together than we had been for a while, even though the unresolved question of children had briefly darkened my heart. Ian was fulfilled at work and I was busy with the work to be done on our new home, and we had settled into as much of a routine as is ever possible within the Regiment.

I started to feel truly comfortable about our life together again. We had more money than ever before after our savings initiative had paid off and once the new Special Services Pay (giving those in the SAS a far better rate of pay than their regular Army counterparts) kicked in. We had a much better social life, we went out drinking regularly with friends to the local pubs, we started to hold dinner parties and went to others. We even started to attend some official Army functions together, something Ian had never been particularly fond of, but which I really enjoyed.

The most memorable was the Summer Ball of the Royal Green Jackets, Ian's old troop, at the Warminster mess. It was a wonderful occasion, a full dinner dance with the women wearing ball gowns and the men in full dress uniform.

I wore a beautiful black taffeta ball gown with hired jewellery, and had my hair done specially. The evening started with a fabulous four-course dinner, which was rounded off with delicate icing sugar baskets filled with chocolates, presented to each of the wives. Then the dancing started. It was a marvellous night, we had official photographs taken and the idea was to keep going until the following morning, when a full breakfast would be served.

There were cocktails, followed by champagne and wine. We drank and danced and danced and drank. The friends who had invited us drank as much as we did, but their capacity wasn't as great as ours and Tim, our host, finally conked out on a settee in the mess. By seven a.m. he was sound asleep and snoring.

The regimental sergeant major had taken against Ian from the moment Ian told him he wanted to join the SAS many years earlier. The RSM had told him, 'You'll never make it, you're not good enough.' Ian felt the RSM had had it in for him from the moment he proved him wrong by passing Selection.

Instead of leaving the dinner dance at a reasonable hour so that everyone could let their hair down and really enjoy themselves, the RSM stayed until morning, watching everything with a look on his face as if there was an unpleasant smell under his nose. When he saw Tim crashed out on the settee, he started getting very vocal about it.

'Look at that!' he told a group of men at the bar. 'It's a disgrace. Wake that man up and get him out of here.' Before Ian could stop me, I was over at the bar giving the RSM a piece of my mind.

'Leave the poor chap alone,' I told him, as people around us gasped. 'It's been a long night, he hosted us brilliantly. Let him be, for God's sake.'

But the RSM wasn't having any of it. He continued to be rude about Tim and said he was shaming the Regiment. In my tired and emotional state I took this as a personal insult and launched into him again.

'I am sorry, but I will not have you insulting my friend in public,' I told the RSM, wagging my finger at him as if he were a naughty boy. It seemed that nobody had ever done that in the mess before. People were agog. I added, 'It isn't on. Who do you think you are, anyway?'

I heard Ian mutter under his breath, 'Oh, girl, you've done it now.'

The RSM was incandescent with rage. 'This is my mess, madam, and I will say what I like and to whom,' he told me, his moustache positively twitching.

'Well it might be your mess but that doesn't give you the right to be bloody rude,' I countered. There was silence all around us.

'Right, madam, I am going to have to ask you to leave the mess immediately,' the RSM said, his face now purple. I could taste a fight in the air and fired up by the drink, I clenched my fists at my side as I had done on that first day at my new school and told him, 'I bloody well shan't. I'll leave with my husband and my friend when he wakes up.'

Ian took one step closer to me, probably to stop me from decking the RSM, and we waited for his response. The RSM, aware that his authority was being questioned in front of the whole mess, turned to Ian and told him, 'I think you had better take your wife home.'

Ian laughed aloud. 'You are asking me to take my wife away, against her will? You are a braver man than me.' He drank from his glass and watched the RSM break out into a sweat. In the face of such defiance, he summoned a sergeant major for back-up.

'Escort these people out of my mess,' he barked. 'They are barred.' The sergeant major, who was something of a man-mountain, placed a hand on Ian's shoulder and said, 'I think the RSM wants you to leave now, sir.'

Ian looked up at this huge sergeant major who suddenly realised with some nervousness that he was trying to evict someone from the SAS, and said, 'Choose your window. Which one do you want to go out of?'

The sergeant major paled and said helplessly, 'I am only obeying the RSM's orders.' I recognised the look in Ian's eyes and realised that the time had come to drag him away before he killed someone.

I picked up my purse and wrap, looked the RSM straight in the eye and told him, 'It's OK. We wouldn't want to stay here any longer anyway.' I grabbed Ian's arm and said, 'Come on, babe, let's get out of here and go somewhere more friendly.'

Ian went over to where Tim was still sleeping, oblivious to the trouble he had caused, and picking him up gently, he slung him over his shoulder. As the three of us left rather unsteadily, I turned at the door and shouted across to the RSM, 'And you can send on my bloody chocolates.'

Within a week, we had received a very stiff letter from the RSM informing us that because of our behaviour we were banned from all future events at the mess. We laughed our heads off. 'What the hell would we want to go there for anyway?' we said. I don't think any of us will ever forget that night.

It had taken me two years to complete all the DIY jobs at the new house, and as I hung the last strip of wallpaper in the spare bedroom and looked out onto the newly completed garden layout, I had an uncanny feeling that Ian might now want to move again.

Sure enough, the minute he walked in the door from his latest mission, he took one look at what I had done and said, 'Great, babe, well done. But I've been thinking. Now that things are going so well, why don't we sell this place while the prices are still high and go for that place we always wanted in the country?'

I glared at him, my eyes blazing. He looked momentarily shamefaced.

'Well, you know you have always wanted to live in the country and so have I,' he added, more pleadingly. 'Think of all the walks we can take with Annie, and all the birds that you'll get there.'

Now he was playing on my emotions. I had always kept a magnificent bird table, laid out with chopped fruit and nuts, seeds and pieces of fat to attract woodpeckers, chaffinches and all manner of garden birds. Friends and relatives joked that the birds in our garden ate better than I did.

'You know you're playing dirty,' I warned him, as he grinned at me cheekily. 'And what about this place? You've hardly spent more than a fortnight in it.'

'Oh, come on, babe,' he pleaded. 'We'll make a fortune on this place now you've done it up so nicely, and then we can get an even better place and spend all the money on holidays and maybe even a new car.'

He looked at me hopefully.

Short of gluing his lips together with wallpaper paste, there was little or nothing I could do to stop him once he had got this far with it in his mind. I knew of old that once he had set his mind on something and had spent a few weeks sitting out in the jungle or in the middle of the desert thinking about it all, working out the profit margins in his head, then there was no going back.

He was very evidently fired up about moving and the capital he hoped it would release for us. He had also decided that it was time we had a new car.

Unless I wanted major grief, then move we would, sooner or later. Sooner, knowing Ian.

'OK, OK,' I told him. 'Just as soon as I get my breath back.'

# 5 | For Better for Worse

ONCE IAN WAS BACK on operational duties I knew there was always a risk that he would have to go away for an extended period of time. I had seen it happen to the other men and I was reluctantly aware that so far we had got off quite lightly.

The longest we had ever been apart was the six months when he had been sent to Northern Ireland just before we got married. I had hated every day of that separation and prayed that he would continue to do the one- to three-month training exercises and missions around the world that were just about bearable.

But one February night in 1987, I had just got in from work when I heard his voice calling me outside the house. 'Jenny, Jen, where are you?' he was shouting. I opened the front door and saw him standing at the gate, just about to come down the garden path. His face looked as if it was lit from within. He looked like the cat that had got the cream.

Rushing towards me, he scooped me up in his arms, lifting me high into the air. 'Mrs Jenny Simpson, allow me to introduce myself,' he said, jubilantly. I landed back on the ground and looked at him quizzically.

'Not rifleman . . . not trooper . . . not even corporal . . . but Sergeant Ian Simpson,' he said, and took a low bow. I couldn't believe my ears, he had been promoted from corporal to sergeant.

'Oh, babe, that's wonderful, wonderful news!' I cried and, holding his head firmly between my hands, I kissed him full on the mouth. He almost blushed. I was thrilled for him.

'They told me this afternoon. I finally got the old tick in the box,' he said. 'The RSM apparently sanctioned it personally. It means we can put all that nonsense behind us for good.'

I was genuinely delighted for him. No one but me knew what he had gone through after the theft charge, how much it had marred the years after the Falklands. Even all these years later I suspected he had been blaming it secretly for his lack of promotion. Now the Regiment had shown that it was forgotten. He had been given the pat on the back at last. We could get on with our lives. It meant more money, more responsibility and a bit of respect. It was no less than he deserved.

I took him inside and we cracked open the bottle of champagne we had been keeping for our next wedding anniversary. I couldn't remember seeing Ian so animated. He couldn't stop talking about how he had been told and what it all meant. We sat laughing and toasting his success with champagne. He was his old self again, carefree and alive. It was a wonderful moment.

'It'll mean more money,' he said. 'We won't have to scrimp and save quite so much. You never know, Jen, we might even be able to afford to get the decorators in next time.'

I threw the champagne cork at him. 'Don't you dare!' I cried. 'That is my job and the only thing that keeps me sane living around you, Sergeant Ian Simpson.'

He smiled but I suddenly knew there was something else he had to tell me. Taking my hands in his, his mood suddenly darkened and he looked into my eyes.

'Thanks for being so enthusiastic, babe. You know how much it means to me,' he said. 'But there is something else. As part of the promotion, I'm off across the water for a while as team commander. It is a fantastic accolade. It will be my first time there as team leader. It means almost as much as the promotion. Please don't be upset.'

'How long?' I gulped.

'Twelve months.' Looking suddenly ashamed, he let the words sink in. What about our holiday this year? And Christmas? And the house move he had got me started on? What the hell was I supposed to do about all that on my own? I wanted to scream: What about my life? Don't I count?

He leaned forward and put his arms around my waist.

'I'll be home every four weeks, babe, for a long weekend,' he said, almost defensively. 'Please don't cry.'

'I'm not crying,' I said angrily, blinking back the tears. The long year alone without him seemed to stretch ahead of me without end. I didn't want to spend it on my own, I wanted my husband by my side. But I also knew that he had to go, it was his job. It was the job he was doing when I married him and nothing I could say or do now would keep him.

'You should be really pleased for me,' he said, unsure of the expression on my face as I weighed it all up in my mind. 'Think what it means.'

I sighed heavily and fell into his arms. 'Oh, babe. I know. I am, really I am. I'm sorry. It's just that I'm really going to miss you. I thought it was all too good to be true.'

He held me to him and we stayed like that for several minutes, neither of us speaking. When I finally looked in his eyes, I could see that his delight at his news was tempered with his own sadness at the thought of all that time apart.

'Well, I'm still selling up the house and moving,' I told him flippantly. 'Especially now you're on sergeant's pay. We could get a bloody mansion. If you think this latest little trick will stop Jenny Simpson getting the brand new house in the country she wanted then you underestimated me. If you're a good boy, I'll send you the new address. If not, then it's back to living in single quarters for you.'

He grinned and kissed my hands.

'Let's go out to dinner to celebrate,' he said. 'My treat. Chinese or Indian?'

So that was how his main tour of duty in Northern Ireland came about in August 1987, six years after we were married. He flew across to this not so civil war at a time when the campaign by the IRA to target British servicemen across Northern Ireland, mainland Britain and Europe was at its height.

One soldier had recently been blown to bits in front of his wife and three children. In Dortmund, Germany, a soldier's wife was shot fourteen times in her car when the IRA gunman mistook her for her husband. Warnings were issued Europe-wide to servicemen and their families to be especially vigilant in the face of such arbitrary terrorism. 'No one is safe,' the message came. 'Be alert at all times. Never let your guard down.'

Ian promised to keep in touch and write as often as possible, so that we could maintain our gypsy fluencing to protect each other from harm. He told me to go ahead with the house move, to put our house on the market and look around for somewhere else. He signed over full legal proxy to me, in case anything happened to him or he wasn't available at a critical moment, and I prepared myself for the long year ahead.

'Twelve months,' I said to myself. 'Twelve months. That's all. And he'll be coming home twelve times during the year. We'll be fine. Everything will be all right.'

Despite the initial upheaval, we both quickly settled into our new routines. We had always had a long-distance relationship, after all, and I had the house move to keep me occupied. He rose to the challenge of being team commander and thoroughly enjoyed his first few months, setting everything up, deciding on targets for surveillance, who would be watching when and where and how best to deploy his men.

His first two trips home that late summer and early autumn were fine, we had quiet weekends together, spending much of the time in bed, the rest out walking the dog or having romantic dinners. It actually felt quite exciting, having a special liaison once a month. I would get my hair done and wear something sexy and look forward to my 'date' with my husband. How many others wives would get so excited about seeing their men? I told myself. Absence makes the heart grow fonder, after all.

Because he was coming home regularly and because he could telephone me every few days if he wanted to, we found that, after the first week or so, we hardly wrote to each other at all. There didn't seem much point. He would tell me all his news when he rang and I would save up mine for when he came home, so that I had something to talk about. I started keeping a notepad in my handbag as an *aide-mémoire* on which I would list the things I wanted to tell him.

But without realising it, by not writing out our thoughts and feelings to each other, by not taking the time to sit down and think carefully about how we both felt about the separation and its disadvantages, we were cutting off the vital, regular contact we had become so reliant on over the years to keep our relationship alive.

By the time Ian's third weekend home was due, I was already beginning to feel the strain of his absence. I had been house-hunting alone for months, but couldn't seem to make a decision about where we should live. We had someone interested in our house and they were pushing me for a response on their latest offer, but I was reluctant to take any steps that would force me into a decision I was not able to share with Ian. I couldn't wait for him to get home so that we could talk it over and I could take him to see the three houses I had identified as possible candidates.

I had the whole weekend planned. He was due home at seven p.m. on Friday and a nice meal, his favourite, 'turf and surf' – steak and king prawn – would be waiting for him. I had been to the hairdresser's and dolled myself up for the night. When we got up on the Saturday, we would drive around and view all the houses I had identified, and then mull over their pros and cons during a pub lunch.

That Saturday night we were due to meet our friends Tony and Linda for a meal, and for Sunday I had invited a few friends and relatives over for a full Sunday roast. It would be great.

The phone rang at 7.30 on Friday evening. I expected it to be Ian calling me to come and collect him from the camp. I heard his voice at the other end of the line and picked up the car keys from the kitchen table.

'You home, babe? I'll be right down.'

'No, Jen, no,' I heard him say. 'I'm really sorry, love, but my weekend off has been cancelled. We've got a big job on, a special operation and something has come up about it. I was just phoning to let you know.'

I tried unsuccessfully to hide the disappointment in my voice. I knew there would be no time to chat, he probably wasn't even meant to have called me. I swallowed hard and gripped the telephone.

'OK, babe,' I said. 'See you when you can next get home then. And Ian . . . please take care.'

I sat alone in the kitchen, my hair piled up onto my head, crying into a glass of red wine. Fingering the chunky bead necklace I was wearing, a gift from America on his last training mission, I ripped it violently from my neck and watched as the brightly coloured beads fell, bouncing, to the floor.

When Ian did come home, after eight weeks away, I wanted nothing more than a few quiet days alone together to remind me how good our marriage could be, to make me realise that the long separations were worth it because of the fantastic relationship we had when he was home. I wanted to laugh with him, play with him, feel and taste him again. I wanted to be truly happy once more.

But within an hour of his arrival, I could tell that the distance between us, coupled with the nature of the work he was doing, was beginning to get to him too. Apologetic as he was about the aborted visit, and anxious to make up for it, I could feel that somehow he wasn't really with me, that his body might have flown in to Hereford to spend a weekend with his wife, but his mind was somewhere else.

His work at that time once again involved intensive surveillance, following IRA terrorists, around day after day, night after night, watching them at close quarters, infiltrating their circle of friends and contacts. It was extremely dangerous work and it required all his concentration. When he woke up each morning he had no idea if that would be the day he was going to be compromised, and each night he dreamt that he had been.

As a soldier in the employ of the British Army, Ian found it extremely difficult to watch these people and know that they might at any time be setting off to plant a bomb that could kill several of his fellow soldiers. The temptation to eliminate the ones he knew were terrorists when he had them literally in his sights was enormous, and the frustration of not being allowed to by law consumed him.

With all this on his mind, he found it extremely difficult to come home and fall back into normal, married life. You can't just flick a switch and put the previous four to eight weeks behind you. It was almost impossible for us both simply to re-tune to each other's wants and needs. He knew and understood that I deserved all his love and attention, but he also needed those few days off for himself, to recover from the mental strains of his work.

I was as frustrated for him as I was for myself. I wanted to be sympathetic and spend as much time as he wanted or needed talking through his worries. But his weekends off were also my weekends off, my quality time away from the stresses and strains of my own job, even if they could not be compared to his. I felt I needed some sympathy and understanding too.

Once I had given him what I hoped was enough time to vent steam, I told him that we needed to go shopping and what I had arranged – Tim and Linda had invited us over for the afternoon and my parents were coming to supper. It was an attempt to bring him back into the real world, to remind him how life could and should be. But he just sat and stared at me with vacant eyes, as if he wasn't really hearing what I had to say.

I was to go through so much of that. Hours and hours of silence. It was an expression of frustration on all levels, and I found it harder to bear than almost anything. I think I would have preferred it if he had got blind, roaring drunk and screamed and shouted. But this zombie sitting in my kitchen wasn't what I wanted or expected at all. It was hardly surprising if I sometimes wondered what it would be like if he didn't come home at all.

Within six or seven months of his tour, I had stopped bothering with the special Friday nights. Several weekends off had been cancelled in a row and I never knew if he would be walking through the door or not. When he did, he was often so estranged, so mentally detached from me and our normal domestic life that it started getting to the point where I thought: Don't bother.

On a couple of occasions, I wasn't even in when he did come home – which didn't go down too well. Not expecting him, or losing track of the weekends, I had gone out with Sue and Anne, or Lisa and her friends for a night's drinking at one of the Hereford pubs. Unable to find me at my mum's or at any of the obvious places, he would sit brooding at home with a few cans of beer until I came back. Then he would play the abandoned husband routine.

I couldn't wait until the twelve-month tour was over, I was ticking off the days on a calendar on the kitchen wall. Three months gone, four, five, six, seven. Only five more months to go. That was twenty weeks, and he should be home five times in that period, God willing. As I counted down the months, anticipating his final return, I tried to remember what it was like when he was based at home. I would never complain about the six-week operations again.

Then on one trip home, I mentioned, in passing, as I was rewiring the kettle, that we could accept a friend's christening invitation for the following August because he would be home by then. His silence made me spin round and face him.

'I thought I had told you,' he said almost nonchalantly. 'The tour has been extended to fifteen months.'

I reached out and ripped the calendar from the wall. I felt like a prisoner who had just been told her ten-year sentence had been extended by another five years. The Bird Lady of Hereford in her own gilded cage. Maybe that is why I loved birds.

I decided there was nothing for it but to go ahead with the house sale, in the absence of any input from Ian, and I chose us a home in a small village outside Hereford. Brand new, detached, with a garden and in a small cul-de-sac of a few other homes, the house was not exactly what I wanted but it would do and somehow house-hunting without Ian yet again was simply no fun. I just hoped he would approve. The weekend he was due to come to view it with me, before we made the final offer, his boss telephoned to say he wasn't able to go because of a job.

'You know we wouldn't cancel his leave unless it was important, Jenny,' he said in response to my silence.

I went ahead and made the offer, had it accepted and signed all the paperwork alone. Ian never set eyes on the place until I drove him up the driveway on his first weekend home after I had moved in. With the help of my family and the removal men, I had it spick and span and filled with all our belongings.

I felt deeply uncomfortable as I showed him around. I could tell he was thinking the same thing, that it was as if I were showing him *my* house, with everything just as *I* wanted it. There was none of the sense I had hoped for of shared wonderment and excitement at exploring our new home together.

It wasn't the house of my dreams by a long chalk but by the time the decision had to be made, it seemed to be the most appropriate in terms of location, price and size and it was also somewhere that I knew would require little maintenance, an aspect of our domestic lives which had by then become totally my responsibility.

Ian said the house was fine and told me he was pleased with my choice, but deep down I wasn't so sure. I missed all my friends and neighbours in town. There were only a few other people around and I was already having second thoughts.

'Let's have a party to christen the house and celebrate your next trip home,' I said brightly. 'I'll organise it, you just make sure you get your arse home that weekend.'

It seemed like a great idea. It would give us both an opportunity to socialise with friends we hadn't seen together as a couple for months, we could meet the new neighbours properly and it would give the house some emotional warmth once it started to become a venue for friends, parties and happy memories.

I went to a lot of trouble with the preparations, sending out invitations, decking out the house with flowers and ornaments, marinating the meat for a barbecue and making up the food and drink. When I picked him up from the camp early that Saturday morning, Ian was in a great mood and looking forward to seeing the house again and helping with the party. I was hugely relieved.

Later that day, two hours before the guests were due to arrive, I was tidying the utility room when I heard his bleeper go off. I stopped folding the washing and held my breath as I listened to him pick up the telephone in the kitchen and dial the number of the camp. I couldn't hear exactly what was being said. The conversation was very brief and was followed by silence.

Then I heard banging – rhythmic, like a football being kicked against a wall. Trembling, I put down the washing and walked slowly into the kitchen, half afraid of what I might find.

The sight which greeted me was one of the saddest of my life. Ian was leaning against the wall by the telephone, banging his head against it again and again, a look of utter despair on his face. There was an emergency in the Province involving a bomb factory in County Down that he had been watching for months. He had been ordered to go back and lead the team in straight away. The helicopter was on the launch pad and he had to leave immediately. He had only been home for a few hours.

Watching his pain, I started to cry. It frightened me to see him like this. It was as if time stopped for a few minutes. We both stood frozen, looking at each other in a moment of intense sorrow and frustration, neither of us able to move towards and comfort the other.

He was, as ever, the first to recover. He held his head for a moment, then ran his hands through his hair and walked out of the room. Without a word he went upstairs and started repacking his kit. I pulled myself together and sat heavily on a kitchen chair. I wanted to run to him, to hold him and tell him it was all right, that I knew he had to go and why, that his disappointment for me should not be a factor. But I was too numb to move. I poured myself a large drink and sat for a few minutes, unable to do anything else.

When I had drained my glass, I stood up and walked into the utility room. Collecting a pile of his neatly washed and pressed clothes, I took them upstairs. Before I knew it, he was gone; the door slammed and that was it. No chance to talk, no time to discuss how we felt. He was back to Northern Ireland and for all I knew I might never see him again. I poured myself another drink and sat by the telephone in the kitchen, dialling the numbers of all our friends and neighbours to tell them I was sorry, but the party was cancelled.

Northern Ireland continued to be a particularly damaging place, emotionally, for us both. It is difficult for anyone else to imagine the frustration Ian went through and I was the one who had to deal with the consequences of it. He felt so helpless dealing with the politics of the place. He would tell me, 'I know the IRA. I can see them every day. I know who they are and what they have done. Yet I am not allowed to arrest them.'

He has always had such a clear-cut, almost childlike view of what is right and what is wrong. In the Falklands it was all so straightforward, all so clear. The Argentinians were the enemy and the British Army could destroy their bases, planes, ammunition stores and all their means of warfare, even if it meant killing some of them in the process.

In the Province it was different. The IRA were the enemy and yet they weren't. It seemed to Ian that if he and his team took out the ringleaders the rest would fall like a pack of cards. But they couldn't because of all the politicians and career servicemen who were trying to make political currency out of every situation, without having the courage to let the lads go in and sort it all out.

Instead Ian had to continue with surveillance and counter-intelligence, evidence-gathering, watching and waiting. Even when he had proof that something was about to happen, or someone had been responsible for a particular crime, there was always some Head Shed who could make or break the order and prevent him from doing what he felt he had been sent there to do, for political reasons.

He spent many of his nights holed up in a ditch, cold and wet, his mind playing tricks on him as he thought he heard or saw something or started imagining dreadful scenarios. He was often completely alone, his troop too far away to talk to and even if they weren't they could only talk in whispers. He'd get terrible cramp and not be able to move to ease his position. He would be on hard rations, going without food or water for hours, and then allowed to eat only cold Army rations after half freezing to death. When it was all over, the Head Sheds would just say, 'OK, let's move you and your troop on to the next one.'

After four weeks without a break he would come home and I would take one look at his eyes and think, Oh great, another fun-filled weekend.

\*      \*      \*

Not all his jobs were so physically and emotionally debilitating. Some were even rewarding in their own way. In one operation in early 1988 he was involved in the covert surveillance of a number of suspected IRA terrorists, including a man called Sean Savage.

Ian and his men were guarding a senior judge in Belfast, an elderly man who had been the subject of terrorist threats before and who, intelligence information suggested, was about to be attacked. The SAS men lived secretly with the judge in his house, taking turns to sleep, eating with him, watching his every move. He was a nice old boy and did not seem to bat an eyelid about the fact that he might be the target of a terrorist attack, he was so used to the danger.

His house was beautiful and he told the men to make themselves at home. His wife cooked them meals, made them tea and coffee and catered to almost all their needs. Far better than lying in a freezing ditch and shitting into a plastic bag, Ian thought. I don't think he ever wanted that job to end.

Then, late one night, while they were watching from the windows in darkness, they saw Savage outside the house. The soldiers went into full alert, hiding the judge in the cellar with his wife and taking up their positions, ready for the contact. Savage appeared to be alone, but they couldn't be sure, and they watched as he stood looking at the house, before walking around the perimeter as if he was looking for the best way in.

Whispering to each other through tiny radio microphones, Ian and his men kept each other informed of the suspect's movements as he walked around and around the big old house. Any minute now, they thought.

But almost as quickly as he had arrived in the residential street, he disappeared, walking hurriedly off towards town, his hands in his pockets. He had, it seemed, been checking the place out.

As far as Ian and his troop were concerned, from that point on, Sean Savage was theirs. Expecting him to come back and finish the job any time, they maintained intelligence on him for the next twenty-four hours and were on full alert, anticipating the moment of contact.

But then the news came that Savage had left Belfast abruptly, after apparently telling friends and family he was having a holiday in southern Ireland. Ian was told that this could be a trick and that they should stay where they were, ready for action.

Three more days of tea and biscuits, central heating and comfort. The lads really thought they had died and gone to heaven. But ever present at the back of their minds was that they had a job to do, to save their host's life in the event of an IRA attack, and the tension built up in them as they felt instinctively that something big was about to happen.

They were right. Savage did reappear at the end of that week and the SAS were watching him, but it wasn't Ian and his men. He had gone to southern Ireland as he had claimed, but instead of taking a holiday in Galway he travelled to Dublin, caught a plane to Paris under the name of Brendan Coyne and flew on to Malaga in Spain, arriving on the evening of Friday 5 March.

He was wearing a pinstripe jacket – the same one Ian had seen him wearing four days earlier – this time concealing a money belt containing £1,660 as well as 1,370 French francs and twenty-six Irish punts. He had flown in on the same flight as Daniel McCann, alias 'Robert Reilly', and the pair met up with Mairead Farrell, alias 'Katherine Smith'. His companions were both dedicated IRA terrorists.

Officials in Gibraltar went into a state of nervous panic after suggestions that the three were planning to plant a large remote-controlled car bomb at the Changing of the Guard ceremony on 8 March, killing as many soldiers as possible and probably maiming dozens of civilian tourists.

Within hours, the Regiment Head Sheds had scrambled about a dozen men from Hereford. They had been told that the their targets were highly dangerous fanatical terrorists, would probably be armed, and might be carrying a remote control device to make the bomb explode. The task ahead of them – in which they were told to arrest, disarm and defuse – was given the codename Operation Flavius.

On the morning of Sunday 6 March, Savage parked his hired white Renault Five in the parade assembly area. Two hours later

Farrell and McCann entered Gibraltar, met up with Savage and all three spent the morning chatting and examining the car.

At just after three p.m., the three suspects separated. Savage walked away from the others and literally bumped into one of the undercover SAS men watching him. Seconds later, the SAS opened fire on McCann and Farrell. Savage was shot a few yards away as he swung round at the sound of the gunfire. All three were killed.

Ian was disappointed that he hadn't been on that job, and so were the men he was working with. They felt that Savage at least had been their target, they had seen him, they knew what he looked like and they would have liked to have been sent to Gibraltar after him.

But from the Regiment's point of view, he accepted that their decision was probably right. The judge still needed protecting, Ian and his team were *in situ* and knew the lie of the land and it made sense to send a fresh team from Hereford to Gibraltar.

I was very relieved that Ian didn't go. When it was discovered afterwards that the terrorists hadn't been armed at all and that there was no bomb in the car, there was a huge controversy and the soldiers involved had to give chapter and verse at an inquest to justify their actions. It was terrible for them and called the whole Regiment into question and disrepute.

Ian took me to Gibraltar on holiday a few years later and, after touring the bars he frequented when stationed there as a young Green Jacket, we went to the scene of the shootings and stood there like tourists, taking photographs of each other and the spot where Ian could so easily have been one of the key players. We laughed and joked about it at the time, but I don't think either of us came away without wondering what might have been.

I tried to settle in to my new life in the country as best I could, and to persuade myself that the journey into town each morning and home again at night was worth it, for the joys of rural living. But the reality was that I was even more isolated there than I had been in town and I wasn't happy.

Yes, there were more birds and far greater varieties. Yes, Annie and I did enjoy long walks together across the fields, but there was no Ian to share them with and it just didn't feel as satisfying as I had hoped it would.

Most of my new neighbours were charming and delightful, although they were largely young families with children. I hadn't yet got to know them well enough to tell them what Ian did, or why he was away. As far as they knew, he had been relocated to Northern Ireland by his company. My family and friends like Sue and Anne were now quite a drive away and that meant that I didn't see them nearly as often as I used to. I felt I had lost the ability just to drop in on people on my way home from work, or have them drop in on me.

My niece Lisa, with whom I had spent many a Friday night when Ian was away, was now living in Jersey, working in a chemist's, and although I wrote to her regularly and spent a small fortune sending her food parcels and gifts, her physical presence was something I missed enormously.

I felt strangely impotent, cut off and alone. There were always books to read and television programmes to watch, and I could go running or to the gym, but my interest in that had tailed off. When I woke up one morning about eight months into Ian's tour with a raging headache, I wondered if I was going to start getting migraines again, or whether it was just the effect of the drink I had had the night before.

Ian was enduring further frustrations across the water, as several operations he had set up and planned weeks in advance went ahead without him, either because he was off for the weekend or because his superior officers chose not to involve him.

The chief reason, he felt, was a personality clash with one of his ruperts, for whom Ian had no respect. It seems the officer was jealous of the adoration Ian enjoyed from some of his men. It is true that the men liked Ian enormously. In some of his career reports, the Head Sheds noted that Ian was often 'idolised' by younger men in his team. There was nothing Ian could do about that, he was a fun bloke to be with, was good at his job and enjoyed taking the newer recruits under his wing, but jealousy about his popularity would surface time and again throughout his career.

In his phone calls and on his trips home Ian started to express anger over some of the minor injustices he was suffering in Northern Ireland. It reminded me of his feelings after the Belize incident. I only hoped he would not allow it to eat him up in the same way.

The worst disappointment for him was his involvement, or lack of it, in the operation to target the Harte brothers, two members of an IRA active service unit near Omagh in south-east Tyrone. The brothers, Gerard, twenty-nine, and Martin, twenty-three, had been pressurised by more senior members of the IRA to get a result in the area after the Loughall incident in 1987 – the SAS's greatest success against the IRA in twenty years in which eight members of an active service unit were killed as they attacked a police station.

The Hartes were suspected of being responsible for the bombing of a bus carrying soldiers of the First Battalion The Light Infantry to their base from Aldergrove airport in Belfast in August 1988. More than 200 pounds of Semtex in a land mine killed eight of the soldiers and injured twenty-seven, many seriously.

The brothers became a priority for surveillance after that and consequently decided to go for a softer target next time, a part-time member of the Ulster Defence Regiment who also worked as a coal merchant, delivering sacks of coal to the villages around Drumnakilly where he lived.

Ian and his men received some very good information that the attack was about to take place and that the Hartes and an accomplice planned to hijack a car with which to follow the coalman around on his beat and attack him when he delivered coal to the local priest's house.

The SAS set up an ambush at the priest's house and waited for the coalman and the IRA to arrive. They lay in ditches hidden by shrubs five yards from the front door. The team waited for a day, but the Hartes never came. The intelligence division put out some feelers and discovered that when the brothers couldn't find the sort of car they wanted to hijack, they decided to go to the pub and get drunk instead.

Ian's troop were pulled off the target, and made some contingency plans in case anything happened while they weren't there. Their information was that the coalman was being watched constantly, and that the attack could happen at any time. It was all down to what they called 'the Paddy factor', whether or not Paddy wanted to go through with it on a particular day.

The following weekend, the last in August, Ian was home for four days and attending our friend's baby's christening, when the Head Sheds decided to force the Hartes' hand. On the Tuesday morning the coalman was replaced by a member of the SAS wearing his overalls. The soldier drove the coal truck to a remote place in the peat bogs, an ideal location for the Hartes to attack. He then pretended that the truck had broken down.

The balaclava-wearing brothers took the bait and soon arrived in a stolen Ford Sierra to attack the lorry with Kalashnikovs. The SAS was waiting for them. The brothers were challenged and shot dead, along with their accomplice and brother-in-law Brian Mullin, twenty-six. An inquest into the deaths several years later heard that 236 rounds were fired at their car by the SAS soldiers waiting for them in the bushes.

It was a tremendous success for the Regiment, since it effectively shut down the East Tyrone brigade of the IRA. The SAS patrol commander who had taken the place of the intended victim was awarded the Distinguished Conduct Medal. Better still, the IRA conducted their own enquiry into the ambush afterwards and a couple of the local 'boyos' ended up shooting each other dead after each accused the other of tipping off the police.

Ian hadn't been bleeped or asked to command the operation, even though he had been on call all weekend. Instead, the operation had been reinforced with nine men from Hereford, not one of them a team commander. The first he knew about the ambush was when he woke up with me the following morning and watched a bulletin on the breakfast television news as I was making the coffee.

He was angry, upset and confused. He felt frustrated and disappointed at not being involved in the conclusion of a job he had planned and controlled, yet he knew that another call home that weekend to take him back to Ireland would have caused considerable distress to me. It had been very important to me that he was home that weekend, so I would not have to attend yet another social function on my own. Either way, Ian couldn't win.

He was also struck by the realisation that, with people like his particular senior officer in charge, he would never achieve the level of success he wanted to within the Regiment. It was not a good weekend.

Ian's response to hurt and disappointment had always been to close in on himself, so much that I couldn't reach him. He started drinking very heavily across the water and would phone me late at night and ramble on incoherently. When he came home he would get drunk and leery with his mates and I would have to endure the macho male act as he sat holding court around the dining table, showing off in front of his friends.

One Sunday I prepared a huge roast lunch for him and his mate Patrick. They had gone to the pub as soon as it opened that morning, got fully tanked up and came back only when I went and dragged them home because the meal was burning. Ian sat at the head of the table and opened a bottle of wine, as I started to dish out the roast potatoes and Yorkshire puddings, one of his favourites.

'What's this shit?' he said suddenly, poking a fork disdainfully into a slightly burnt Yorkshire pudding. His mate giggled at his nerve.

'It's your bloody lunch,' I said, hacking at the joint of meat and placing a thick slice on his plate. He turned up his nose and pushed his plate away.

'Well, I'm not eating that shit,' he told Patrick, laughing. 'And you don't have to either, mate. Have another drink.'

All I can remember is seeing red. Something snapped inside my head. I walked into the kitchen to count to ten and calm down, but Ian came staggering after me, bottle of wine in hand, to complain further. Almost as soon as he opened his mouth, I swung my arm back as far as I could without wrenching my shoulder socket and then launched it, fist clenched, straight at Ian's face.

The look of surprise in his eyes in the split second before contact was worth every minute I had slaved over that lunch.

Caught off guard and off balance, he tumbled backwards as my fist connected with his jaw. Still clutching the bottle of wine, which spilled its contents all over the front of his favourite white shirt, he fell – almost in slow motion – down towards the kitchen floor.

His feet slipped from under him, his body turned and twisted slightly to try to save himself, but there was nothing he could do. His shoulders hit the floor with a thump and the rest of his torso followed. He ended up with backside smack in the dog's heavy china bowl, which was full of water.

It took him several seconds to recover. He lifted his head and, rubbing his bruised jaw in which there was a clear indentation from the large gold ring I was wearing, he looked up at me in astonishment.

'What the fuck did you do that for?' he said, still rubbing his jaw.

I stood over him, my right fist still clenched.

'Don't you ever dare criticise my cooking again,' I said, fuming. 'Now get back to the table and eat your meal or I'll deck you a second time.'

With water dripping from the seat of his trousers and a dog biscuit stuck to his hair, he did as he was told. The meal was eaten in subdued silence.

There was so much I wanted to say to him on his next weekend home and I hoped there were things he would want to say to me, but when he walked into the house he put his bergen in the hall and locked himself away in his study.

OK, I thought, if this is how it's going to be for a couple of hours until he has got used to being back and stopped sulking, then I'll just have to wait until he is ready to come out and talk. He'll come out soon. It will be all right. He'll tell me he is sorry and we'll have a cuddle and go to bed. The radio was on and I sang along to the music as I busied myself with the housework.

But the hours went by and nothing changed. Ian completely

ignored me when I told him lunch was ready, so I put it on the desk where he was sitting, staring at the wall with a blank expression on his face.

It was evening when he came out of the study, and he headed straight for bed. When I joined him a little later he pretended he was asleep, his back turned to me. He didn't make one attempt to touch or hold me, and when I tried to cuddle him, he moved away. I silently cried myself to sleep and hoped that everything would be better in the morning.

I woke at six a.m. alone. The house was empty and his running gear was missing, along with Annie, so I assumed he had gone for a run with her.

Right, I thought, a good Geordie breakfast is what he needs, so I got dressed and started frying up sausage, bacon and eggs, ready for when he got back. By the time he returned, his breakfast was black and crispy from heating too long in the oven. He hardly said a word, and sat down to read the Sunday newspapers.

Once again, something inside my head just snapped. I stood up, grabbed the newspaper he was reading, threw it to the floor and said, 'Right, you bastard, you bloody well talk to me or this is the end of us. What is going on inside your head?' Then I slapped him full on the face, really hard, and stood shaking over him, wondering what reaction I would get. His skin reddened where my palm had made contact.

I had never hit him before and now in the space of two weekends home he was qualifying for a place in a battered husband's refuge. He sat staring up at me, blinking, and then said, very quietly and with a look in his eyes that made me melt, 'I'm sorry, Jen. Come here and give us a cuddle.'

He put his arms around my waist and pulled me to him, and I buried my face in his hair. When I had finished telling him how much I loved and missed him, the old Ian that I knew and loved looked up at me with an impish grin and said, 'Any chance of some breakfast?' I chased him all around the house with a rolled-up newspaper.

My shock tactics weren't always so successful, however, and sometimes he would go back to Northern Ireland as estranged from me as when he had arrived. A lot depended on how strong I was feeling, and whether I was prepared for the battle, or just felt like letting him shut me and everyone else out. On the worst weekends it was almost as if he wasn't there. I would just get on with my life, go out, have a drink, have friends over, or watch a movie while he sat silently in his study staring at the wall or went out on his own for a long walk with the dog.

But over the years I had developed the belief that I had to bring him out of himself in some way, to get him to open up and talk to me about his feelings, otherwise our relationship would never move forward. I had learned that unless I stopped his thoughts festering inside, they would destroy him, even if I didn't always want to be there to witness the results of my amateur therapy.

I would bully Ian into talking to me about what he was feeling. When he went for a long walk, I went with him and chatted on about family matters until he found himself drawn into the conversation automatically. By the time we got home, we would be holding hands.

On one occasion when he was behaving like a zombie, I took up him to our friend's caravan at Borth. I packed up tins of Army rations – meat stew, beans and tinned vegetables – took a couple of bottles of wine and a bottle of Jack Daniels and bundled him into the car. He hardly said a word to me all the way there, but when he got out of the car at the beach and inhaled the fresh salt air, he seemed to wake up. He took the dog for a long walk by the sea while I threw all my ingredients into a huge saucepan and opened the wine, ready for his return.

I lit a candle and when he got back he was his old self again. We had a lovely supper, eating my hastily prepared concoction, and spent the rest of the weekend cuddling up, going for long walks and eating fish and chips on the sea front for supper. It really blew the cobwebs away and when he went back, he was a new man.

Fighting Ian's demons was hard work, and there were times during that year when I honestly didn't mind him going back to that place from where I knew he might never come home. Just occasionally, when I didn't have the energy to face his moods, or was feeling too miserable myself to court any more trouble, I felt that if he was there forever neither of us would really have minded.

He was doing what he believed in, all the lads together, fighting the enemy in their own little world where good and evil battle it out. In his own way he was quite happy. It was just so mentally and physically absorbing that he couldn't handle anything else, even me. His unhappiness only really came out when, like a fish out of water, he was flipped out of the pond onto the bank and had to lie there gasping for air.

Many members of the Regiment stay single, or have one failed relationship after another, because the time away from the job is in some ways much harder for them than anything they face at work. Suddenly they have to deal with real life, real emotions, and learn how not to hurt other people's feelings. They can't just be themselves in their own little world, looking after Number One. They are not used to the demands on their time, attentions and emotions.

Just as I sometimes felt that I didn't want Ian home if he couldn't handle it, I am sure he would have felt more comfortable staying in the pond, swimming around with all the other fish.

Most of his jobs were over quickly, in and out in a matter of weeks or months. The Falklands had been longer and more intensive, but Northern Ireland was the hardest to bear of all. Not only was it so dangerous, the place where he looked death in the eye every day, but it was also so concentrated.

Little did the people committing atrocities over there realise that the violence they dished out was in turn dished out at home by the men who were trying to control it. Not shootings or bombings, of course, but mental and physical violence of a kind that suddenly erupts for no reason and simply cannot be prepared for.

The only people who knew what this combination of factors did to the men were their wives, torn between wanting to help them and wanting to help themselves. If a wife couldn't find the balance, as I very nearly couldn't at times, then the marriage was over. It is not surprising so many fell by the wayside.

My saving grace was the arrival back in Hereford of Lisa. She returned from Jersey and we held a surprise party for her. Afterwards, she and I took Annie for a long walk across the fields.

'I've been thinking, Auntie Jenny,' she started, and I knew something was about to follow. I pushed back the wisps of brown hair from her face and examined it carefully.

'I've been thinking that I would like to come back and go to college here, to do secretarial studies,' she said.

Fine, I thought. Her mother lives in Liverpool, and my parents are too set in their ways to take her in. I think I know what's coming.

'I know it would be hard for me to get in when I don't even live here, but, well, I am positive that you could arrange it for me.' I stopped in my tracks and stared at her.

'And once I got my place, I would only start off living with you for a few months,' she hurried on. 'Then I'd move out just as soon as I had got myself a bed-sit.'

It took me weeks to arrange. Through a series of telephone calls, letters and even verbal threats, the Geordie charm finally worked and Lisa got offered a place at the local technical college. She moved in and my house suddenly seemed smaller and less empty.

She was a pain in the arse, of course, show me a teenager who isn't. She had her set ways and annoying habits. She had to have a bath every day, at a certain time, even if it meant I couldn't have one because all the hot water had gone. She wouldn't consider having a shower to save money. She was constantly on the phone, didn't help much with the housework, stayed out late and woke me up when she came in, and she ate me out of house and home.

But I was glad of her company and grateful for her youthfulness. Her high spirits kept me buoyant, she understood the loneliness I felt when Ian was away and she had the good sense to keep out of the way when he came home for one of his moody weekends.

She also appreciated that it wasn't just the emotional mind games Ian's absence in Northern Ireland played on me. There was the sheer bloody fear of what might happen to him when he was out there.

After the Sea King crash, I never wanted to go through that dreadful experience of watching and waiting again, not knowing if Ian was alive or dead, but it very nearly happened again in March 1988 after the funeral procession of the three IRA members killed in Gibraltar.

That Saturday afternoon I was home with Lisa, doing the ironing, when the phone rang. It was Johno, a friend of ours from the Army Air Corps, who was based in Germany. 'Is everything all right?' he asked cautiously. My mind flashed back to a similar telephone call in 1982.

'Yes, fine,' I said. 'Why?'

'Ian's OK, then? Is he home at the moment?'

'No,' I said. 'He is across the water.'

Johno was quiet for a moment.

'What is the matter Johno, tell me?' I said, my voice rising. Lisa stood up and came to my side at the ironing board, her face etched with worry.

'It's just something we just saw here on the television news,' Johno said, choosing his words carefully. 'A couple of plain-clothed soldiers who blundered into the IRA funeral cortege from that Gibraltar job have been killed by a lynch mob and . . .'

'What?' I almost shouted into the receiver.

'Well, one of them looked just like Ian.'

My mind galloped through what he had said.

'It can't have been,' I told him. 'It can't have been. I'd have heard.'

Lisa had been listening at the ear piece and went to turn the television on. She flicked the channels but the screen showed images of sport and an old black-and-white movie.

'Don't worry, Johno,' I told our friend. 'It can't have been Ian, really. I am sure he is fine. I'll call up the camp and call you back.'

I telephoned the camp but they said they hadn't had any unusual news from Belfast. I replaced the receiver and watched the television screen as Lisa flicked through the channels once more. A few minutes later, the BBC announced a newsflash. The jerky images taken by a news cameraman in the crowd at Milltown cemetery showed a car containing the two soldiers being surrounded by an angry mob.

I peered at the myriad of moving faces, terrified I might recognise my husband's, but it was all too unclear. Then, one image flashed up on the screen for a couple of seconds. A man who looked incredibly like Ian had drawn his gun and fired in desperation and was being pulled from the car and beaten. He was dragged away by men waving guns.

Lisa gasped and held her hands to her mouth. I stood stock still and stared and stared at the screen, transfixed by the sight. The newsflash ended and the announcer said that both the soldiers involved were believed to have been shot dead.

The telephone rang. It was another of Ian's friends, Tom, who was calling from Liverpool. He had watched the newsflash too and believed it to be Ian. I wondered if both these men, who knew Ian better than I did in some ways, could possibly be right when my heart was telling me they were wrong.

'It wasn't Ian,' I said, convinced finally that I was speaking the truth.

The face I had seen on the screen had fooled me for a minute as fear crept into my heart, but as my mind paused and replayed the image over again, I suddenly realised that the man waving the gun had been right-handed. Ian is left-handed. Hearing myself tell Tom that Ian wasn't the man reassured us both.

The telephone rang later that afternoon as the camp confirmed what I knew to be true, that Ian was safe. He called me himself half an hour later and teased me for even thinking that it could have been him.

'Honestly, Jen, you are silly,' he said. 'The soldiers who died were corporals in the Signals Regiment. And anyway, I wouldn't have been so bloody stupid as to have turned up waving a gun like that in the middle of an IRA funeral, whichever hand I was using.'

I think Lisa was more upset than I was about the incident. Shocked at what she had seen and terrified that it might have been Ian, she spent much of the evening in tears, first for me, then for the men who died and, finally, for their widows and family.

'What if they had been watching the news,' she sobbed. 'And had recognised their husbands?' I bade the widows a silent prayer.

\*       \*       \*

The fifteen months dragged slowly by and Ian's trips home did little to bind us together. In some ways they drove us further apart. We went through a particularly bad patch when Ian didn't come home at all for a while and I suspected that he just didn't want to. By this time, he was regularly drinking himself into oblivion, so much so that one of his younger troop members took him to one side and told him to get a grip on himself.

When he did come home for a weekend, he would often be abusive. I found myself wishing once again that he had stayed away. I knew that his moods and sudden outbursts were slowly destroying us but I didn't know what I could do to stop it and often felt too tired to try.

It was about this time that the fights started. I was fed up with playing the brave little woman waiting at home and he was just exhausted. He admitted years later that it was never my fault that the arguments started. He always picked them. But once we got going, I gave as good as I got and we would be screaming the place down within minutes of him walking in the front door.

By this time, I believed Ian when he told me – in the heat of yet another row – that he didn't care about me or the house or 'jackshit'. He didn't want to be in Northern Ireland, he didn't want to be with me, he didn't know what he wanted. I gave up trying to second-guess him and, for a while, we lost all control. He was often drunk, I was no longer budgeting properly or taking care of myself or the house, and we were fighting almost all the time.

On the nights he came home unexpectedly and I was out, he wrongly accused me of seeing someone else. He even suggested that he might start doing the same over there. One weekend when I went to an office function, after which he was meant to be picking me up, he drank several pints of cider while I was out and when I telephoned to ask for a lift he shouted for me to get one of my 'boyfriends' to drop me home. I burst into tears and caught a taxi to The Swan to cry on the shoulders of Mandy and Terry. Terry went round to see Ian to try to sort it out, but he found him unconscious and then brought me home. Ian and I slept on opposite sides of the bed.

In the heat of our many arguments I would often reach out and slap his face in anger and he started to punch me back. I would kick and scream and bite and fight, and he would have to sit on me on the floor, pinning my arms to my sides until I calmed down and stopped hitting and scratching him.

The battles of wills would take hours. He would hold me down, using all his strength and weight to keep me still, and I would lie there, crushed, waiting for my moment to try to break free. It was like an extraordinary wrestling match and would only end when Ian grew so tired of pinning me down that he would jump up and walk out of the house, or lock himself in his study, just to get away. Then I would lie where I was on the floor, crying and rubbing my bruises. I bruise very easily and my body would be black and blue for weeks on end.

I had begun to convince myself that our marriage was on the rocks. I felt that there was little or no point carrying on. Things were getting dangerously violent, we were losing control and I wanted to get away. I wanted to be free of Ian and his moods. I wanted to have a normal life with a normal husband and start to feel human again.

Matters came to a head during one particularly heated argument, which had started over nothing at all – an outburst by him about the enormous telephone bill. The telephone had been my lifeline since I moved to the country. I would spend hours on the phone in the evenings, chatting to Sue and Anne, my family and other friends. Now he was complaining about how much it cost and I was shouting back that he didn't understand.

He suddenly spun round and shouted at me, 'Why don't you just bugger off then, if I am such an insensitive bastard?'

I stopped and stared at him. 'Yes, Ian, why don't I?' I said quietly.

It was his turn to stop and stare.

'Well, give me one good reason why I shouldn't?' I asked, hoping for an argument as to why I should stay, though I wasn't really sure I wanted to hear it. 'Let's face it, the whole bloody thing has turned to rat shit.'

He sat down heavily in a chair and bowed his head. I thought he might cry. He ran his hands through his thick black hair – now flecked with grey – and looked back up at me.

'Well, what are you saying?' he asked, unexpectedly quiet now.

I took a deep breath and spoke the words my mind had been telling me for months. 'I'm saying there is no point in going on if all we can do is fight and hit each other all the time,'

I wondered at the courage of my own words, but felt compelled to speak them. He looked shocked, genuinely taken aback and stared at me for what seemed like ages without saying anything.

I broke the silence. 'What I am saying is, unless things improve vastly, I think our marriage could be in serious trouble.'

Without speaking he stood up and, grabbing his coat, headed for the front door. I leaned back against the kitchen table, wanting to run after him, to tell him that I loved him and wanted him back the way he used to be. But I couldn't move. My head was ruling my heart for once and it was telling me to let him go.

As soon as the door slammed, I felt my knees give way. I reached for the gin bottle and a glass and sat down to pour myself a drink. My mascara was streaking down my face before I had even finished the first glass.

So that was it. A fight to end all fights and then he was gone. I might never see him again. It had happened a dozen times to friends of mine and now it was happening to me. I was going to be just another of the abandoned Hereford Wives, the most elite of all the nation's dumped women.

I was asleep on the sofa when Ian came home and I felt his lips brush my cheek. I opened my eyes to find him kneeling next to me, his eyes as red as mine from crying.

'I love you, Jen,' he said, taking my hand in his, 'I don't know why I am doing this to us because I do still love you. I realise that now. I just need some time to get my head together. It's this job. It's doing my head in. I'm so sorry.'

I sat up and took his hands in mine. I kissed them and pulled him to me and we lay together on the sofa, hugging each other, silently willing our marriage back together again.

I felt suddenly guilty, as if I had somehow let him down. Wasn't he doing his best, fighting the enemy, the IRA, for us all and having to deal with the mental consequences on his own when he came home to me? Wasn't my job to comfort and console him? Had I not berated other wives for not being compassionate enough with their men, understanding their special needs and giving them all the support they needed?

What he needed was my special care, the comfort only I could give him. His outbursts were a cry for help, a childlike tantrum at the frustration and tension he was feeling. I scolded myself for my selfishness and made myself promise to keep my marriage vows.

'We both deserve so much better than this, babe,' I finally said, taking him by the hand and pulling him to his feet. 'Come to bed and let me make it up to you.' I dried my eyes and led him up the stairs.

We spent the rest of the weekend like a different couple. The unspeakable had been spoken, the gauntlet had been thrown and we had both realised that neither of us was prepared to pick it up. We did have a marriage worth saving after all. We always knew we had but it had taken the threat of losing it to bring it home.

How does that Joni Mitchell song go? 'You don't know what you've got 'til it's gone.' Coming close to losing our marriage had taught us its value. We knew we were made for each other, we had known it from that first night after the Paludrine Club. We had just needed a reminder, that was all. We were going to be fine.

# 6 | In Sickness and in Health

THE NEXT TIME Ian was due home, he was to stay for almost a week and I couldn't wait. Was this the end of the bad times? I wondered hopefully as I drove into the camp to pick him up. He flew in early one Saturday morning, arriving by helicopter at the base and I took him straight home. Lying in bed later that morning, he told me, 'I am so glad to be home, girl, this is great. Today is the first day of the rest of our lives.'

I breathed a huge sigh of relief. Fingers crossed, there would be none of the petty bickering, anger or jealousy that had poisoned some of our most precious moments together recently. Maybe he had meant what he said.

But within a few hours, I knew that my hopes would be dashed. There was nothing specific at first, just a general clamming up on his part, and a growing suspicion in my mind that all was not well. He started to drink and the sharpness returned to his tone. He began to comment on what I was wearing and how I had arranged my hair.

'There's something different about it,' he slurred. 'Anyone would think you were dressing up specially for someone else.' He accused me of changing my perfume and he said I was wearing more make-up.

I had done nothing to provoke his jealousy, but his mind had been affected by the isolation across the water and there was nothing I could do to stop him thinking that I was having an affair with someone or was dressing more suggestively than I had previously been.

It didn't occur to him for one minute that my special attempts to look good might have been for his benefit and his alone. And when I pointed this out to him, he laughed in my face. No amount of pleading on my part could convince him.

Infidelity was common within the Regiment: wives bored at home, fed up with feeling lonely and unloved, flattered by charmers who are excited by the prospect of stealing an SAS officer's wife from under his very nose; soldiers alone and under pressure abroad, seeking solace in women and booze in some Godforsaken bar; relationships that became more serious after the initial fling, women falling pregnant, men not knowing what to do for the best.

How many SAS men counted back to the alleged date of conception when a child was born 'prematurely'? How many wives discovered their husbands had illegitimate children scattered half-way around the globe?

Just as I had seen some of the wives fooling around at home, Ian had seen the men playing away and it didn't take much imagination or paranoia to start thinking that it could be happening to your spouse too.

By the time Ian dropped me off at work that Monday, his mood had metamorphosed. All the promises and assurances of his previous weekend home had been forgotten. He was surly, abusive and prickly.

When he picked me up from work that night, he sullenly watched me as I walked towards the car. The first thing he said when I got in was, 'I hope he appreciates how you are dressing up for him.' Fine, I thought. Terrific. I wasn't dressed any differently from normal, but as he was rarely there to see how I would usually dress for work, he had started to imagine that I was dressing up for someone else. I decided not to rise to the bait and we drove home in silence.

By the end of the week he was extremely uptight and I was a nervous wreck, wondering exactly when all the frustration and jealousy bubbling inside him would erupt. I had endured a headache for two days and was tired of all the mind games he was making me play. If I could just get him through the week, I started thinking, then he would be back in Northern Ireland and he could take it out on some IRA terrorist and not me. So much for our truce.

I knew the signs to look for. Each night when I got home from work I checked the look in his eyes. I knew from past experience that sometimes I didn't get much of a warning, and that glazed look would be my last glimpse before the violence would explode. I felt on edge the whole time, as if I was constantly stepping carefully around a land mine, that if I made one false move I would misjudge my footing and it would all blow up in my face.

His last night home was particularly strained. Lisa was still living with us and I had invited a girlfriend for dinner and to stay the night, in the vain hope that some pleasant company might defuse the atmosphere. It didn't. Ian sat at the table playing with his food, jumping down my throat at the slightest comment and pouring himself too much wine. I could have cut the air with a knife, it was so thick with tense expectation.

Not surprisingly, both our guests decided to turn in early, sensing Ian's mood. We were left alone together in the lounge, watching television and having a night cap. He was still in his jeans and sweater, I was in a T-shirt ready for bed.

Half-way through the Ten O'Clock News, an item came on about the latest IRA atrocity in Belfast. An off-duty RUC officer had been gunned down in the hallway of his own home, as his wife and four children looked on. Two of the children had been hit by the bullets sprayed from the guns and were critically ill in hospital. Their mother was filmed being led hysterically from the house, her dress stained with the blood of her husband and small children, after she had cradled them in her arms. We watched the devastating images in silence before Ian picked up the remote control and clicked off the set.

'Why can't someone stop those bastards?' I said, almost casually, standing up to leave the room, ready to turn in. I don't even know why I said it. It was an off-the-cuff remark, a meaningless, rhetorical question that required no answer, no reaction. It was just an expression of the frustration felt by anyone watching the broadcast at the inability to put an end to the bloodshed.

When it came, it came from nowhere. Before I knew it, Ian had leapt to his feet and was looking at me like a crazy man. He grabbed my neck and chin, yanked my face inches from his own and spat,

'You haven't got a fucking clue, have you?' His eyes were not his own.

I was paralysed by shock and fear. Unable to respond or even struggle, I was as limp as a rag doll when his hands grabbed two fistfuls of my hair and smashed my head into the wall behind him. I felt my hair tearing at the roots as it strained to support my head, and my eyes filled with tears. A burning pain spread across my forehead.

Getting a better grip, he pushed my head down to my knees and started to drag me across the room. I was doubled up, my knees bent, my legs straining to get a foothold. I screamed and tried to ease his grip with my fingers as handfuls of hair parted company with my scalp.

He pulled me across the floor, the carpet burning my bare flesh. I couldn't lift my head, but I could see we were heading for the stairs. 'Ian!' I shouted. 'Ian, stop!' I struggled to break free, but he only increased the pressure as he roughly bumped me up the first few steps. I felt every stair-tread. I tried to pull back from his grip, but his brute force overpowered me.

My head, knees and elbows cracked against the walls and banisters. The rough stair carpet grated my skin. I was crying from a combination of pain and sadness that the man I loved was doing this to me. When I did manage to raise my head and look up at his face, I saw a look of venom in his eyes that I will never forget for as long as I live. His jaw was set and he was glowering at me from above. It was the face of a man in torment.

I felt frightened and alone. I had never thought that he would hurt me like this. I tried to remind myself that inside he was hurting just as much as I was. I couldn't help wondering what was going to happen to me when he got me to the top of the stairs.

By the time he had pulled me almost to the landing I had stopped resisting him. He was far too strong for me and my only chance of escape was to let him think I was giving up the fight. His clenched fists were still buried in my hair and I was half-kneeling, half-standing on the top step. I looked down and saw blood all over my T-shirt. My nose was bleeding.

Suddenly, he released his grip. I fought to regain my balance. My hands found the banister just in time. I turned my tear-stained face to his, my eyes pleading for mercy. Ian had not reached out to stop me from falling. He stood looking down at me, his eyes blank and distant now. I held my breath. Without speaking, he turned abruptly and walked away in silence, slamming the bedroom door behind him.

Collapsing, I gasped for breath. Wiping the blood and tears from my face, I picked myself up. Gingerly I ran my hands down my arms and legs, feeling for broken bones. As none were immediately evident, I smoothed back the broken skin on my knuckles and picked myself up. I limped down the stairs and into the kitchen where I reached for the gin bottle and poured myself a large drink.

It was 10.30 p.m. It had all been over in a matter of minutes, although it felt so much longer. I sat crying into my glass at the kitchen table until the early hours, a wad of bloody tissues pressed to my nose. There wasn't a sound elsewhere in the house, neither Lisa nor my other house guest had come to see if I was all right, and Ian remained shut away in the bedroom.

I closed the kitchen door and tried to cry quietly so as not to wake anyone, but great, gulping sobs spluttered from my mouth spasmodically. I relived the sequence of events over and over in my mind, shivering at the memory. I was cold but too frightened to go upstairs to get any clothes, so I wrapped Ian's overcoat around my shoulders and pulled my skinned and bruised legs up under me on the chair.

Every bone in my body ached, my scalp burned. My long blonde hair was twisted into a knotted tangle on my head. I had to hold the gin glass with both hands to stop the contents from spilling.

I felt as desolate as I had ever felt in my life. I couldn't believe what had just happened, how much Ian had hurt me. Whatever else had gone on before, even the occasional slap, it had never gone as far as this. I was frightened and confused. Where would we go from here? Where could we go? Was this how marital violence started, now he had crossed the barrier would there be any going back? I had seen and read about battered wives and heard them say they never left because they still loved their men. Was that what would happen to us? A downward spiral of abuse?

I did still love him, in spite of myself. I even understood where all his anger had come from and why it had erupted at that particular moment. It had been my fault, partially, I told myself. There was no excuse for what he did, but if I hadn't opened my big Geordie gob then it might never have happened. It is not as if I hadn't seen it coming.

But I was angry too, angry and upset that he had hurt me. I wanted to punish him, to hurt him back in some way. I didn't know what to do for the best, how to respond. All I knew was that there was no going back from that night. We had crossed into new territory that neither of us had ever expected to reach. I knew I had to try to find a way back.

As first light showed through the kitchen curtains, I drained my glass and pulled myself to my feet. My eyes felt gritty and sore from all my tears. I climbed the stairs and crawled silently into bed beside Ian. He was sleeping like a baby, curled up in the foetal position over my side of the bed, his arms draped around my pillow. I resisted the urge to reach down and kiss his cheek and slid under the covers alongside him.

'Goodnight, babe,' I whispered. 'I love you.'

That morning I was up with the lark and making breakfast, trying not to let on how much my back, shoulder and hip ached from the previous night. Neither Lisa nor our other guest said a word to me about it. They must have heard what went on, must have glimpsed the grazes and bruises under my dressing gown, but they said nothing. It was an unspoken understanding between us and I was grateful to them for their silence.

After they had gone I heard Ian moving around upstairs, and then the shower running in the bathroom. He seemed to take ages to get dressed and come downstairs, as I sat waiting, my hands gripped around a mug of coffee in anticipation.

Eventually I heard his footsteps on the stairs and tensed myself as I looked up to meet his eyes as he walked into the room. He lowered his eyes quickly but not before I could see his pain and read his shame. I felt instinctively then that his attack had been a one-off. That he was as hurt as I was by it. I knew I had to make the first move, to show him the way forward from here.

I pulled myself to my feet and asked him if he would like some breakfast.

'Yeah, great,' he said, relief lifting the corners of his mouth. He poured us both a fresh mug of coffee and as I stood at the cooker, frying up some bacon, he came up behind me, slipped his hands around my waist and buried his face in my neck.

'I love you, Jenny Simpson,' he said quietly. I stood still staring out of the window and watching the birds on my bird table.

Flipping the bacon rashers over onto the other side, I said softly, 'I know you do, babe, I know.'

Neither of us ever spoke of it again and we had a calm final day together at home until he left for the camp and the helicopter ride back across the water. I went to bed early that night, alone again and grateful for the freedom that gave me. I cried myself to sleep.

I would never have wished that night upon myself or anyone, but in a way it had to happen, it was a catalyst. I couldn't help but hope that it was a turning point from which he would have to come back to me. That thinking back on what he had done to me while he was alone with his thoughts in Northern Ireland, he would realise that he had hit rock bottom and that, unless he took some serious steps to get himself back together mentally, he was about to lose his mind, and his wife.

I spent that week very quietly, doing nothing more than going to work and coming straight home again each night, numb inside and still hurting from the great purple bruises that had started to emerge very visibly on the surface of my skin. I hardly spoke a word to Lisa, I didn't have time for any of the girls at work, and explained my mood to Sue and Anne by complaining that I thought I must be getting the flu. When I got home at night, I shut myself in my bedroom and lay on the bed, staring at the ceiling and waiting for the telephone to ring.

He didn't call all week and I wondered if he ever would. He wasn't due home for another four to six weeks and I hoped that all the yellowing bruises would have faded by then. Maybe that would be just enough time, enough time for the immediacy of what had happened to fade as well, I thought.

I was so glad when Friday came. Before the clock even struck five p.m., I had my coat on and was out of the office door. Lisa was in Liverpool at her mother's all weekend, so I had the house to myself and my brooding. I turned the key in the lock and opened the door to see Ian's face. He was sitting on the stairs in his camouflage kit, waiting for me.

He stood up as soon as I got in and pulled me towards him.

'I've come home for a while, babe,' he said. 'So we can sort all this out. I should never have hurt you so. Something just exploded in my head. It wasn't me, I didn't think of you as you. I can't really explain it any better than that, but I can promise that it will never happen again. I've told my CO I needed some personal time and that I wouldn't be back until I was ready. I love you and I want to make things better. There isn't a bad bone in your body and you don't deserve any of this. Please forgive me and help me to sort this mess out.' He had obviously been preparing his speech.

I stood unresponsively in his arms and let his words sink in. It wasn't his offer to sort things out that stunned me. It was the fact that he had come home, in the middle of his tour, without thinking of the consequences. We both knew he could have been binned for telling the CO that he wasn't going back until he was ready.

As tangibly as if he had punched me in the face, I was hit with the sudden realisation that, for the first time in his life, Ian was putting me before the Regiment.

I pulled away from him and looked up into his gypsy green eyes, which were moist. He had meant every word. He really did want to make a go of it. I reached up and kissed him and flung my arms around his neck.

'Oh, Ian, babe, that's wonderful,' I said, fighting back the tears and holding him close. 'Welcome home.'

\* \* \*

We spent the next four days together, talking things over, walking and sleeping and loving together in a way that we both thought we had forgotten.

'I don't want to lose you, Jenny. I hope I'm not too late,' he told me earnestly in bed one afternoon.

I told him I thought our marriage was salvageable, but that I needed more than a few days of his time for him to prove it to me. He was nearing the end of his tour. His days in Northern Ireland were numbered and he promised me faithfully that from that moment on, we would never fight like we had that night. He was mortified that he had hurt me so, and he begged me to trust him again. I told him I would try.

He wrote to me afterwards that he couldn't believe I had put up with it. 'The dark days are gone, babe,' he said. 'That stranger who was here has finally moved on. I'm glad you hung around waiting for him to leave. I feel very differently now. It is strange how you become a different person in different circumstances.'

In another letter, he said, 'So sorry for the anger and the physical blows. Can you ever forgive me? All I can say is that it wasn't me, it was someone else. I would never hurt you.'

The arguments we had were almost all confined to his time across the water, so it is not surprising I never had any great love for the place. Ian is extraordinarily fond of it and says we should tour Ireland one day, north and south, when everything has calmed down. He says I would love the people and the countryside and the crack, but I think he knows he'll have a tough job getting me over there.

When the peace talks looked for a moment like they were going to do some good and the IRA ceasefire was first announced, I watched several Belfast widows on the television news asking what the point of it all was unless it could bring their husbands back. My heart went out to them. I felt I knew something of what they meant. Ian may not have been killed in Northern Ireland, but something inside him died over there during those long, cold nights lying in ditches, and no one can ever bring that back to me either.

It was Northern Ireland, not Ian, that made him drag me up the stairs by my hair, it was the poison of working there that made him step over the boundaries he had previously respected, and it was his fear of death there that has lost to me forever that unspoken trust between husband and wife. And it is because of the nature of the work he did there that what little peace we had away from it all was later to be shattered irrevocably.

The violence wasn't the only consequence of his time in Northern Ireland. Ian's nightmares first started to become more than an occasional problem a few weeks after the end of the Falklands War, but by the time he was on his fifteen-month tour of duty in the Province, they were becoming a regular occurrence. I would wake in the middle of the night to hear him murmuring in his sleep, and would look across the bed to see him tossing and turning restlessly, mouthing words that he couldn't bring himself to say aloud, even in repose.

Sometimes words and phrases would emerge suddenly, bursting forth with a savagery that made me jump. They were never very coherent. A name, a sentence, a half-strangled cry of something hidden deep in his subconscious. I would sit up in bed, watching and listening, wondering if there was anything I could or should be doing to help him. I had suffered from insomnia and restlessness at night for years and I was used to the random nature of the attacks, but those night terrors of his were relentless in their frequency and intensity and I could hardly begin to imagine what his mind was making him relive.

Paul's name and mine were the two which escaped from his lips most often. In his waking moments Ian liked to think that Paul had survived the helicopter crash and was washed up on a desert island somewhere, where he was lying on his back, sunbathing and drinking cocktails with a few South American beauties at his beck and call, not caring if he was ever rescued. But at night, when he eventually allowed his mind to relax – after his usual hour or so of lying awake, wide-eyed, in the dark – he would dream of Paul's body at the bottom of the sea, being washed backwards and forwards by the rhythm of the waves, his arms outstretched as if pleading for help.

Ian would then wake, sweating and sitting bolt upright in bed. In his mind he would be standing on the deck of HMS *Intrepid* once more, looking out to sea, wishing he had taken a boat or hijacked a helicopter or swum out to where the crash had happened to rescue his friend.

Northern Ireland did nothing for his peace of mind at night. The time alone with his thoughts, the concentration required for surveillance, seemed to rekindle the terrors he had experienced after the Falklands. Not long after the shootings in Gibraltar, the Milltown cemetery incident and all the related operations, he was home for a weekend. It was one of those times when I couldn't seem to reach him and he spent hours and hours sitting silently in his study, staring at the wall, hardly responding to anything I suggested.

Trying to ignore his mood, I spent the evening watching a video in the lounge. I heard him go up to bed early and it was an hour or two later that I joined him. As I so often did when he was home, I propped myself up on the pillows to watch him sleep. He always looked so peaceful, as if he didn't have a care in the world. I whispered how much I loved him, kissed his cheek and turned the light off. I felt exhausted from the stress of his visit home.

I was awoken by screaming a few hours later and sat up to switch on the light. Ian was lying on the bed next to me, a pillow clutched to his chest, his face waxy white and covered in sweat. His eyes were wide open – he was staring up at the ceiling like a deranged man – but I knew he couldn't see me.

'No! No!' he moaned and buried his face in his pillow, his hands flailing in the air around his head, grappling with an unknown terror. I had no idea what to do, I just sat staring at him, my own eyes filling with tears. At last I took a deep breath and said his name as softly and gently as I could, moving slowly towards him.

'Ian, Ian it's me, Jen. I'm here, babe. It's OK, I'm here.'

He didn't seem to hear me as he tossed his head from side to side, his whole body glistening with sweat. He looked up in anguish. I reached for his hands, but he started to push me away.

'Ian! Ian! It's me, Jenny. Look at me!' I commanded.

He stopped moving and looked up into my eyes. Suddenly he folded and his body went limp. I held him to my breast as he recovered himself. He fell back to sleep again in minutes, drained. I lay awake for much of the rest of the night, wondering if I should talk to someone about what he was going through.

Ian had always been dismissive of counselling. He was too self-contained to seek help. He believed counselling was an American phenomenon which revolved around – as he put it – 'people examining their own navels'.

His opinion of it was not improved when a psychological team arrived on a Selection course he was working on, when he was on Training Wing. The psychiatrists interviewed the candidates and those training them. After psychometric testing and hours and hours of questioning, the official line came down from above – the shrinks say you are all saner than most 'normal' people. As Ian knew personally that several of the failed candidates were complete nutters and that some of his fellows on Training Wing were far from what any respectable psychiatrist could call hinged, he lost any respect he might have had for such testing methods.

It was part of his job on Training Wing to identify the fruitcakes, the macho mule heads who only wanted to join the SAS so that they could jump through windows with all the black kit on. It was his specific task to bin anyone who lost their nerve in the jungle or on the Brecon Beacons or who seemed unstable, people who could jeopardise the lives of a whole troop through either foolish heroics or cowardice.

In the Falklands he once had to use a rifle butt on a fellow soldier who had frozen during an assault. He found a butt in the head did wonders to bring the young soldier to his senses. And in Fiji, when he was walking his own mental tightrope, he watched a fellow member of the Regiment have a nervous breakdown as his previous fastidious nature became an obsession about cleanliness and made him completely psychologically reject the dirty, sweaty conditions in the rainforest. The poor guy was binned.

So Ian had become quite an expert at spotting loose screws in other people – he just wasn't very good at identifying them in himself. And after seeing people he knew and respected go to pieces, he vowed he would never seek help for himself, even though he and I both knew in our hearts that it would probably do him some good.

Even if there had been a psychiatrist at the camp, someone people like us would have been able to go to if we had any problems, I'm not sure anyone would have visited him. It was as if to admit to having any problems was a sign of weakness, an indication of an inability to do the job, a failure to cope with all that went with it and still come out of it the macho male. Maybe everyone in the Regiment went through this, I thought as I lay stroking Ian's hair the night of the bad dream, maybe we weren't alone.

I never knew because none of us ever spoke of the psychological strain, and even damage that a life in the SAS causes. Ian would have killed me if he knew I had said anything to anyone else, and the others would have been the same. It was strictly taboo, any suggestion of being unable to cope. It wasn't just a question of macho pride, it was more serious than that. Any member of the Regiment who shows a hint of mental instability risks being binned, kicked out for good. So none of us dared mention it, the truth that dare not speak its name.

On the night of Ian's dream I fell asleep eventually and woke to an empty bed. Ian was out, gone for one of his long walks, and I didn't know when he would be back. I wondered if I should speak to him about the previous night, tell him I was worried, ask him to go and get some help. When he did return, the look on his face told me not to ask too much. His jaw-line was set and I could tell he wasn't in the mood for my amateur psychoanalysis. I said nothing.

It was several weeks later, during a quiet meal out together, that he felt able to talk about it for the first time. He always found it hard to discuss his nightmares and often told me, when I asked, that I really didn't want to know. But I knew that the last one must have been important, more vivid than the rest, and I wanted to coax it out of him.

'Do you remember that bad dream you had the last time you were home?' I asked, as gently as I could. He nodded and swirled the beer round in his glass. 'Do you want to tell me about it?'

'Oh, it was just the usual, you know,' he said dismissively, looking up and smiling. 'All blood, guts and screaming. You don't want to know.'

'But I do, Ian, I really do. Tell me about it, it was the worst yet.'

He drank from his glass and placed it carefully on the table.

'OK,' he said. 'If you must know, I was in Derry. It was dusk and I was undercover, following some boyo. He headed down some alleyways and back streets I didn't recognise. I knew I had to follow him or I would lose him, but I didn't know where the others were to back me up.

'I tried to radio for assistance, but I couldn't get any response, and still this bloke was walking fast around these alleyways. It was night-time and I had no idea where I was now. I started to get worried. He seemed to be deliberately twisting and turning in these dark streets. I wondered where the back-up was.' He paused.

'Go on,' I said, watching him picking at nothing at all on the tablecloth.

'He rounded a corner and I followed him and there, in front of me, was his whole gang, waiting. All the evil bastards I had ever followed, all facing me in this dead end alley, all smiling. I heard a step behind me and two more closed in, cutting off my escape route. I had a weapon but I knew I didn't stand a chance against eight of them, and they knew that I knew. They were laughing at me, smoking cigarettes and laughing. I knew then that I was a dead man.'

He gulped down his drink before adding, 'It was the knowing it was going to happen, but not knowing when or how, or how long it would take. I couldn't stand the helplessness of it. I wanted it to be over there and then and I lunged for them, hoping they would take me out. But they knew what I was up to and they wouldn't play my game. They grabbed me and put a hood over my head and tied my hands. "It's not that easy, mate," one of them said. "We want a little chat first." I had hoped that the end would come then, but hearing his words I realised that my ordeal was only just beginning.' Ian gulped hard and took another drink.

'I was led away and put into a car. They were still chuckling and I was lying on the floor of the car, being driven away from any chance of rescue, knowing what was to come. That was when I woke up.'

His eyes were glassy. I knew how hard it had been for him to tell me. I reached across the table and held his hand in mine.

'Have you ever had that dream before?' I asked.

'Yes.'

'Is it always like that?'

'No, I mean, it always starts the same and then each time I have the dream it takes me one step further.' He looked up at me, the strain of it etched on his face.

'It is so real, Jen,' he said. 'I don't know that it is a dream at the time. It feels real. It sounds real. I can even smell the peat-smoke of Derry and taste it in the back of my throat. Each time I go through it I wonder if this is the night the dream is going to end and I am going to die.'

I chose my words very carefully.

'If I came with you,' I said slowly, 'would you please consider going to see someone ... I mean, seek some professional help about these dreams, Ian? I think, I think it might help.'

But the shutters came down. It was as if something in the back of his eyes switched off and I was no longer allowed the brief glimpse into his soul. He finished his drink and asked the waiter for the bill.

Leaning across the table, he whispered, almost menacingly, 'If you think I'm letting some nosy Parker fish around inside my head, you're more insane than I am. Now, shall we go?'

Ian dreamt a lot about the jungle camps in Brunei and Belize, being sucked dry by mosquitoes and leeches, spending days and nights crawling through swamps and insect nests. But some of his best dreams were about the jungle too, of fishing peacefully by a river and reeling in a huge silvery fish with the anticipation of how it would make a much more appetising supper than the dried snake or ants' nest paste he might have had once his ration pack had gone, or lying on the jungle floor, looking up at the lush green canopy overhead and feeling at peace with the world.

He would always have nightmares on his first few days out in jungle camp, as he acclimatised to the conditions, and the lads he was with would throw things at his A-frame to get him to stop screaming out in the night. Once he had got through that stage, he would start to sleep like he had never slept before, uninterrupted unconsciousness, from which he would wake feeling incredibly refreshed.

He had a close encounter with an elephant once, on an exercise in Africa, and he sometimes dreamt of elephants rushing him. That dream was the easiest for me to spot and almost always made me laugh. He would suddenly start twitching his lower limbs, like a puppy dreaming of chasing cats, and would then sit up and cry out, 'Sh-i-i-i-t!' as he caught sight of the charging elephant and started to do a runner.

Once he had realised it was a dream and opened his eyes to see me looking at him bemused, he would apologise and flop back down onto the pillow.

'Nellie the elephant again, I presume?' I would joke, and he'd nod and roll over to turn on the light.

Some of his nightmares were about being ill. His body mimicked the effects of the ague I had nursed him through – shivering as if with malarial fever – and I would stroke his forehead as I had done then, and cover him with blankets, until he drifted off into a deeper sleep as I held him in my arms.

With his track record in free-fall, it is perhaps not surprising that he also often dreamt about falling from a plane with a malfunctioning parachute. In the dream he is falling and falling through space and pulling and pulling on his cord, but it doesn't work. Those dreams always ended with a sudden movement from Ian, as if an electric shock had been applied to his body, which would jolt me and the bed, and which signified the moment when his reserve parachute jerked him to safety at the last minute, just as he could see the ground coming up fast towards him.

After a few years of living with his nightmares, I began to understand that they were only really at their worst when he felt under pressure at home or at work and needed to cry out for my help. Initially, I worried about them as they continued to dominate our nights, but eventually I came to accept them as he did.

'A lot of the guys cry out in their sleep,' he reassured me. 'It happens all the time, it goes with the job.'

My fears were further allayed when I asked my doctor about them casually and he told me that it was when Ian stopped having nightmares that I was to worry.

'At least, this way, the stress is coming out somewhere, even if it is only in his subconscious,' the doctor said. 'It is when people bottle it all up so successfully that they can't even allow themselves to dream about things that the real problems begin.'

I took special comfort from that because, increasingly, Ian wasn't alone in his disturbed nights. My sleep patterns were almost as bad, although instead of having the screaming abdabs, I would get up quietly and walk about in my sleep. I had sleepwalked since I was a child but it got worse when Ian started to go away on dangerous missions. Within a few years of the Falklands, I was getting to be a regular night-time rambler.

It got to the point when Ian never knew what he would wake up and find. He came home from a job in the early hours of the morning and was astonished to find all the houseplants outside the house, and the furniture thrown all over the place. He thought we must have been burgled or something terrible had happened and he rushed upstairs to find me fast asleep in bed, snoring like a fat baby. He woke me up to ask me what had happened, but I couldn't remember anything. I must have got up in my sleep, rearranged the entire house and carefully laid all the houseplants in a row outside the front door, all as naked as the day I was born. Thank goodness we had understanding neighbours.

Another morning, I woke up feeling really dreadful. My head hurt all over and I couldn't seem to open my eyes properly. When I looked in the mirror, I couldn't believe what I saw. I looked like I had just gone ten rounds with Mike Tyson, my face was black and blue all over, my eyes and nose were swollen and bruised.

Ian was away on a job, and I had been completely alone and couldn't remember for the life of me what had happened in the night. I could only assume that I must have gone for a walk and fallen over, hitting my head against something as I fell.

Similar night-time bruises have appeared on several other occasions. When Ian is there to witness it, he is as shocked as me when he sees my face in the morning. I think in the back of his mind he worries that he may have beaten me up in the night and then blanked it from his mind. I am sure that isn't what happened because I know I would have remembered, and I tell him so. But he still ministers to my bruises with a special gentleness.

Because of his own nightmares, he is pretty sympathetic to my night walking and helps get me back into bed if he wakes and finds me gone. Generally speaking, he can lead me back to the bedroom without me protesting and I go straight off to sleep, but sometimes he says I sit bolt upright in bed, still asleep but staring at him with my eyes wide open, which he finds very disturbing.

I don't know what is going through my head at these times, and Ian can only guess, but we both suspect that I am trying to accept that he really is there, beside me in bed at our home in Hereford and not lying dead at the bottom of the South Atlantic or falling from a plane or being tortured by the IRA. I just stare and stare at him, as if I am expecting him to disappear if I even blink. He says he finds it deeply unnerving.

I rarely remember what I dream about. It is as if I blank it from my memory deliberately, or maybe my mind is so busy getting me up and walking me about, that it doesn't have very much time to create imaginative mental scenarios. But there is one dream that I can remember. It recurs time and again and I have come to know and accept it, it always leaves me feeling strangely at peace.

I am at St Martin's Church, in the graveyard. It is a beautiful summer's day and I am holding a bunch of flowers to put in Paul Bunker's urn. I am completely alone, and walking towards the six yew trees and the low wall that mark the start of the Regimental plot behind the church. In the distance I can see Hereford Cathedral and overhead puffy white clouds are set amid the blue sky.

As I walk along the path, enjoying the warm sun on my back, I start to read the names on some of the neat white headstones lining my route. Name after name. All young men, many of them friends

179

of Ian's. The ultimate basha (sleeping quarters) for those that didn't make it home.

Their number and rank appears first, underlined by their name, followed by an acknowledgement of their membership of the SAS and the date and age at which they died.

I stop at one I know and reread the inscription.

24332940

Sergeant A I Slater MM

22 SAS Regiment

2 December 1984    Aged 31

*'His work on earth is done. He gave his all'*

It gives so little information. It says nothing of the man Al Slater or his achievements or even how he died. Al was someone Ian knew from parachute training. He was known to millions of television viewers as the NCO training officer in the BBC television series 'The Paras'.

We were staying with a close friend of Al's in December 1984 when the phone rang at three a.m. to tell him that Al had been shot dead during a gun battle with the IRA in Fermanagh, Northern Ireland. He and his men inadvertently intercepted an IRA bomb squad and were ambushed. Despite being mortally wounded, Al managed to return fire. Two IRA men died, two were arrested and 1000 pounds of explosives were recovered. Al, who was single, was awarded the Military Medal posthumously. Ian and I later became very friendly with his parents, Ira and Peggy, a lovely Scottish couple whom we met at a Regiment wedding and who made us wish we had known Al better when he was alive.

As I stand looking at his headstone in my dream, as I have done a dozen times in my waking hours, I listen to the rustling of the trees and start to read the inscriptions on some of other graves, which speak of loving fathers, husbands and sons. 'To the world you were a soldier but to me you were the world,' says one.

I think about the widows and their children, the mothers and fathers whose sons were lost. I wish for the wives' sake that they could be buried alongside their men in this special place, but it is a military cemetery and it is only possible to have your ashes scattered over your husband's grave or be buried in a plot in the civilian part nearby. One widow whose husband was killed in the Falklands helicopter crash later died and had her ashes scattered over the South Atlantic.

The whispering through the trees starts to sound like voices, like names read and ranks given. I can hear eulogies and prayers said quietly over coffins, I can hear the quiet sobbing of a woman, overcome with grief. Lost in my distant thoughts and dreams, I hear a little boy laughing and I look to see a child standing over by the wall, the memorial wall to the men who died in the helicopter crash. I smile and follow him, he seems to beckon, and I walk over towards Paul Bunker's urn.

The child smiles back at me and starts to hide behind the gravestones. He is small and agile and I can't keep up with him. I lose sight of him just as I come round from behind a tree to the memorial wall. I look and look but he is gone, although I can still hear his distant laughter. Sighing, I walk past the winged dagger plaque and the 'pilgrims' poem from the regimental clock and towards Paul's plaque, where I stand for a moment and read the inscription.

24145047
Cpl P A Bunker
26.1.54 – 19.5.82

Underneath, written on the small stone urn, are the words I had suggested to Vanda when she was wondering how best to express her feelings, 'Paul, Apart but always together, Vanda'. I remove the fading flowers I had put there a few weeks before and lift out the small inner pot. I am filling it with water from a nearby standpipe when I hear the boy's laughter again. Cupping my hands to my eyes, I look up and see him standing, hands on hips like Peter Pan, on an old headstone in the civilian part of the cemetery.

He is smiling and laughing and I suddenly realise he looks a lot like Paul. It occurs to me that it could be Paul as a young boy, and I decide to call out his name to see if he responds. Just as I open my mouth, the boy jumps down behind the headstone and disappears from view. Seconds later, a huge bird that I cannot identify, takes to the air close by. I can hear its enormous wings flapping slowly as they lift the creature up into the air and towards the sun.

I am blinded by the sunlight as I try to follow its path upwards. For a moment it is gone. Then I hear the familiar clatter of a helicopter, the blades whirring overhead, as it swoops low over the graveyard in preparation for landing at the camp to deposit the latest troop back from a mission.

Within a few seconds, the boy, the bird and the helicopter are gone, and I am left standing alone, feeling quite calm. It is at that moment that I wake up, rather reluctantly, wishing I could stay asleep and dream the dream again.


Sometimes I talk to Ian in my sleep. Mostly, it is about trivial domestic matters or about something to do with my work, but occasionally, when my guard is down, I talk to him about his job and what I am feeling about it, going against the grain of everything we had ever been taught about complete secrecy. I am always unhappy when he tells me that I have done it again. I worry that if I talk about the job he will begin to think that I know too much about it. The last thing I want to do is deter him from opening up to me. It is very frustrating because I feel like I am betwixt and between.

Ian has never been great at telling me what he is thinking or how he is feeling about his work, but I think I probably know more than most SAS wives. He tells me the basic facts of where he is going and what he is doing, but no operational details, and I often have to wait until weeks after he is back from a job to find out what really went on. Much of what I know is gleaned from overhearing his conversations with other people, mates in the Regiment or our other friends, who ask more questions than I do and who don't get their heads snapped off for doing so.

We wives do not sit down together and talk about what is going on in our husbands' work, we are all too afraid that we might let a cat out of the bag. If I were to sit with Karen or Vanda in the old days and say, 'Wasn't it great about the Pebble Island raid?' or, 'Did you hear what happened to Dave in the jungle?' only to discover that they hadn't been told about those incidents, it would inevitably cause unnecessary worry and distress.

The easiest thing to do was to bolster each other as best we could, without going into specifics. But, in a way, our silence and circumspection perpetuated the myth of the Regiment – the tough façade, the stiff upper lip. By glossing over the issues with our men at home and pretending everything was fine with the other wives, we left ourselves with little outlet for the release of the tremendous pressure that builds up within a Regimental marriage.

With no one professional to talk to, and the need for secrecy preventing us confiding in our friends and family, the tendency was to bottle it all up as much as the men did, to talk about anything but the worries caused by our husbands' dangerous work, to dust it all under the carpet.

Not surprisingly, the stresses and strains eventually blew many marriages wide apart. Few wives could go the distance alone and some of those who did like me found themselves resorting to the only help that was immediately to hand – a bottle.

I had always enjoyed a drink, and so had Ian. For many years, particularly after his bad time across the water, he almost had a problem with it. But he was never a great one for holding his alcohol and eventually, what with months on end in the jungle and training for free-fall and exercises, he slowed right down on his drinking.

But I didn't have the same reasons to stop as he had. In fact, I felt as if I had every reason to continue. He was still going away as much as ever, leaving me largely to fend for myself, and what with his nightmares waking me up night after night and my own memories of the helicopter crash and Northern Ireland, when he was home I had been forced to live in daily fear.

I found solace in alcohol. I wasn't an alcoholic. I could stop whenever I wanted to, and often did for days on end when Ian was home and we had no particular reason to drink. But I was a heavy social drinker, enjoying it more and more as a means of instantly achieving the 'feel good factor', which to me meant feeling like a normal human being again, away from the special pressures I had at home.

It was the loneliness most of all, the overwhelming sense of isolation and unhappiness at being on my own for so much of the time. With no children, and nothing but Annie and occasionally Lisa for company, my weekends and evenings after work were spent largely with my own thoughts and fears.

Not that I felt sorry for myself, I knew I had married a good man and I had a good idea what I was getting when I married him, but I don't think I had ever really appreciated quite how stressful and emotionally damaging it would sometimes be to be married to the SAS, for that is how it felt, as if I was married not just to Ian, but to the Regiment, to its traditions and values, its way of life and sense of duty. Sometimes, just sometimes, that was a hard burden for a simple fun-loving Geordie girl to bear.

Ian's concerns for me were touching. He worried for my health as I lost more and more weight. I had always been quite skinny but I got even thinner. I just wasn't hungry most of the time, which was great for the diet. I told him I was fine and promised him I was eating. I didn't consider it a problem and I asked him not to fuss.

He worried that I was home alone too much, dwelling on his absence. 'Don't isolate yourself so much, babe,' he warned me in one letter from Florida. 'Don't sit at home getting yourself into a state. Get out and see the girls, go and see your family. Try and pull yourself out of this . . . I want to know that you're eating properly and taking care of yourself. Please don't let us go back to the bad times.'

I resented his fussing. I felt he was making too much of it. But in truth I had cut myself off from my friends and family. It was easy to do, living in the country. I largely ignored his requests to get out and about. Annie and I and we were happy at home in our little world, I thought. If Ian wanted to come home and share it with us every now and again that was up to him.

I made light of it as best I could, and tried to make his homecomings so entertaining and special that he wouldn't worry about me so much and would look forward to coming back. It was always such an emotional build-up for me, each time he came home from a long trip away, and I tried my best to live up to the occasion.

On one trip home from a tour of duty in Northern Ireland, I was going to meet him at Birmingham Airport. A few days beforehand, I remembered that he had once dared to mention that one of his sexual fantasies when he was away was of me wearing a fur coat and little else underneath. I borrowed a fur coat from a girlfriend at work who had been left it by her aunt, put a basque, stockings and suspenders on underneath and drove to the airport.

The look on his face when he came into the Arrivals hall and saw me standing there in the fur coat, my hands across my chest and a twinkle in my eye, was priceless. He was with a whole group of lads and he was terrified that I might have been drinking for Dutch courage and would flash everything in the middle of the airport to the whole crowd.

He pushed ahead of the rest of them, grabbed my arm and said, 'Do you want to get us arrested or what?' I laughed and moved as if to open the coat. He slapped his hands across mine.

He frog-marched me out of the airport and to the car park, where our car was waiting for us. My feet hardly touched the ground, he got me out of there so fast. He was trying his best to look angry, but I could see he was excited and rather bemused.

When we got to the car and he was fumbling for the key, I gave him a quick flash, and he went weak at the knees. He bundled me into the car and we headed out of the airport. It had taken me two hours to get there, but it took us six hours to get back. Well, he had been gone for a couple of weeks.

Generally speaking, as soon as we got home it was straight into bed while dinner was cooking. I usually had a casserole bubbling away in the slow cooker, so that we had some time to catch up. I would always eat well when he was home, being with him gave me an appetite again and I always gained the weight I lost while he was away.

'There, you see,' I would tell him as I finished up my plate. 'There is nothing wrong with my appetite. I just pine for you when you're not here.'

But that didn't stop him worrying, or thinking that I wasn't taking good enough care of myself while he was away. He wrote about it endlessly and asked my family and friends to keep an eye on me. I though it was sweet that he was concerned, but I wasn't worried, I knew I could look after myself. I had to. He had never been around.

One of the times I really could have done with his care and concern, he was away on desert training. I had taken Annie jogging one afternoon and tripped on a paving stone, landing smack on my face in the gravel road. I broke some teeth, cut my mouth very badly and split my lip. I looked in a right state. I got myself to a neighbour's house and they took me straight to the hospital to get me patched up. When we got back, they asked me if they could contact Ian so he could come home and look after me. My face was so badly swollen that I couldn't see or eat properly so I would need to be spoon fed.

But I refused to let them call him. They simply didn't understand, it is not that simple in the SAS. Any normal husband may be able to pop home from the office to take care of his sick wife or ask for a few days off to attend to something back at the house. But Ian was probably lying up in the middle of the Arabian desert, days from civilisation, his only contact with the outside world a satellite radio link that cost hundreds of dollars each time it was used and was only meant to be used to call for emergency assistance.

He couldn't call me and I couldn't just pick up the phone and say, 'Hiya, babe, do you think you could possibiy come home, I've bashed my face.' It just wasn't possible and it wouldn't have been fair to worry him.

I just had to get on with it, on my own. I didn't even tell him about it until he got home a few weeks later, by which time my face was almost completely back to normal and I had had my teeth repaired. He scolded me for not getting word to him at the time, but he never suggested for one minute that he would have dropped everything in the desert and come home to help me.

The only time I ever did ask him to come home, he wanted to very much, but he wasn't allowed to. I had gone to bed on my own one night about two a.m. and must have been sleepwalking again, because I woke at five wearing different clothes, my face hurting dreadfully.

I looked in the mirror and my face was black and blue, even worse than it had been when I fell over in the street. I had chipped my cheekbone somehow and my face was grossly swollen on one side. I must have gone walkabout, fallen over and somehow got myself back to bed.

I was feeling pretty sorry for myself and I suddenly got it into my head that I wanted Ian to come home and take care of me. It wouldn't have been that difficult, he was in the same country at least, four hours' drive away, in London for the weekend, staying at a military barracks in central London. I picked up the telephone and dialled the number Ian had left me. I was eventually transferred through to his barracks and heard his voice.

'I've fallen over and hurt myself badly, babe. I need you here,' I said breathlessly into the receiver. There was silence on the other end of the line. 'It is the only time I have ever asked,' I reminded him tearfully.

'I'll have to go and see the CO,' Ian said cautiously. 'I don't know if he'll let me go, the Duke arrives today and everything is arranged. But I'll try.'

He went to see his CO immediately and told him that his wife had had a bad fall and had hurt herself. 'Is she in hospital?' the CO asked.

Ian said, 'No, but she must be pretty badly hurt if she has asked me to drop everything and come home. She never has before.'

The CO told him, 'You can go home tomorrow, after the visit.' And that was that. Ian knew he couldn't argue and if he went AWOL, he would be binned.

He telephoned to tell me the news and I was dreadfully upset. I had really wanted him by my side that day and I had never felt so abandoned. I spent the day miserably and went to bed early, feeling terrible. Ian had a miserable day too and left the barracks as soon as he could, at six the next morning, to arrive on our doorstep at just after nine o'clock. He pressed the doorbell and called through the door, 'Is Mike Tyson there?'

When I opened the door, he took one look at my face and his mouth fell open. 'My God!' he said. 'You look bloody awful!' I burst into tears and he hugged me, leading me inside to look more closely at my injuries. I was so glad to see him, to have him with me – even if it was only for a day or so – and I told him so.

He turned me round to the light and examined my face. Frowning suddenly, he said, 'Are you seeing someone else and he knocked you around?'

I laughed, even though it hurt, but when looked in his eyes I realised he was deadly serious.

'What?' I said, incredulously.

'Jenny, your face looks like you've been bloody beaten up, not fallen over,' he repeated. 'I can't believe you could have done this much damage just falling over.'

He stared at me accusingly. Tears started to well in my eyes.

'You can just turn straight round and drive back to London, you bastard,' I told him, pointing to the door. 'You don't come when I need you and when you do turn up you accuse me of seeing someone else? You've got a bloody nerve, Simpson.'

He looked suddenly sheepish and realised he had jumped to the wrong conclusions. He pulled me to him and apologised profusely.

'You're right. I'm so sorry, babe. I'm tired, that's all. And I've been so worried about you for the past twenty-four hours. Now let's forget it and get you up to the bathroom and put something on those bruises, eh?'

I let the matter drop and hugged him back.

'Anyway, if you think I look bad,' I told him, smilingly as we climbed the stairs. 'You should see the other fella.'

We both fell about laughing, me holding my face to stop it hurting so, and him laughing even more because of my grimaces.

# 7 | Let No Man Put Asunder

HIS VOICE WAS UNUSUALLY STRAINED.

'Can you come over?' he said. 'We need to talk.'

It was March 1989 and Ian had recently completed his final tour of Northern Ireland and was about to go away for three months' jungle training, when he telephoned me from the camp. My heart was racing as I drove through the gates. It was unheard of for him to summon me and I wondered what it could all mean.

He was waiting for me in the sergeants' mess.

'There is no easy way to tell you this, Jen,' he said, walking towards me and taking my hand. I thought my heart would burst through my chest as he fetched us both a cup of coffee and led me outside to a table on the patio.

'There has been a security leak.' He waited for his words to sink in. 'A junior security officer from the RUC left his address book with my name and home telephone number in it on the back seat of a staff car in Belfast and it has somehow got into the hands of the boyos.'

The boyos. I knew what the expression meant. My mouth was dry.

'They now know who I am and . . .', he paused, 'where we live.'

There were a thousand questions I wanted to ask but I couldn't speak. I stared hard at his face, peered deep into his green eyes and watched as a small bead of sweat formed on his temple.

The IRA, the dreaded enemy, were suddenly with us, in our minds, in our home. Ian knew he had to try to reassure me so he carried on.

'Now, you're not to worry, Jen. We mustn't let the buggers grind us down. I'd like to get you away from the house for a while. I will make some enquiries about a safe house, or perhaps you could go to your mother's for a few weeks because there are going to have to be a few changes made at the house and it will take a while for you to get used to them all.'

My mind swam and my legs felt weak. I was glad I was sitting down.

'We're going to get the best protection there is, so you're not to worry,' he told me. 'This address book has been missing for months apparently and if they had wanted to get me they would have done by now. We only found out about it because the cheeky sods handed it back to some of our chaps with a message which basically said how much they enjoyed reading it.'

I started to tremble. After all this time of seeing how the constant threat of death in Northern Ireland affected Ian, I knew in that instant what it felt like to be living within the sights. It all seemed so unreal. I was half-listening to what he was saying while my imagination ran riot. I thought of Annie alone at home and wondered if I would come back from work once day to find her poisoned on the kitchen floor and the boyos waiting for me.

Ian was telling me that the colonel of the camp had asked to see him to explain what steps were being taken to protect us. He said he would have to go.

He walked me back to my car and gave me a hug. 'We mustn't let the bastards win, Jen,' he said. 'That is what they want. We'll just have to get used to the changes in our lifestyle and get on with it. OK?'

He went to see the colonel, who was sitting behind his large desk. I had never much liked the man and I could imagine his patronising look as he told Ian that there was nothing to worry about.

'This is one of the risks of the job and it doesn't mean that you have to be any more vigilant than you would normally be,' he told him. 'The key thing is for you and your wife not to over-react.'

Ian knew he spoke for us both when he erupted, 'Don't overreact?

I am away for three months, the IRA know where I live and my wife is sitting alone in that house. Just exactly how do you expect us to react?'

The colonel reddened and started shuffling papers on his desk as if he were ready for Ian to leave. 'All I mean,' he said, rising from his chair, 'is that you are the target, not your wife. You are trained to deal with that, you deal with it every day, so there is no point worrying unduly. I don't think there is any need for a safe house at this stage.'

The door was opened and Ian was about to be dismissed unceremoniously. As he was leaving, he turned to the colonel and said, 'They don't have a picture of me, do they?'

The colonel shook his head. 'No, of course not. It was just an address book.'

'Then how the hell will they know if it is me or someone else in my house if they come round? One of my brothers-in-law or a neighbour might be there and they could think it is me and have a crack at them. I don't want Jenny to witness that and I certainly don't want to have her hurt in the process. And you tell me not to overreact.' He stormed out.

Back in my office that afternoon, I tried to take it all in. I had wanted to stay with Ian and talk it through, but he was busy seeing the colonel and preparing to take a troop off to the jungle and neither of us could really spare the time off work. Half of me wasn't even sure I wanted to go home that night but I knew that I had to behave as if nothing had happened, go straight home and see that it was all still the same.

I couldn't talk about it to anyone, not even Sue and Anne. Oh sure, they would be understanding and sympathetic, but I didn't even know what it meant for me, why should I frighten them as well? If Ian and I were targets, couldn't I be targeted at work, couldn't anyone who came to see me at my home suddenly be in danger too? How I longed to speak to Ian some more and find out what it all meant.

When I did get home, I found him busy packing his bergen and sorting out his kit. The house was full of its usual sights and smells, warm and welcoming, and Annie rushed up to lick me to death. I felt strangely reassured.

Ian stopped what he was doing and also came running to greet me. He held me tightly in his arms for several minutes without speaking. It was just what I needed.

'What did the CO say?' I asked when we had pulled away from each other, not expecting much from the response.

'He told me not to overreact,' Ian replied. 'He said there wasn't any need for you to go to a safe house.' He studied my face for reactions.

'I don't know what to think,' I said, deliberately. 'I've been thinking of little else all afternoon. But I know I would hate to live in a safe house without you and with policemen all around me, and I couldn't stand it at Mum's, so perhaps this is best.'

'I don't know, Jen,' he said, looking concerned. 'I don't think I want you here on your own while I am away. It will be fine at your mum's. It's only for a few weeks and then I'll be back and we can face this together.'

I shook my head. 'No, Ian, you said the address book had been missing for months. This will be no different to what it was like when you were away before. Just because I know about it now, shouldn't make any difference. What did you tell me? Don't let the buggers grind you down. Well, I won't, and if staying in my own home despite them is the first step towards that, then I want to take it.'

He hugged me once again and stroked my hair as he tried to decide what to do for the best. 'Maybe we should ask Lisa to come back and stay with you for a while,' he said, but I shook my head vehemently.

'No, I don't want her getting involved in all this,' I said.

'I just wish I wasn't going away again, not right now,' he said. 'Perhaps I should ask for some special dispensation, ask if I can stay home for a while instead.'

I stood back from him aghast. 'Ian Simpson,' I cried. 'Don't you dare! You love going to the jungle, you've been looking forward to this for weeks, and anyway, if you start altering your plans too then they will be grinding us down, won't they?'

Later that night, as I stood at the kitchen sink peeling potatoes for supper, I looked out onto the conifer hedge in the back garden and wondered if I would ever know if anyone was lying in it, watching us, as Ian had laid in a hundred hedges in his lifetime, watching other people.

I told myself I was being stupid, pulled down the blind, and poured us both large drinks. We spent a quiet evening together talking it over and reassuring each other that everything would be all right. We went to bed early, but despite all my assurances to Ian, I couldn't sleep.

I went to work as usual the next morning, but having hardly slept a wink, I felt exhausted. Not long after I got in, my telephone rang. A stranger's voice said, 'Jenny Simpson?'

I felt suddenly uneasy, then stupid. This is what Ian meant about grinding us down, I thought, I was already paranoid about the slightest thing. Keep it together, Jenny. The voice turned out to be that of Bill, the Regimental Security Officer, who asked if he could come to see me later that morning and if it was possible for me to second an office at my workplace where we could talk.

I thought about the small office next to the part-time bank that we had on site at the firm. What day was it? No, the bank wasn't open today, the office would be free. I told him there was somewhere private we could talk and he said he would be with me in an hour.

He arrived at eleven o'clock sharp with two men he introduced as Major Gerald Cooper from the Home Office and his assistant, Corporal Smith. I ushered them into the office and we sat down.

I had never met Bill before, but I liked him instantly. He wasn't a man of many words, but he had a young, open face and a reassuring air about him, like that of an older brother looking after his kid sister's interests. Major Cooper was very distinguished, about fifty-five, silver-haired and in a dark suit, very much the officer. The spotty little corporal didn't say a word throughout the meeting, but scribbled down notes of what was said.

'I have to tell you gentleman,' I said, as soon as we had sat around a small table, 'this whole thing scares the living daylights out of me and you coming here like this is doing nothing to calm my nerves.'

I found myself trembling as I spoke and I pressed my hands together between my knees in the hope that they wouldn't notice.

'Now you really mustn't worry, my dear,' the major said, paternally. 'These leaks happen all the time and are very rarely acted upon. We are going to monitor the situation very carefully, but our initial assessment of the risk is that this is not nearly as serious as you might imagine.'

How serious is not serious? I thought, but I buttoned my lip.

'And anyway,' he said, 'it is your husband who is the target, not you, so you have nothing to worry about personally.'

'I beg to differ,' I said, as politely as I could and mimicking his accent. 'But not only would I have a great deal to worry about personally if they killed my husband, but I am not at all convinced that these people give a monkey's who they shoot or blow up. They might just put a bomb under the car and hope that they get one of us.'

The Major had heard it all before. I wondered how many anxious wives he had briefed in just this sort of situation. He seemed to have an answer for everything and I was more reassured than I thought I would be. He told me that, from a few days' time, I would be surrounded by the very latest in high-tech security equipment, that the house and car would be well protected, that I would have panic alarms and a direct line to the police.

We talked for over an hour before he left, shaking me warmly by the hand and congratulating me on being so calm.

'Calm? I am trembling from head to toe inside,' I told him.

He laughed and, squeezing my hand, he said, 'Then you are extremely good at hiding your fear, my dear, and that is exactly the sort of Army wife this country needs.'

They made an appointment for two men from the local Special Branch of Hereford Police to come the following morning and advise me on general security matters and install a temporary panic alarm. They would be followed by a team of Home Office security advisers and a surveyor who would come for most of the day and install a high-tech security system that would then come under the control of the local Special Branch.

*       *       *

Ian left on the Friday morning of that week. His bergen had been packed and in the hallway for two days and although I had seen it sitting there a hundred times before, this time its departure filled me with foreboding.

My concerns about the security leak had been just about bearable when he was around to protect me and Annie and make it all seem as if it was all right. What would it be like when I was on my own again? I did not sleep terribly well when he was away at the best of times. Would I now think every creak in the middle of the night was the IRA coming to shoot me in my bed? Would I ever have the courage to turn the car ignition on again, thinking that the very turning of the key might trigger an explosive device?

We hugged in the doorway and he held onto me a little longer than usual. I could sense his unease at leaving me alone.

'Don't you worry about me, chooch,' I told him, giving him my broadest smile. 'If any of the buggers come by I'll just give them your address in Belize.'

He was grateful for my humour and hugged me again.

'See you in three months, then,' he said, and waited for my tears. But I was determined not to cry. I looked up at him and smiled.

'Three months, eh? Better than fifteen months any day, and I promised I would never complain about these jobs again, remember.'

He could tell I wasn't going to break. Not in front of him, anyway. So he kissed me goodbye, gave me one last hug and left.

I closed the door and leaned against it, my eyes pressed tightly shut.

'Come on now, girl, get on with it,' I told myself brusquely.

Two hours later, I heard the cars. Our house was one of four in a cul-de-sac off a country lane and the only sounds you ever hear are the neighbours' cars going in and out of their drives at staggered intervals. This was unusual, five cars all at once, slowing down as they neared the entrance to the cul-de-sac and then stopping. I looked out of the bedroom window and saw them lined up in the lane, all blue Home Office-issue Fords, virtually blocking the road.

'Jesus Christ,' I said, as one by one, four men in crombies stepped out of their cars carrying briefcases. They couldn't have been more conspicuous if they tried. Four smartly dressed, clean shaven 'suits' walked in a neat line towards my front door, followed by the fifth, wearing a duffle-coat, who was obviously the surveyor.

I flew down the stairs to open the door and let them in before they rang the bell and set off Annie barking. Too late, I thought, as I heard the bell go. The dog leapt up at the door, doing her best impersonation of a pack of meat-starved Doberman pinschers. I yanked on her collar and locked her in the kitchen, from where she launched into her Hound of the Baskervilles routine.

By the time I had opened the door, the surveyor had stepped back several paces. 'Is that dog tethered?' he asked me nervously. 'Only I have been bitten before, you see.' I nodded as the head Home Office man introduced himself to me. 'Gordon Burns,' he held out his hand, 'Special Services Division.' He was neat and compact, a precise man, the one in charge of the costing, I presumed.

His colleagues filed in after him one by one and made their way into the living room, shaking me by the hand as they passed. They all seemed very similar, wearing almost identical clothing and the same smiles.

The surveyor was still standing back from the porch, wincing as Annie's barking and scratching grew ever more ferocious with the scent of four strange men in the house. 'It's OK,' I said, holding the door open wider. 'She's locked in the kitchen and I'll put her in the garage once you are inside.' He stepped gingerly through the doorway.

As I went to shut the front door, I saw Mary, my neighbour, on her front door step, her arms folded quizzically across her dressing gown. 'Is everything all right, Jenny?' she called out.

'Yes, um, fine,' I replied. 'Don't worry, they are just some workmen who have come to do some, er, work.' I shut the door before I could register the disbelief on her face.

We stood around awkwardly, my Home Office men and I, examining each other for a few seconds, before they started looking around the living room. I had spent the previous evening cleaning and vacuuming as if my life depended on it, but the five pairs of Government eyes scanning the room made me wish I had done even more. I felt strangely guilty, like you do when the Customs men at the airport ask if you have anything to declare.

'Well, then,' I said. 'Who would like a cup of coffee?' Five heads shook in unison. Mr Burns explained that they wanted to measure up the whole house, from top to bottom, identify the key electrical and lighting circuits and talk to me about which rooms I used most and at what times.

Fine, I thought. Let's get it over with. We proceeded round the house in a human crocodile for what seemed like hours, me telling them where and when I used which rooms, pointing out the light switches and electrical sockets, they following closely behind, almost tripping over each other and me as they measured and scribbled, lifted carpets and peered into cupboards.

I felt very uncomfortable telling these strangers what time I generally got up, how long I spent in the bathroom, what I had for breakfast and what time I left for work. Sometimes on a Saturday morning when Ian wasn't home, I would lie in bed for hours and I wondered guiltily if some dreadful fate would befall me as I heard myself claiming that I was always an early riser.

'We'll be installing panic alarms in every room you use,' said one of the men, as he lay on the floor under the bed. 'There will be security lighting front and rear, special doors and windows and a video entry system.'

'You will have a new front door that doesn't have a letter box,' another man added. 'All your mail from now on will be security screened before it even gets here but when it does, it will be delivered to a special bombproof mailbox in the front porch.'

A third, who was in my airing cupboard, told me, 'You will have to take your car to the camp and have a UCBT alarm system fitted in the next few days.'

'UCBT?' I asked, naively.

'It stands for Under Car Booby Trap.'

I shivered.

The fourth man, who was on a ladder peering up into the attic, told me, 'We'll teach you how to use everything. Remember, the police would much rather be called out on a false alarm than be called out to pick up the pieces.'

The nervy surveyor reeled in his tape measure and asked me where I thought I would like the master control box placed. I didn't have a clue and was actually feeling rather tired of their company by then. 'Place it where you like,' I said wearily and shut myself in the bathroom, to sit on the edge of the bath with my head in my hands.

So this is what it felt like to be protected. I had never felt so insecure. With all their talk of panic alarms and special locks, I was turning into a raving paranoiac. How could I ever feel comfortable in my own home again?

They left four hours later having checked over the temporary security system already installed by the SB, the control box for which looked like a large plastic milk crate and was shoved under the bed. I tried not to dwell to much on their talk of warnings and security codes and waved them goodbye as they promised to return the following Monday morning with the real thing.

I closed the door and let Annie in from the garage, throwing my arms around her big furry neck. 'You're all the protection I need, aren't you girl?' I told her, as she licked my face. 'Come on, let's get some lunch.'

I had just kicked off my shoes and collapsed onto the sofa with a sandwich when the doorbell rang again. 'Oh no, not more of them,' I thought, as I stood up to shut Annie away.

Standing on the doorstep was Bob, the Regiment's latest Families Officer, a nice enough chap although I had only met him a couple of times before. He was accompanied by a very severe-looking woman in a mac.

'Hiya, Jenny,' Bob said breezily. 'Can we come in?' I ushered them into the living room and we all sat down. Too hungry now to care, I waded into my sandwich and watched them both carefully.

'Just thought we'd drop in and see how it all went this morning,' said Bob. The woman remained silent.

'Oh it was fine,' I replied. 'If you like five strangers in your house, prodding and poking and looking under every carpet.'

I saw his face fall and wished I hadn't been so harsh. 'Oh, it's

OK,' I said. 'They were fine, very nice actually, and they explained to me everything they would be doing next Monday when they come to fit the final system in. I am glad they came.'

He looked happier and asked me how I was feeling about it all. I might have told him but I didn't feel like opening up in front of this strange woman who had not said a word to me yet and was sitting with her hands in her pockets.

Putting down my empty plate, I asked her, 'By the way, who are you?'

She stiffened and answered, 'I am the adjutant.'

'And why are you here?' I asked her.

'I am his boss and I am here to make sure he briefs you properly,' she said. Bob looked like a naughty schoolboy under her gaze.

Snotty bitch. Here she was, fresh out of training college, assigned to the Regiment to learn the ropes and sitting in my house as if she owned the place. Well, I didn't want her there and I made that quite clear. I told Bob I had things to do and stood up to show them out. When I shut the door this time, I was determined not to open it to anyone else again that day.

I spent the weekend quietly, dreading Monday. After another bad night's sleep I got up on Sunday and decided to spend the day really cleaning the house from top to bottom so that none of my guests could accuse me of being a bad housewife. I spent the morning as usual, preparing lunch, and then carried the vacuum cleaner upstairs to get the fluff out from under the bed. They were going to be on their hands and knees under there after all.

I tried to think about anything other than the security leak as I pushed the suction hose in and out under the bed. Perhaps I would phone Lisa and her husband Kevin, I thought, and invite them over to Sunday lunch. She always loved my Yorkshire puddings and I could do with the company. Yes, I'd call them as soon as I was finished, I decided.

I moved towards the window and vacuumed the carpet by the skirting board. One of the men had told me the previous day that all the skirting boards would have to come off and I wondered why I was bothering if they were going to make that much mess. It was a crisp morning and I looked out of the window into the garden to see if the bird table needed refilling. What I saw there made my heart stop.

Two men in black were kneeling on the lawn, ten feet apart, their guns pointed up at the window. I froze. Reaching down slowly, I turned the machine off. Suddenly I could hear Annie barking furiously downstairs. I backed away from the window inch by inch. Feeling my way with my hands, I reversed out onto the landing and stood there shaking and trying to remember what it was I was supposed to do.

The door bell rang, startling me. Annie was on her back legs at the front door, going demented. Surely the neighbours will have noticed something. Surely Annie's barking will alert them and they'll call the police?

I crept down the stairs and urgently whispered her name. Pulling her towards me I sat on the bottom step, shivering with her in my arms. The bell rang again and again, and I could hear a man's voice calling out my name. 'Open the door,' the voice said. 'This is the police.'

The police? Had someone called them? I peered cautiously through the net curtains of the window at the bottom of the stairs and saw, to my enormous relief, that my cul-de-sac was full of uniformed and plain-clothes officers, all standing by their panda cars, several with guns pointing at the house. I rushed to the door and turned the lock. The door flew open and an armed sergeant from Special Branch burst in, grabbing hold of me by the arm and looking around him anxiously.

'Are you all right?' he asked, as he pulled me into the safety of the study.

'Yes, yes. I am fine,' I exhaled. 'There were men, men in the garden with guns.'

He radioed this information to his colleagues and asked me more. 'Where? When? How many?'

I told him what I had seen. He looked at me closely as if he was trying to take in what I had said.

'Did you activate the security alarm?' he asked.

'No,' I said, confused.

He studied my face carefully. 'Why didn't you answer the telephone and give the appropriate security code?' he asked.

'I didn't hear it ring,' I said. 'I was vacuuming.'

He waved some men in and helped them search the house for any terrorists that might have been holding me hostage. He looked in cupboards and under beds, and kept coming back down to me in the hallway to check if I was still all right.

Finally, he took my arm and led me into the kitchen. Standing by the sink, he pointed into the garden with his radio and said, as gently as he could, 'Mrs Simpson, were those the two men you saw in the garden?'

I looked at him quizzically and then outside. Sure enough, the two men I had seen were still in position, covering the back of the house, only from down here I could see they were wearing black baseball caps with the words POLICE on them.

Suddenly it all clicked into place. The giant milk crate under the bed. The vacuum cleaner. In my quest to be fluff-free, I had accidentally triggered one of the most dramatic rescue operations in Hereford, and mobilised an entire Special Branch team to save me from death or kidnapping.

Not only that, but the entire village was now in on the secret and my immediate neighbours were scared witless over the whole operation. I had never been so embarrassed in my whole life. How could I have been so stupid? I wanted the ground to swallow me up there and then.

To their credit, the boys in blue were wonderful. 'Never mind, Mrs S,' the sergeant told me. 'It was a wonderful practice drill for when the real thing happens. Just be a bit more careful next time you get out the Hoover.' I was mortified. Talk about crying 'Wolf!' I wondered how quickly they would react if I ever did have to call them out in a real emergency. I imagined the sergeant raising his eyes to the heavens the next time the alarm went off and thinking, Oh God, not another false alarm over at the dotty housewife's.

I closed the front door as the last of the policemen drove away, and went into the kitchen, closely followed by Annie. She licked my hand and I looked down at her big brown eyes. 'What a plonker I am, Annie,' I told her as I got on with the lunch.

If the neighbours didn't think I was off my rocker by then, they certainly did the next morning when, at eight a.m. sharp, the Home Office workmen arrived in force. Filing into my home in overalls, carrying giant rolls of cable, security lights and boxes filled with electrical gizmos, they moved in and took over. Instantly I felt as if I was in the way, so I ended up sitting up on the kitchen worktop, nursing a large mug of coffee and a digestive biscuit.

Within hours they had ripped up all the carpets, had the floorboards up in the attic, and replaced the doors and windows with the like of which I had only ever seen in 'Prisoner Cell Block H'. The windows were blast-proofed, a video entry system was installed and panic alarms were fitted in every room.

They seemed to fit alarms to just about everything, as well as security lights and special locks. It was the kind of security for which an American politician would give his favourite bodyguard. If a neighbourhood cat decided to creep across our front lawn at night for a pee, the house and garden would light up like Wembley Stadium.

I felt somehow numbed at this mass invasion of my home. It would have been better if Ian had been there to help me through it, but he wasn't, and I just had to get on with it and cope like he had told me to. None of these people were here to hurt me. They were trying to help, to make me feel safe. But the longer it went on, and the more my house was torn apart in front of my eyes, the more it felt like a very bad dream.

They had almost finished. The front door was the last thing to be installed. Steel-plated underneath a wood veneer, it was to be my best defence against anyone kicking the door in or trying to shoot their way through it, I was told. Nice thought.

It was a freezing day and the wind was blowing through the house like a gale. It seemed to take the workmen hours to unscrew the old hinges and put the new ones on and I couldn't find anywhere warm to sit.

Trying to lift it onto its hinges, they dropped the new door. It smashed down onto the concrete front step and the steel-plating buckled so much that it would no longer fit snugly in the door-frame. The men stood around and scratched their heads for a while before telling me it would be a couple of hours more before they could get a replacement delivered.

That is just about it, I thought. I was so cold I decided to get in the car and get away from them all for a while. The car took ages to warm up and I didn't know where I was going or what I was going to do when I got there, I just knew I had to get away from the house for a while, and go somewhere to get warm.

I drove past the local supermarket with all its lights blazing and turned into the car park. I didn't need any shopping, but I wandered in, felt the heat of the place and grabbed a shopping trolley.

Walking up and down the aisles, I was lost in a world of my own. I looked around at all the people going past me, people who were leading ordinary lives with normal jobs and families; people who had no security leak threatening them; housewives whose homes were comforting sanctuaries against the outside world; women whose husbands came home each night at six o'clock and whose most frightening experience was watching the horror video they rented out on a Saturday night to have with their Chinese take-away.

I thought of Ian in Belize, setting up his A-frame in some jungle camp with his mates, their supper bubbling gently over the fire. I wanted him there with me, my body ached for his touch and his reassurance. I couldn't imagine spending that first night alone in the house, the panic alarm by my bed, the demons in my mind tormenting me. I'd get a bottle of gin, I thought, and drink myself into oblivion. It was the only way I knew to numb the pain.

I felt a hand on my arm. 'Are you all right?' said a concerned young man in a supermarket overall. It was only then that I realised that my face was wet with my tears and that people were staring at me.

I wiped my face with the back of my hand and said, 'Yes, I'm fine, sorry'. Abandoning the empty trolley, I fled from the store and sat in the car, head in hands, sobbing for all I was worth.

\* \* \*

A few days later, I received a call from the camp telling me to bring my car in to have the security alarm fitted. I hadn't been looking forward to the call and I drove my Ford Sierra past the camp gates reluctantly, wishing I did not have to go through with it.

It was as if there would never be a car bomb as long as I didn't have the alarm fitted. Once the thing was in, and I was going to have to check it day and night, I felt that there would always be the possibility of a bomb or at least that it would always be at the forefront of my mind.

I booked the car in and left it for the day, catching a bus into town to do some shopping. Try as I might as I wandered around Hereford, I couldn't concentrate on what I was meant to be buying or where I was supposed to be going. All I could see in my mind were images of cars blown to pieces by bombs in Northern Ireland and mainland bombing campaigns, of the tangled metal and the devastation in the area where the target vehicles had been parked – windows blown in, craters in the road, blood on the pavements.

The house security was different somehow. It was my own environment, my home, and if I pressed the panic alarms someone would come. But the car was independent of that, and much easier to target. I didn't want to go back to the camp to collect the Sierra. Why couldn't I just leave it there forever, and catch buses and taxis everywhere from now on? They were hardly likely to blow up a bus just to get me. Or were they? I found myself walking into the pub where I first met Ian, the Booth Hall, and ordering a large gin and tonic to steady my nerves. I noticed that my hand was shaking as I picked up the glass.

By the time I got back to the camp it was nearly dark. How I hated the nights drawing in, I thought as I identified myself to one of the security staff and waited for my car to be brought out to me. I was tired and cold and I just wanted to get home.

The fitter drove round to the front of the workshop and stepped out of the car. 'Right, Mrs Simpson,' he said. 'All done, now you just have to learn how to use it.' I felt suddenly colder and shivered.

'The car has been fitted with a UCBT Detector,' he said. 'The

UCBT stands for Under Car Booby Trap.' Yes, I thought. I know.

'It is really quite simple but it is not a substitute for a physical examination of the car. You must always check your vehicle yourself first and for that reason, we give you this . . .', he handed me what looked like a small silver compact case, 'and this,' he held out a high-powered torch. I held the compact in my hand and looked perplexed.

'That is a special extendable mirror for checking under the car,' he said, smiling. 'You open it like this.' He flipped it open as if it were a communicator out of *Star Trek*. 'You pull out this little handle here . . .', the handle extended into a long telescopic rod, '. . . and then, using the torch so you can see what you are doing, you walk along all sides of the car holding the mirror firmly down on the ground, enabling you to see any device that has been attached to the underside of the vehicle.'

As I had no idea whatsoever what the underside of a vehicle was meant to look like, how the hell was I supposed to spot anything that wasn't meant to be there? I thought to myself, but I didn't think the time was right to voice my concerns. At least the mirror would be useful for putting on my lipstick.

'If you see anything at all suspicious,' the fitter went on, 'get down on your hands and knees with the torch and have another quick check before calling the police. Sometimes something that looks strange in the reflection can look quite normal when you see it close up.'

I tried to imagine what on earth I was supposed to be looking for. A small, shiny black ball engraved with the words BOMB and a smoking fuse, perhaps? Or a pack of dynamite bound tightly with tape and a timer device ticking dangerously away next to it? This was ridiculous.

The fitter was carrying on with his routine. 'Once you have checked the vehicle over, you then turn to the alarm as a second line of defence. The car is fitted with a very strong magnet underneath and a mercury tilt switch which detects the slightest movement. There are eight detectors fitted in the car at various points, which are designed to detect any suspicious metal object placed underneath the car. Fitted close to the steering wheel here . . .' he pointed to a small display panel with horizontal flashing red, green and orange lights, '. . . is your LED control panel. The system is armed and disarmed by the ignition.

'When you first open the door, all three lights will come on like this,' he opened the door and the three lights duly came on. 'When the red and the green lights are flashing that means the system is on standby and will not arm until the final door or boot lid is closed.

'Once you have closed all the doors, all three lights will flash for twenty seconds before the single constant green light stays on in the middle, which will tell you that the system is working and armed. If there are no lights at all, then there is something wrong with the system, and you should take extra care and do a check yourself.'

I tried very hard to take in all that he was telling me in the disappearing light. The torch in his hand was still on and as he gesticulated his instructions, it flashed wildly around the inside of the car and up into his face.

'You should always check the status of the lights before touching or entering the vehicle,' he was saying. 'Most of these devices are activated by timers, but some can be triggered by the movement of the vehicle, or even flash guns pointed at them from a distance.' I was now shivering with cold.

'When you return to an armed vehicle, you must look through the driver's door window and down at the control panel each time,' the fitter carried on regardless. 'The single green light in the middle of the panel means that the system is armed and nothing untoward has been detected. A single green light coupled with the single amber light means that the door or boot has been tampered with.

'A single red light with a flashing green light means danger, the magnetic alarm has been activated. The number of times the green light flashes will indicate which of the eight sensors has been activated. An audible alarm will sound as soon as you open the door.'

He had already lost me.

'If the amber light is flashing on its own, that means the battery is low and has interfered with the power supply, but if the red light and the flashing amber light are both on, that means the alarm had been activated before the battery ran down.'

He stopped suddenly and shone the torch directly into my face. 'Do you understand what I am saying?'

I wanted to tell him that no, I didn't understand and I didn't want to understand. That the flashing lights meant nothing to me, that I wished the bloody thing had never been fitted in the first place and that I just wanted to get home and pour myself a drink. But I nodded meekly and smiled.

'We issue you with this *aide-mémoire*,' he said, handing me a credit-card-sized plastic instruction sheet with all the possible permutations of flashing lights and what they meant printed out in neat rows. 'The main thing to remember is that if the red light is on, at any time, you should call the police. And try not to panic when you see it light up. It is important that you don't slam the doors or disturb the vehicle. Just walk away from it as calmly as possible and get help. Oh, and try and make sure no one else interferes with it either.'

I nodded again, hoping he was finished.

'Any problems, bring the car back and I'll run through it with you again. If that's all OK for now, I'll bid you goodnight.'

I jumped into the car and turned the ignition key. The control panel seemed to be flashing all its lights at once, but I couldn't care less. I would figure it all out tomorrow. The IRA were hardly likely to have planted a bomb under my car at the camp. I drove out through the gates as fast as I could. I had never felt more in need of a drink in my life.

The system took me weeks to get used to but eventually I mastered it. After a while, it became almost second nature – mirror, signal, manoeuvre, I called it. And I was right, the mirror did come in handy for doing my make-up. It always seemed to be the first thing I put my hand on when I reached into my handbag.

By the time I left work one night six weeks later, after doing some overtime to get some accounts finished, I had almost come to accept it completely as part of my way of life. It was dark when I came out of the office and into the firm's car park. As I walked up to the car I glanced in at the control panel and stopped dead in my tracks.

The red light was on and the green light was flashing. I felt the adrenaline course through my veins. Red light, green light flashing. That was it wasn't it? A bomb? I dropped my handbag to the ground and tipped out its contents hastily, searching for the torch, the mirror and the *aide-mémoire*.

I flicked on the torch and shone it at the plastic card. Red light on, green light flashing, what did it say? 'DANGER – MAGNETIC ALARM'. I froze. I stood up slowly and watched the green light. How many times was it flashing. One blink. Two. Three. Four. Five. Stop. Sensor five had been activated. Where the hell was sensor five? I flashed the torch down at the card again and flipped it over in my hand, panicking. It didn't tell me which sensor was which. Damn.

Grabbing the mirror, I got down on my hands and knees and started crawling around the car, looking up at the underside of the vehicle with the torch and checking it with the mirror. I swore out loud as I snagged my tights. I couldn't see a bloody thing. What if it goes off now? I wouldn't even have a decent pair of tights on. Perhaps I should back off and call the police? My breathing was coming shallow and fast.

Looking up across the deserted car park I saw a light shining in the security lodge. Billy, the chief security officer, could be seen moving around inside. I sighed heavily. He was a sweet old man and someone I had known for years, he would know what to do. I ran over to his lodge and, bursting open the door, arrived breathless and pale.

My words rushed out in a confused jumble. I looked up at his astonished face as I told him, 'Billy, I need your help. My husband is in the SAS and I've got this special alarm fitted to my car and, well, I think there may be a bomb under it.'

He was wonderful, completely calm. He switched off the small television set in his office, sat down in his chair and looked at me as if I had just dropped in from Mars. 'Just a minute, young lady,' he said, pulling a chewing gum from its wrapper and folding it onto his tongue. 'Run that by me one more time.'

Once he had understood what I was trying to tell him, he did all that I asked him to and more. Sitting me down to let me catch my breath, he rang the camp in the hope of speaking to someone who could come and take a look at the car. They had all gone home, but the switchboard operator told him to call the local Special Branch. I dialled the home number of one of the police officers I had met at the start of the security alert and he instructed Billy to go round the car carefully with the mirror and torch and check it over.

It took almost two hours before Billy and I were finally satisfied that my car was safe. We rang the police back to tell them and a young detective constable told him, 'Yes, that's what I thought you'd say. Don't worry, it happens all the time. The alarms are sometimes triggered by another car parking close by and upsetting the magnetic field.' Great, I thought, feeling ten years older. In gratitude to Billy for his kindness, I gave him my spare extendible mirror and he was really touched. By the time I got home it was past eleven o'clock.

The alarm broke down on me several times after that, despite being put in for a service every time it did it. It got to the point where I didn't even bother to take it back to the garage. The thing was clearly temperamental and that was all there was to it.

I still went through all the necessary motions, mirror, signal, manoeuvre, only I didn't feel quite as panicky about it all any more. On one occasion at the local supermarket, I was down on my hands and knees under the car checking it after the display panel had indicated something in sensor one, when I suddenly looked round to see a middle-aged woman crawling around on the ground next to me.

'Is it a hard or a soft one?' she said, squinting at me through thick spectacles.

I asked her what she meant.

'Your contact lens, dear, the one you've lost.'

When Ian first told me about the leak we both thought that the Home Office would move me to a safe house, take me somewhere out of danger, where I would be watched and cared for by professionals until Ian could get home and take over. When we were told that would be too expensive and that they would protect my home instead, I had been genuinely relieved. I hadn't relished the thought of a personal security guard night and day, however comforting it might have been.

But once the men had gone and I was left alone in the house, staring at the panic alarms, checking the car with the mirror every day, I started to feel increasingly vulnerable and exposed.

It didn't help that the IRA had restarted a mainland campaign against servicemen and their families, and I couldn't help but watch the news stories about the killings and bombings with a renewed sense of horror. In September 1989, ten Marine bandsmen had been blown up at the Royal Marines School of Music in Deal, Kent. In 1990, IRA gunmen shot dead two Australian tourists in Roermond, Holland, believing them to be British servicemen. In July 1990, Ian Gow, the Conservative MP for Eastbourne and junior minister for Northern Ireland was murdered by an IRA car bomb at his home in Sussex.

There were several other attacks on British soldiers and civilians that year, twelve bombs in all, including one at Wembley in north London which killed an Army sergeant. Paddington and Victoria railway stations were targeted, and bombs were planted in the London Stock Exchange and at the Carlton Club. Sir Peter Terry, former governor of Gibraltar, was shot in the face and body at his home in Stafford, his wife was slightly wounded. Even 10 Downing Street came under mortar attack in February 1991.

SAS missions against the IRA had become much more high-profile after the successful ambush of the IRA attack on the Loughall police station in 1987. IRA members continued to die at the hands of the Regiment, including the Gibraltar 'Death on the Rock' incident. Where previously, the Regiment's operations were never openly discussed, they suddenly became the hot topic of news, and those affiliated with the SAS knew that it was only a matter of time before the IRA tried to get back at the men they knew were their deadliest foes.

Ian would have been an ideal target for them. He had worked undercover across the water for so long that he had come to know many of the key players and had been personally responsible for

ABOVE: Ian in Fiji on jungle training exercises in 1983

LEFT: Cartoon I had made up for Ian when he missed the Drop Zone during a parachute jump near Hereford and ended up on the main Cardiff to London railway line

Browning nine-millimetre automatic pistol similar to the one I learned how to use in the Killing House at Stirling Lines

ABOVE: Ian returning
to Northern Ireland
from Stirling Lines,
1987

RIGHT: The photograph
of me and Zorba that
Ian carries around the
world

LEFT:
Ian preparing to jump
from the plane during
exercises in Florida, 1987

ABOVE: (left to right), Sean Savage Mairead Farrell and Daniel McCann, the three IRA terrorists shot dead in the Gibraltar 'Death on the Rock' attack in 1988, days after Ian had been watching Savage in Belfast

LEFT AND BELOW: Official photographs of the shot IRA terrorists in Gibraltar

ABOVE: Our snap-shots of the garage where the shooting took place in Gibraltar and the flats from which witnesses saw what happened

RIGHT: Ian outside the Wembley bar in Gibraltar which had been his favourite watering hole when he was a young rifleman in the Royal Green Jackets stationed in Gibraltar

LEFT: Ian and me at Buckingham Palace in 1990 after he received the Queen's Gallantry Medal for his work in Northern Ireland from the Queen

BELOW: Ian and me at the Royal Green Jackets' Summer Ball, Warminster, 1989

RIGHT: Video grab from the only film footage shot of the SAS behind enemy lines, Iraq, 1991. The picture shows Ian, on the right, helping an injured Iraqi soldier to a waiting helicopter and safety

INSET: SAS soldiers in a specially converted vehicle with the roll bars removed and replaced by a gun, similar to the Land Rover in which Ian nearly lost his life during the Gulf War, 1991

RIGHT: Ian (top left) giving first aid to a wounded Iraqi soldier during the Gulf War. The soldier, who was only sixteen, thanked him repeatedly and promised to bring his family to meet him one day

Who Dares Wins:
Ian and me on the Log
Ride at Alton Towers,
1992. Guess who got
the wettest?

12 5 92
The Worlds
Biggest Log
Ride

Alton Towers

the arrest and imprisonment of some of them. He undoubtedly represented a major threat to their operations and they would have taken great satisfaction in killing him or his wife.

The whole thing worried me tremendously for a very long time, at least a year, and much more than I had expected it to. Ian telephoned almost daily to reassure me when he could – the bills were horrendous – but when he came home from one trip it seemed it was only to prepare for the next one, so I was left to cope with it on my own.

As I watched all the news bulletins, I couldn't help but feel that it could be our turn next and imagined the news crews filming our house and talking about my death or Ian's as flippantly as they seemed to talk about the rest. My imagination was doing a very good job of driving me slowly round the bend.

I couldn't sleep, I couldn't eat. I felt wretched and had never felt so alone. Every stranger I saw I wondered about. Was that man across the street a terrorist? Why was he looking at me like that? How long had that car been behind me in the traffic jam? Wasn't it the one I had seen earlier that morning?

I carried the fear around inside me all the time, wondering if each day would be my last; trying to contain my panic each time I turned the key in the lock of my own front door; afraid to answer the telephone or open the door. It was affecting my work and my looks. I felt permanently exhausted. I knew I had to snap out of it somehow, but I didn't have the energy.

Matters were not helped when, late one Sunday night, not long after our phone number had been changed, the telephone rang. I watched it ringing for a few seconds and then picked it up, thinking it might be Ian or Lisa.

'Hello?' I said quietly into the receiver.

Nothing.

'Hello, hello,' I repeated. I could tell that someone was there but wasn't saying anything. I slammed the phone down and stood staring at it in disbelief. This was it. They must have got the new number.

Seconds later the phone rang again. I hesitated, not sure what to do.

Nervously, I picked it up, my hands trembling as I cradled the receiver.

'Hello?' I said. Silence. 'Hello? Hello? . . . Who is this?' I demanded.

No-one spoke and I cut the call off with my hand. As I stood staring at the panic alarm on the wall by my side, I remembered my last false alarm.

The telephone rang again, making me jump. I stood looking at it for what seemed like ages, willing it to stop. Finally, I picked it up, my hand cupped over the mouthpiece so that the caller would not hear my fast breathing.

There was silence. I didn't speak and strained to hear any background noise. When the voice came, it was unexpected. It was a young male voice, but without the Belfast accent I had half-expected to hear.

'We are coming to get you,' the voice said, almost matter-of-factly. 'We know where you are and we're coming for you now.'

I slammed the phone down and burst into tears.

I grabbed my address book and found the number of Ruth and Jerry, close friends of ours who live in Leominster, about seven miles away. Jerry is a local police sergeant, he would know what to do. Shaking with fear, I picked up the phone and dialled the number. It rang twice before Jerry answered.

'Jerry?' I sobbed into the phone. 'It's Jenny. Sorry to ring you so late but . . .'

He interrupted. 'What's the matter, Jenny? Is something up?'

'I know this sounds crazy,' I said. 'But someone just called and said they were coming to get me . . . Could you possibly come over?'

Ian had already told Jerry privately about the security leak and had asked him to keep an eye on me. Jerry told me he would be round straight away and not to answer the phone again. I thanked him and replaced the receiver. He was round within minutes. I heard his car pull into the driveway and opened the door, running out to meet him. He had brought Ruth with him, and I fell into her arms. I felt like a little girl, all alone and frightened of the dark.

These wonderful friends stayed for two hours, calming me down, telling me it was probably just a crank call and promising to speak to the Special Branch in the morning. Ruth made me a hot drink and put me to bed, and they both stayed until I had almost cried myself to sleep.

They let themselves out and I heard the door click shut. I was too tired to sleep, but too scared to get up. I tossed and turned all night, wondering whether it would be possible to call Ian in the morning at his jungle base. It would be wonderful just to hear his voice.

The following morning, Jerry and Ruth were on my doorstep very early. They looked exhausted and I told them so.

'I should think so,' said Jerry. 'We have been parked outside your house all night, keeping an eye on things for you.'

I was staggered. I couldn't believe their kindness. Ruth said they had driven home after leaving me but Jerry told her he was worried and wanted to stake out the house for the night. She told him if he went, she was going too, and so they made up flasks of coffee, wrapped up warm and sat in their Isuzu Jeep at the end of my drive until seven a.m.

Jerry called the Special Branch that morning from my house and, after a preliminary investigation, they surmised that the most likely possibility was that a crank had accidentally dialled my number, realised that he had reached a woman alone and had called back to frighten me. We all agreed that the crank had done a very good job. But the police could not rule out the possibility that the call had come from the IRA and the thought chilled me to the marrow.

For weeks afterwards, I kept thinking, Don't be stupid, pull yourself together, but I couldn't get the worry out of my head. During daylight it was just about bearable but, as always, the nights were the harder to face. I would lie in bed listening to the ticking of the clock, watching the shadows on the wall and jumping at every sound or wind whistle in the house. I would drift off for half an hour, then wake up again in a panic, thinking I had heard a strange noise. If I heard a car approach in the lane, I imagined it contained hooded gunmen with no other purpose in mind than to kill me.

I would run through the security procedures in my head. Am I close enough to that panic alarm? If I hit it will they come quickly enough? How long will I have? I took to wedging a chair against the bedroom door to give me more time and I wished I had the nine millimetre Browning pistol I had trained with. If the security lights turned on outside because of a neighbourhood cat, I would leap up and peer out to see if there was anything sinister. I even took to wearing a T-shirt in bed, forsaking my previous dislike of night wear.

In the daytime, I wanted to fill the house with friends, but then I worried in case they might be innocently involved in any attack on the house. If they did come, I had to warn their children not to touch any of the panic buttons with their little fingers.

It affected the minutiae of my life, the very fabric of my everyday existence. I gradually came to realise that the fortress around me which was designed to protect me from the threat of terrorism had become a prison in which I was the sole inmate. It had completely taken away the peace of mind I had always enjoyed in my own home and I thought for a while that I was losing my sanity.

But one day, quite without warning, I woke up and thought to myself that I was no longer going to be a victim. I decided that I was tired of feeling defenceless. I stood up and said to myself out loud, 'Get on with it, girl. Remember what Ian said. Don't let the bastards grind you down.' I put on a favourite CD, got dressed and decided that from that day on I would lick this thing. It did take a long time, but I beat it in the end.

One of the most significant psychological breakthroughs for me was our decision, when it came to changing the car that year, not to have the UCBT alarm installed again. I would still check the underneath of the vehicle each time and look out for anything suspicious, but I no longer wanted my life made a misery by the display panel of flashing lights. I became quite a fatalist, believing that if something was going to happen, it was going to happen, and there wasn't very much I could do about it.

We couldn't make the same decision about the house, so we continued to have the protection there. But ultimately I came to see it as an advantage and not a disadvantage. I mean, how many girls get given a free make-up mirror by the MoD? Suffice to say, when it came to getting rid of the house, the security system was one hell of a selling point.

The whole experience was pretty ghastly and one that I would not wish upon my worst enemy. It was frightening and miserable and it did nothing to soothe my nerves or slow down my drinking.

But, in many ways, and especially after the bad patch we went through during Ian's tour of Northern Ireland, it bound us together. It reminded us of the important things in life, and made us realise how very much each one of us meant to the other. Having survived the violence and the arguments relatively intact, we were determined not to let the IRA tear us apart.

How they would have hated to think that their terror campaign, and their direct threat against us, only served to make us stronger, and better able to cope with whatever the future held.

# 8 | Forsaking All Others

'HOW DO YOU FANCY A NEW DRESS?' Ian asked me long distance from Florida in the spring of 1990. I was sitting at home in bed, a book and a drink in my hand, enjoying one of our many late night telephone calls while he was away on free-fall training.

'What do you mean?' I asked. I could tell he was bursting to tell me something, he was never any good at keeping things from me.

'I received a telegram from London today, Jen,' he said, excitedly. 'They're giving me the QGM, the Queen's Gallantry Medal, for that last trip to Northern Ireland. Me and another bloke from the Regiment. It means we'll get to go to Buckingham Palace and meet the Queen.'

I was thrilled, knowing how much it meant to him. From his earliest childhood days, Ian had been an ardent Royalist. One of his uncles had been Lord Mountbatten's bodyguard for a period and he never failed to tell people about it. The Royal Family inspired a loyalty and devotion in him that I rarely saw in relation to anything else. For Queen and country, that was what joining the SAS had been all about for him. He might as well have had the Union Jack tattooed on his heart.

He sounded like a little boy on the phone, telling me all about it and pretending that it was all for my benefit and not for his. 'It will be wonderful for you,' he said. 'Who would ever have thought that a feisty little tomboy from Hetton-le-Hole would be meeting the Queen one day.' But despite his best endeavours, he was unable to hide how much he was looking forward to it too.

'They said that I can only take two people with me, though,' he sounded disappointed. 'You obviously get to come, babe, and I couldn't go without Mum, but I really would have loved Dad to come along as well. I think it would have meant a lot to him.'

Ian adored his father, although he had never been one to express it, and I knew how much he would have enjoyed having him there when he received his medal. The two men had never really been able to open up to each other, even though Ian's father is tremendously proud of his son and Ian has enormous respect for what his dad did as a bomber pilot in the World War II.

They have a lovely relationship, though, very affable and easy-going. Ian is always the joker, making light of everything and his father, with his dry sense of humour, makes a perfect foil.

I told Ian that if he wanted, I wouldn't go to the Palace, so that his father could go, but he wouldn't hear of it.

'No, babe. Absolutely not. I want you there, by my side. God knows, you deserve this medal as much as I do.'

I had never been a devotee of the Royal Family like Ian. Where I came from, they had always seemed so distant and out of reach, they might as well have been from another planet. When Ian spoke of fighting for his Queen and country, it meant little or nothing to me. What did the Queen know about my husband and what he went through, what we both went through in her name? I had always wondered.

But now I felt differently. It looked as if she did know, that someone somewhere had put Ian's name forward and she now wanted to give him a medal. I thought about her as I had seen her on television documentaries, sitting at a desk in her twin set and pearls, signing papers her private secretaries handed to her. Had she sat like that, in her grandly decorated room, when Ian's name and what he had done had been raised? Or had some lackey gone through the list for her? Either way, in a few months' time she was going to be face to face with my husband, handing him the medal that he so rightly deserved.

I was hugely proud but I wasn't planning on making any more of it than it was. I was delighted for Ian's sake and I was pleased that the Regiment had nominated him and put the past behind them, but that was as far as it went in my mind. Little Jenny Simpson from

County Durham wasn't planning on being bowled over by something as trivial as a trip to London to see the Queen.

That was, until the morning of the big day, when I was suddenly as nervous as a kitten. It made my wedding day feel like a breeze. Ian and I drove down to London the previous day and stayed at his parents' home. On the morning of the ceremony, we went to a military barracks in central London to get ready and to change into our best clothes.

It was strange seeing Ian in his full dress uniform. He hardly ever wears it and it looked a little tight to me, but I tried not to laugh. I wore a purple dress, with a matching hat and shoes, and a beige coat. It cost me a fortune and I told myself I would get good use out of it, but I knew that I would probably never wear it again and didn't mind a bit.

We helped each other get ready and were just about to leave to pick up Ian's mother when his CO dropped by and asked if he could have a word with Ian. How nice, I thought, the CO is wishing him well and congratulating him on his achievement. I waited nervously in the room we had changed in, ready for the off.

Ian returned with a look on his face that I hadn't expected. It was one of anger.

'What's the matter, babe?' I asked.

'Those bloody bastards,' he said. 'Can't they even let today go by without ruining it?' His jaw was clenched and he looked as if he could hit someone.

'Ian, what is it?' I asked, worried now.

'It's the security thing,' he said. 'The CO just popped in to tell me that one of the national newspapers has got wind of the fact that two of the people receiving medals from the Queen today are 22 SAS and they are threatening to publish our names. The CO is trying to get a D-Notice served, some Government order banning them from doing so because of the threat we are under, but he said he just thought he should let me know.'

I sat down hard on the bed. 'What does it mean?' I asked.

Ian smashed his fist into the wall. 'It means nothing,' he said, 'absolutely bloody nothing. We've still got to go and get the medal, there's nothing we can do about it, and telling us about it has only served to spoil our day.' He sat down next to me and put his head in his hands.

'Oh, babe, no it hasn't,' I told him, stroking his hair. 'Come on, let's try to forget about it and go and get your mum. It's going to be a wonderful day. You're meeting the Queen, remember? Let's not let the bastards get to us now, not today.'

I forced him to his feet, brushed down his dress uniform and gave him a kiss. 'Sergeant Ian Simpson, you look drop dead gorgeous,' I told him and, despite himself, he smiled.

We collected his mother who looked splendid in red and black, and drove to Buckingham Palace, pulling up at the main gates. The press were there in force, cameras clicking. It was the day cricketer Freddy Truman got his OBE and there was a lot of media interest. We joined the small queue of traffic at the gates and watched as each party was directed across the wide gravel forecourt in front of the Palace towards the inner courtyard.

I could hardly wait. I had watched on television as various members of the Royal Family celebrated a marriage or some other special occasion on the balcony above us or drove out in golden carriages from the covered porch, now I wanted to see it all for myself.

When it was our turn to introduce ourselves, the guard leaned into the car and asked who we were.

'Ian Simpson, 22 SAS,' Ian said proudly, expecting to be ushered across the courtyard like the rest.

Instead the guard looked at us aghast, and replied, 'Get round the back, quick. My orders are that you've got to go through the back door, to avoid the cameras.' Ian's face fell.

I could hardly believe it. We had been waiting in this queue, Ian in full dress uniform, for a full fifteen minutes and only when we were at the gates were we ushered to the back of the building, like some also-rans. Ian looked as if someone had just punched him in the stomach. His mother was utterly bewildered.

'Come on now, babe,' I told Ian. 'It doesn't matter. Let's just do as we're told.' He reversed the car back and we drove round to a side gate in Birdcage Walk. They waved us through and told us where to park the car. A footman led the way to a small door in the side of the building. Strain as I might, I couldn't see round to the balcony any more.

'Well, now, this is exciting, isn't it?' I told Ian and his mum as I grabbed each of their arms. 'I shouldn't think many people get to see the back stairs of Buckingham Palace. We might even see the royal loo.'

But even my bravado started to fail me when we had to weave our way through the vast building towards the hall where the awards ceremony was being held. I had expected palatial splendour from corner to corner but as we were led through the servant's quarters, we had to step over buckets, mops and piles of dirty laundry. It was really quite grotty.

Ian didn't say a word. 'Great,' I thought. 'This is lovely. Everyone else gets to go through the front door and we get the tradesmen's entrance. So much for the miner's daughter making a big impression.'

We were eventually shown into a huge room where all the other guests were waiting. All I could see at first was a sea of hats – the dress hats of the ladies and the top hats or military caps of the men. An usher took Ian's name and asked us to sit at the back.

'You are to go last of all, for security reasons,' he said and Ian nodded resignedly. There was another member of the Regiment there and Ian said hello. He and his wife had also been told to wait at the back.

The ceremony started when the trumpeters with their beautiful gold embossed costumes suddenly blasted a fanfare and the Queen walked in, smiling at everyone and looking just like she did on the television, only considerably smaller.

'She's much shorter than she looks on the stamps,' I whispered to Ian, trying to lighten his mood. He squeezed my hand and smiled.

One by one the names were called out by an ornately dressed footman wearing a wig, and the recipients formed an orderly queue to approach the Queen. It was a very well-oiled machine. Each person got a nod and a smile and a few words, and was then given their medal and moved on so the Queen could go through exactly the same process with the next.

As we sat waiting, I looked up and around me and noticed that even this room seemed rather shabby. Some of the wallpaper was peeling and the curtains obviously had not been cleaned in ages. There were footmen standing all around in their fantastically embroidered costumes and the hall was lined with lots of wonderful paintings and furniture, but it all looked like a film set that needed a new lick of paint. Perhaps I should offer my services, I thought.

A rather eccentric-looking old woman sitting at the back near to us wandered up to the dais to receive an award for her work with the Red Cross. She was muttering to herself under her breath the whole ceremony, her lipstick was smeared all over her mouth and, as she stood up to collect her medal, it became immediately apparent to Ian and me that she was drunk.

Staggering back from the royal dais, she caught sight of Ian's winged dagger and tottered up to him rather unsteadily.

'Are you with the Red Cross too?' she asked, breathing fumes of alcohol over us both. Ian smiled and patted her arm. 'That's right, love,' he said, and she staggered on her way, smiling.

After over an hour of watching and waiting, it was finally Ian's turn to receive his medal. He stood briskly to attention when his name was called and looked down at me briefly to wink. I could see that the morning's disappointments were completely forgotten as he approached the dais, his eyes ablaze with anticipation.

Sitting in my seat, I strained to watch as he moved closer and closer. To my great surprise, I suddenly found that I had a huge lump in my throat and my eyes were filling with tears. I was so proud of him and of what he had achieved. I could feel the emotion welling up inside me and felt as if I might burst. By the time he was almost at the dais, I was on my feet, anxious not to miss a second of his big moment. When he walked up to the Queen and shook her hand, I could have run up and kissed the sovereign herself.

Sitting to the other side of me was a woman and her small son, who had spent much of the morning fidgeting and banging my leg. As I watched Ian standing directly in front of the Queen, I wanted to say to the little boy, 'Keep still, shut up. Can't you see? My husband is talking to the Queen.' But I held my tongue.

Then I heard the woman whisper to her son, 'That man is in the SAS.'

'Who are the SAS, Mummy?' the little boy replied.

She said, 'They are the really brave men.'

I was completely choked. I looked down at her and she smiled.

Ian accepted his medal, shook the Queen's hand again and chatted for a moment, and then the ceremony was suddenly over. He was the last one in the line and a fanfare marked the end of the event. Ian was ushered to the side of Her Majesty and stood to attention as she left the room, smiling and waving to the crowd. He appeared for a moment to be part of her personal guard.

He walked back down the room towards us and his eyes were alight. I couldn't control myself any longer and the tears spilled onto my cheeks.

'Congratulations, darling. That was wonderful. I am so very, very proud of you,' I told him. His mother was too overcome with emotion to speak as she gave her son a hug.

'Well?' I asked him. 'What did she say? What was she like?'

He blinked hard as if to capture the moment forever in his mind. 'It was amazing,' he said. 'I was standing face to face with the Queen of England. She was wonderful but her eyes were old and tired. She looked as if she had the weight of the world on her shoulders. She held out her hand and I took it and it was tiny and very bony. She asked me how long I had been back from Northern Ireland and I said, "About twelve months Ma'am." She said, "And what do you think of the situation there now?" I couldn't think what to say really so I just said, "We're getting there, Ma'am."

'Then she asked me, "Do you think you'll be going back?" and I told her I thought it was best I got back there soon to sort it all out.'

I couldn't believe my ears. 'You cheeky sod,' I told him, laughing. 'We won't be invited back for tea then.'

We stepped outside and had our photographs taken round the side, away from the others, where we were able to laugh and relax

a little. I told Ian that he looked like Benny Hill in his tight uniform
and lifted my hand in the famous Benny Hill salute with my tongue
out. He said I looked stupid in a dress and we were continuing to
insult each other when the photographer called out, 'This way please,'
and the shutter clicked.

We had the photograph framed and it hangs on the wall in Ian's
study. It is one of his most prized possessions.

I know he had been very moved by the whole occasion but within
a few minutes of stepping out into the daylight, he behaved as if he
didn't give a monkey's. As far as you could tell from looking at him,
you would think that he would rather be lying in the jungle somewhere thinking, Who can I stab next? than shaking hands with the
Queen of England.

We met up with his father and had a slap-up lunch to celebrate.
After the meal, Ian phoned the barracks and the CO told him the
D-Notice had been served on Fleet Street. His name and that of
the other Regiment soldier would not be appearing in the papers
the next day.

We still bought them to check the following morning, and found
only two small paragraphs in one of them saying that two SAS men
had been honoured along with Freddy Truman. We breathed a sigh
of relief. The boyos hadn't spoiled our day after all.


That wonderful spring day at Buckingham Palace in 1990 was highly
significant to me for many reasons but mainly because at the time
I came to think of it as the climax of Ian's time in the Regiment.
He only had a few years left to go before he would be forcibly retired
at forty, I had got him through the Falklands and Northern Ireland
alive and we had the rest of our lives to look forward to.

The world seemed relatively stable, I couldn't imagine another
Falklands situation now, and Ian had stayed the course with the
Regiment he loved almost in spite of himself. It felt very important
to us both, this medal from the Queen. It was so much more than
just an honourable accolade from Her Majesty, even if the inscription

did read 'Ian Simpson, Royal Green Jackets' and not '22 SAS' (an anomaly that Al Slater's father campaigned unsuccessfully for years to change – his son had been killed by the IRA and yet his posthumous award didn't even recognise that he was in the SAS).

Despite the Regiment's continual reluctance to publicly admit that it even exists, we both knew Ian's medal was its way of acknowledging his personal gallantry, his courage and his fortitude. We were convinced it had a lot to do with the security scare and all that we had been put through afterwards and it felt right and proper that he should have been so honoured. Now we had the rest of our lives to look forward to.

Unbeknown to me though, Ian had other plans – plans that he knew would horrify and appall me if I were to discover them. He had decided that he would like to work permanently in Northern Ireland, taking on a special position of security forces liaison officer between the British Army and the RUC.

It would mean us both moving over there for his final three or four years, living under the sort of anti-terrorist conditions that would make the security arrangements we had on our house seem like an welcoming party for the IRA.

He applied for the job behind my back, deciding that he would only tell me if he got it. He had always said that however old he was, he still felt like a twenty-five-year-old with his hair alight, running around the world putting out fires. Northern Ireland, however much pain it had put us through, was somewhere to which he had become addicted. It was a fire he very much wanted to help put out. He hoped to see his final days out across the water and then pick up a highly paid security job somewhere abroad, anywhere his special expertise was needed.

Not realising that his plans included Northern Ireland, I assumed that the only promotion or position he would now be able to go for would be that of troop sergeant major. After he had been awarded the QGM I had every reason to think he would qualify. I was looking forward to the prestige and the extra pay. Being a sergeant major's wife is a major social coup in a small town like Hereford. I had always wanted to see those badges on Ian's shoulder where I felt they belonged, although I would have hated the cocktail circuits that went with it and, knowing me, would probably have caused quite a stir over the gin slings.

I knew he would leave the Regiment at forty and had long assumed that we would take off together into the sunset to live and work abroad, preferably in America, the retirement destination of my dreams. There was plenty of work out there for ex-SAS men and I loved the country, the people and the climate. It seemed to be all working out at last and I had never been happier.

So there we were at the Palace, a visible symbol of recognition in a satin-lined presentation box in Ian's hand, smiling at the camera but expecting very different things of our future. But there was going to be no quick answer to Ian's request for the Northern Ireland job, and I wasn't expecting any sudden promotion anyway, so we were content enough then to savour the moment and dream our respective dreams.

We had other things to think about for our future, too. After nine years of marriage, surviving the good, the bad and the very ugly, we had found ourselves slowly changing our minds about the possibility of having children.

Until this time, sincerely believing that the decision we had made before had been the right one, we had – apart from that brief mention in Spain – rarely given it a second thought. Although I had been terribly lonely so much of the time that Ian was away, and a baby would have been something to keep my mind occupied, neither of us would have wanted to share a second of the precious time we had together with anyone else. It was ours and ours alone. And when the security scare started, one of Ian's first comments to me had been, 'Thank God we never had kids. At least I only have you to worry about now.' I agreed. I don't think I could have slept a wink at night thinking that our children might have been IRA targets.

Ian was still travelling and the same rules still applied. He had never wanted to be just a 'weekend father' – or in his case a 'once-in-a-blue-moon father' – or someone who was compromised emotionally on a mission because he was thinking of his kids.

I don't think either of us would have thought twice about our decision again, but earlier that year, in an unexpected turn of events, the idea was suddenly forced upon us during a holiday in America.

Vasectomies are not always fail-safe, and we had been warned by the doctor who performed the operation eight years earlier that it might only last seven years. Yet it did not occur to me that pregnancy could be the cause of my missed period until I spotted a pregnancy testing kit when we were shopping in a chemist and stopped dead in my tracks.

'What would you say if I told you I might be pregnant,' I asked Ian the following morning in bed. I expected to see disappointment, anger or distress register in his face, instead I got a look of surprise and excitement.

'You're kidding, Jen? Really? Is it possible?' he asked, jumping to his feet, his face lighting up.

'Well, it is not impossible,' I said, cautiously. 'The doctor did warn us that the snip might not last forever. Though God knows how we would cope if I were.'

Ian reached over and pulled me to him, holding me tight. 'I'm happy if you are,' he said. 'If you want it then let's go for it. I'll do all I can to help.'

I studied his face for the tell-tale signs that he was lying and found none. Tears spilled from my eyes as I hugged him back.

'Oh Ian, do you really mean it?' I asked. 'I mean, what if I am? Can you imagine what it would be like? Aren't there still all the same reasons why we shouldn't?'

He laughed at my nervousness. 'No, babe. I'm older now, and wiser. In a few years' time I'll be free of the Regiment and we can have a life together. All those reasons have disappeared now. I think it would be great.'

We were staying with a friend of ours called Geoff and, Ian being Ian, he told him the news straightaway by asking him to be a god-father. He even went out and bought some Havana cigars.

I watched the two of them strutting around Geoff's apartment, puffing away and discussing babies' names. It all seemed like a strange dream. Here I was, nearly forty years old and possibly expecting a baby. How would we manage after all these years of being alone? What would I do at home with a baby while Ian was working? Didn't being an older mother bring risks to my health and the baby's? I was scared and excited and happy all at the same time.

The twinkle in Ian's eye was wonderful to see. I had never realised how much he had been thinking about being a father in recent years, when he was away on missions, as I realised now that I had been thinking about it myself, lying in bed alone at night. There was always David in the back of his mind, but the hoped-for truce with his ex-wife had never really happened and consequently he could not watch David grow up. His mother saw her grandson regularly and occasionally showed Ian photographs, but Ian looked at them with a sense of great sadness that the boy in the pictures was a stranger.

Ian embraced the role of would-be father wholeheartedly. He made sure I took it easy, kept my feet up and ate properly. 'We don't want you and the baby to come to any harm,' he told me, tucking a blanket around my feet and handing me yet another ham sandwich. 'And remember, no more drinking and you've got to start eating for two from now on.'

I think I was in shock, really. I just sat there and did as I was told, my mind spinning with all the possibilities and consequences of being a pregnant old lady, for that is how I felt. My head and heart were jostling with each other for command. The emotions I felt ranged from utter despair and resentment at the end of our special time alone together to elation at the thought of having something of my very own, something that was also a part of Ian, to hold and love and keep by my side when he was away.

How awesome it would feel to have someone who loved and needed and relied on me twenty-four hours a day, seven days a week, I thought. Ian certainly never had, he had always been that independent gypsy I had first met in the Booth Hall, and I had grown accustomed to being alone, never learning what it felt like to be indispensable to someone.

Ian and Geoff were uncontrollable. They were hyping each other up more and more about the forthcoming baby. They were convinced it would be a boy and had provisionally nick-named him Rambo. They were already planning desert and jungle training camps for him, complete with a mini A-frame, miniature uniform and toy gun. I listened to them laughingly, and thought that if it were a boy we might just call him Paul.

On the night after Ian had told Geoff our news, he announced that he was taking his friend out for a celebration drink 'to wet the baby's head'. He made me something to eat, tucked me in and told me not to wait up. They were half flying when they left the apartment so God knows what state they would be in when they came back, I thought, as I slid down the bed and prepared to watch a sloppy movie with a cup of cocoa and a box of chocolates.

It was after one a.m. when they came staggering home, bursting into the apartment singing their heads off, half-empty beer bottles in hand. 'Yes, sir that's my baby, no sir I don't mean maybe,' Geoff was chorusing as they switched on the light.

Ian took one look at my tear-stained face and stood stock still.

'What's the matter, Jen?' he asked, removing the Havana cigar from his mouth.

I looked at the two of them standing in front of me, their motion frozen as they awaited my response and wondered how on earth I was going to tell them.

'Geoff isn't going to be a godfather after all,' I said and ran from the room in tears, slamming the bedroom door behind me.

We were both so disappointed. My body clock had, it seemed, been affected by jet-lag and the time change and not by a developing foetus at all. It was the strangest sensation, suddenly having to accept that I wasn't pregnant. I had almost convinced myself that I was, that my body felt different, special somehow and unusual. The fact that I wasn't left me feeling almost bereaved, as if I had literally lost a baby. Ian felt much the same way, as if something physical had been lost, when really there had been nothing there in the first place.

The rest of the holiday was spent quietly, not one of us mentioning it again. Geoff did his best to cheer us up, but we were beyond comforting. To me it seemed like the end of the world, but I did my best to hide my feelings for everyone's sake, and spent much of my time hiding behind my sunglasses, counting the days to our flight home.

Before I knew it, the holiday was over and we were back in Hereford. As soon as he had unpacked his holiday clothes and I had started on the washing, Ian was packing his bergen again for three months' jungle training in Malaya. We both knew it was coming, we had known before the holiday and had accepted it as part of the routine, but now it seemed such poor timing.

There was little time to talk and not enough desire from either side to discuss anything so painful as the 'lost' baby in such a short space of time. We spent the next two days circling round each other, avoiding contact both physically and emotionally, skirting round the issues. I finished his washing, helped him with his packing and stood in the hallway, waiting to kiss him goodbye.

'I'm sorry I've got to go away right now,' he said, his bergen by his feet. 'I wish we had more time together to, you know, talk.'

'I know, I know, babe.' I said. 'It doesn't matter. We'll have some time when you get back. Now you'd better get going or you'll miss your ride.'

He knew I was dismissing him, anxious to close the door on him and the issue, to be alone once again with my thoughts and tears. But he was reluctant to let me go. He felt there was something more he should do or say.

'Is there anything I can do while I am away?' he asked. 'Would you like me to ask Lisa to come and stay. Or speak to you mum, or Sue and Anne?'

I shook my head. 'No, no, it's fine, babe. I'm fine, really. Now come on and get out of my hair so that I can finish up the housework and get an early night.'

He kissed me goodbye and held me for a few seconds longer than normal and then he was gone. I shut the door and exhaled for what seemed like the first time in days.

Ian started to write me letters home again from that trip, something he hadn't done for a while. A week after he had gone I got home from work to find the familiar blue paper of an airmail letter in my mailbox. I found solace in the paper as I held it in my hand and scanned his spidery scrawl. His first letter said, 'It was a horrible parting wasn't it? I was more upset for you because I know it was difficult this time for you, to let me go.'

Two or three letters later, half-way through his trip, he raised the subject of my phantom pregnancy as delicately as he could. He wrote:

> On the question of children, you're right, I have given it considerable thought and would like to try for a family. I have no idea what the score is on a vasectomy reversal and how successful it would be but if we are going to try for our own, let's do it soon.
>
> If it fails (and there are no guarantees) then we can consider adopting or whatever. What do you say? Funny how you come to decisions. You spend a long time thinking, avoiding etc, then it just seems the right thing to do.
>
> I think we've been together long enough to give it a go, eh? I think we would also make smashing parents. I also think it would be the answer to my restlessness.

As I read and reread his letter in the final weeks of his tour, my mind was swimming with fear and excitement. Did he really mean it or was he just feeling sorry for me? What sort of family life could we really offer a child, with Ian away so much? What if the vasectomy wasn't reversible? Were we too old for adoption? What would the social services say about Ian's job and the security scare? Who in their right mind would let us be parents?

I decided to make enquiries immediately, starting with the private clinic where Ian had the operation all those years before. It was the last week in July 1990 and there was no time to lose.

A week later, in the early hours of Thursday 2 August, Saddam Hussein's Iraqi army invaded Kuwait. The sudden invasion was something few could have predicted and most never anticipated.

I was dressing to go to work that morning, with the radio on in the background, when I heard the news. I stopped, half-way through buttoning up my skirt, and listened pensively to the brief bulletin about Iraqi tanks rolling over the Kuwaiti border at dawn, putting British and American citizens' lives at risk and posing a threat to international oil interests.

I sank to the bed in dismay. Something deep within me told me in that instant that all thoughts of having a family would now have to go on hold.

Ian was still away, although he was flying back over the Middle East that very day after his jungle exercises in Malaya. When he got home, we were supposed to be having a holiday together, a few weeks alone to discuss having children, and to investigate how to go about it. I had been planning it for weeks, but I felt instinctively that world events had once again overtaken any personal plans we might have had.

I was expecting Ian home later that afternoon, but his arrival was delayed. His special RAF flight was forced to land at Dubai in the United Arab Emirates when the Iraqi invasion was first announced and the whole squadron sat on the tarmac for three hours, wondering if they would be allowed home or whether the Regiment would send them straight to the crisis area. Eventually, to their great relief, they were allowed to fly on home.

I met him at the camp that night and he was already firing on all cylinders. Forgotten were the romantic letters, the promises of some private time together, of better things to come. Try as he might to hide the fire in his eyes, I recognised it instantly and had long ago acknowledged its supremacy. I knew that when he looked like this, there was nothing I could do to hold him down until the crisis was over.

Within days of the invasion, the newspaper and television reports and bulletins were busy profiling Saddam Hussein, whom they dubbed 'The Butcher of Baghdad'. The propaganda machine warned of the possibilities of full-scale chemical warfare, and spoke of Saddam Hussein's brutal secret police and the regime of fear he ran in his country.

Try as I might, I couldn't help feeling a growing sense of foreboding. Even though the Middle East seemed so far away, I couldn't contain my unease. Ian was addicted to the television coverage of the crisis, although he was more sceptical about his possible involvement in any Middle East war. He told me the invasion wasn't such a big deal, that it was an Arab thing and as we hadn't got involved in the Iraq–Iran War, we would not start to get involved now.

But I knew what he was really hoping for, and I had a creeping suspicion in my mind that he was merely trying to placate me. Night after night when I got in from work, we watched the television news together, following every step taken by the peace brokers King Hussein of Jordan and James Baker, the American statesman, as they did their best to defuse the tension in the region. As the news bulletins started to drum on more and more about America's concerns, oil and the cost to the Arab economy, there was no escaping the sense that something big was about to happen.

The Regiment called Ian into camp for contingency planning and he spent weeks on end with the rest of his squadron, knee deep in maps of the Kuwaiti and Iraqi desert. He came home and told me how it was all going, but he said that if anything did happen, it would be a largely UN and American show, he still wasn't sure if the British or Special Forces would get involved. It seems Norman Schwarzkopf, the Commander-in-Chief of the American forces, who was running the UN's military planning and preparation for the war wasn't a big fan of Special Forces after he had had some bad experiences with them in Vietnam. There was no guarantee that they would be used at all, and even if they were, there would only be two squadrons going and there was no certainty that one would be his.

But as the weeks rolled on and Margaret Thatcher became more and more vociferous in her verbal attacks on Saddam Hussein, we could both feel the tension building. I knew in my heart that it was only a matter of time before the woman who had sent my husband to the South Atlantic all those years before would send him off again to newer and more dangerous territory.

By the time the Iraqis and the Americans emerged from talks in Geneva having achieved nothing, Ian was almost beside himself with excitement. A fluent Arab speaker and by this time one of the Regiment's most senior and experienced men, he was convinced that his unique combination of talents would be required. 'Any day now,' he told me. 'Any day now and I'll get the call.' I felt like ripping the telephone plug out of the wall.

'Your Arabic is rusty and you are too old to go gallivanting around the desert like some latter-day Lawrence of Arabia,' I scoffed. Inside, I was feeling far from jovial.

The 'situation' was all anyone seemed to talk about in Hereford. It was just like during the early days of the Falklands Conflict. The men were all hoping that they would be the ones chosen to go and were rushing around town buying up kit, and the wives were all at home, praying for a diplomatic solution.

Then Saddam announced that all the Western ex-pats in Iraq and Kuwait would be held as 'human shields' and that, if necessary, he would tie them to the front of the Republican Guard tanks. I heard the news and winced. I knew that Mrs Thatcher wouldn't stand for that. Sure enough, within days, Ian was committed.

I came home from work one balmy night in September with nothing more than a barbecue in mind. I had stopped at the supermarket on the way home to get a couple of steaks and some wine. We would have a few drinks and fire up the barbie and have a lovely night together in the garden, I thought. Just for one night, I wanted to forget what it was that my heart knew was about to happen.

It was too late. Ian's bergen was in the hall when I opened the front door. I heard him upstairs slamming wardrobe doors shut and my heart started pounding in my chest.

Surely they would let us have one last night? Surely he wasn't going right away? But when I saw him running down the stairs with his hands full of kit, I knew we had no time.

My face said it all and he stopped for a moment and looked apologetic. 'Got to go, love, the transport is waiting. I am already late,' he said.

'Not even time for a nice fat juicy steak?' I said, holding up the shopping.

'Put it in the freezer and I'll have it when I get back,' he replied. Cramming a few last-minute things into his bergen, he wedged the front door open with it and turned to kiss me goodbye. I tried to fight back the tears, and nearly lost the battle. They welled up in my eyes as he held me tightly to him.

'Come on now, angel eyes,' he said. 'This isn't like you. What's up?'

What's up? I wanted to scream, what's up? You are about to go away to war and God knows what in that mad country on the other side of the world and you might never come back. How much longer do we have to wait to have a life and a family? But I wiped my eyes and said, 'Sorry, chooch. It must be the thought of that steak going to waste.'

He kissed my nose and turned to look outside. A mate from the Regiment hooted the horn of his car as he pulled up in the driveway.

'I'm only going for a few weeks and it is just for a recce,' he said, trying to reassure me. 'We're not even going anywhere near the trouble zone. We're just going to do some desert training and stand by in case.'

In case of what, I thought.

'Don't forget to write, and send me some mints,' he said as he hugged me once more. 'I love you, you know that, babe, and when all this is over, we'll take that holiday I promised you. I just need to go and get my suntan started first.'

'Go on, get out of here,' I scolded. 'The sooner you go the sooner you'll be back and the sooner we can book that holiday. And don't come back too brown or you'll be sunbathing on your own.'

He pinched my cheek and then he was gone. Bergen on his back, he was running up the driveway as I had seen him do a hundred times before. He got into his mate's car and they both waved cheerily as the car reversed up the drive and sped off.

I stood in the doorway in the late evening sun and listened to the engine fading in the distance. Long after I could hear it no more, I shut the door.

*       *       *

Despite his promise of 'just a few weeks', Ian was away for more than three months, topping up his tan. While I sat shivering in wintry conditions at home, he was practising jumping out of planes and living in the desert.

The SAS Land Rovers and other vehicles were shipped out ahead and the squadrons followed in a dedicated C130 transporter plane from RAF Lyneham. Their brief was that they weren't officially there, I wasn't even meant to know exactly where Ian was: if anyone asked we were told to say he was just on desert training somewhere in the Middle East. They would have been too high-profile amongst all the thousands of other soldiers and airmen setting up camp there, so a different country was chosen.

The SAS were to be out there in rotation and Ian's squadron replaced G Squadron. The idea was that they would all get the opportunity to hone up their desert training so that if the Allied offensive suddenly began and they were dropped behind Iraqi lines, they would have had recent practice in the basics of desert survival.

They had to re-familiarise themselves with vehicle operations because it had been decided in the contingency planning that almost all of their missions would be vehicle mounted – going into Iraq across the desert in Land Rovers and trucks, rather than being dropped in alone by air. So it was back to basics, learning about engine maintenance, mechanics and servicing, something I found hysterical because Ian hardly knew how to open the bonnet of our Vauxhall Cavalier at home.

It had been two years since Ian had last been in the desert, when he went to Jordan for training, and the terrain where they were was quite different to that in Jordan and different again to Iraq. In the Emirates it was mostly soft sand dunes, but further north – where they would be going – the ground was rocky and hard. There was little chance of digging themselves in, and they quickly learned that they would have to rely on natural features for cover, caves and dried wadis, along with their special camouflage nets.

The soldiers had to re-acclimatise to the very arid conditions, maintain their fitness levels and learn how to care for the equipment when there was so much sand about. Ian practised his Arabic on the local militia, trying to bring it up to speed for use in encounters with Bedouins in the Iraqi desert, who might be able to tell him of Iraqi troop movements and other useful information.

The plan was to lie up in the day and only move at night, so they retrained in how to move across the desert in the darkness and not be spotted from the ground or the air by day. Even in training, they were often compromised, almost always by young Arab goat-herders who roam the deserts with their herds and have eyes like hawks'. They would notice if a single rock had been moved out of place in their domain, and could easily alert the enemy.

I could tell from Ian's letters that he was loving every minute of it. It was all the lads together, technically in training but practising for a very real situation. The command structure was good and the men got their desert skills up to scratch very quickly. Many of them had never seen action as Ian had in the Falklands and hoped this would be their big chance. Even after what he had gone through in the South Atlantic, Ian was bitten by the bug too and the whole squadron became more and more hyped up about what they might be about to do.

As the weeks rolled by and a full-scale Allied involvement in the crisis looked increasingly certain, I got back into the sort of routine I had set up for myself during the Falklands War – working all day, home in the evening to make up the parcels I was sending Ian and to write him letters and cards. I waited at home for news, watching the wall-to-wall television coverage of the military build-up and praying to God every night that He would bring Ian home safely from this war too.

It was hard to concentrate at work, though it was a particularly busy time for me. The wages department at my company was being computerised and I suddenly found myself working two or three hours' overtime a night and at weekends to try to get the system on-line. I would come home exhausted from my day's exertions, make myself something to eat, pour myself a drink and crawl into bed with my airmail letters and brown paper.

But no matter how tired I was, I found it very difficult to sleep at night. My nightmares were full of visions of Ian in the desert and the television images of Hussein patting the head of Stuart Lockwood, the young British boy being held as a human shield. My mind flashed up the pictures I had seen of the results of the chemical warfare Saddam had used on the Kurds and my dreams returned me time and again to the cemetery at St Martin's Church, this time filled with new rows of white gravestones.

I wrote to Ian almost every day, filling my letters with news and domestic information from home, trying to make light of his absence so that he wouldn't worry about me. It was strange having him so far away on a war footing again. He once told me that when he was away he liked to think of me singing in the kitchen while I prepared supper, or as I did the polishing around the house. It made him happy. I described myself singing away to my favourite Country and Western songs, making up nice things to eat to keep in the freezer until he came home. Because the weather was so bad, I seldom left the house except to go to work or walk the dog, and I described how beautiful the snow looked and how the birds had never been happier with the special high-protein, high-fat food I laid out for them each morning to ward off the effects of the cold.

As Ian and I both felt the war looming closer and closer, the pain of our separation worsened and we stopped pretending in our letters that we weren't missing each other pretty badly. There is nothing like an impending war to concentrate the mind. I wished I had been more upbeat in our last few days together. I kicked myself for getting so upset about the issue of children at the expense of some quality time with Ian, and prayed that we would still have the rest of our lives to spend side by side.

However much he was enjoying the work, from the tone of his letters home to me, I could tell that Ian felt the same way. He even wrote me a poem while he was watching and waiting, thinking about going to war again and what it might all mean. A friend of his came across it in his locker and told him to send it to me. I have it framed on a wall at home, I love it so much. It is beautiful and I am touched each time I reread it to think that he could be moved to poetry by our separation. Part of it reads:

> At times our lives pass untouched, like ships,
> Course unknown, no destination, no route planned
> Yet a common bond cuts through the fog of uncertainty
> And I touch you and all is clear.
> My life turns many corners, challenging and tormenting me
> And, believing in false hopes and destiny, I continue
> Hoping I know the answers, onwards goes the pursuit
> When suddenly, like a child losing a cherished toy
> It is gone and I return to my love.
> My strength is you, for you are everything
> I pray I return the commitment you have shown
> And insecurity, like the night, disappears
> Into shining light and happiness, for I love you so.

Preparing for war made Ian think about things he wouldn't normally consider, like the absence of his son David from his life. On 11 October he wrote to me:

> Sitting out amongst the camels and things and have a bit of time to write you a letter. Been away from 'civilisation' since the 7th so I hope to have a letter awaiting my return in a couple of days' time. I have thought about David again on this trip. I regret not having sent him things from my trips despite you-know-who's objections. To me it all seems so late. I get a bit sad about it all, but not depressed. I've got you and I wouldn't have got you both. I thank God I did the right thing all those years ago.
>
> Hello, the camels are back again. Saw a desert rat last night. You get to see a lot out here. Not much else happening so I'm going to try to get a couple of hours' sleep before tonight. I've been sleeping really well out here. Fairly cool at night. You would definitely enjoy the climate. I suppose when this is all over, there will be lots of work out here for us whiteys, eh? Loads of dosh, girl. Thinking of you and our home. Hope the mail is reaching you OK. I will write later in the week. All is well here. Soon be finished and home to you.

The combination of the circumstances, impending middle age and
the possibility of children had fully concentrated both our minds
on the lives we had led in the past and the ones we hoped to lead
in the future. Ian wasn't the only poet in the family. The poem I
wrote to him in reply summed up what I felt about his wanderlust.
I have often wondered if it is the Romany in him that prevents him
from ever staying in one place for very long. I wrote:

> Tell me only this, in thoughts so far from home
> Do the seasons change? Do they come and go?
> Have you ever wondered when your sun goes down
> That I am just awaking, and still am on my own.
> So many miles away, what answer can you find?
> Do you need to wander? Does it give you peace of mind?
> Can I understand how alone you feel? But I must wait and see
> And you must find your answer, and then come home to me.

He loved it and kept it, neatly folded, in a wad of his favourite
letters and photographs close to his heart.

There was meant to be a weight and size limit on all parcels sent
to the Gulf, the wives were sent a note about it from the camp, but
I wasn't planning on taking any notice of that. Ian would get whatever
he wanted when he wanted it as far as I was concerned.

The mail had to delivered to the MoD Lodge at the camp before
being sent on to the Gulf. One day during November, I was walking
into the camp and there was a rupert driving out, someone I knew
of old. He took one look at the huge parcel under my arm and
stopped to speak to me.

'You are aware that there is a weight limit on parcels going out,
are you, Mrs Simpson?' he said rather snootily.

I looked at him disdainfully and replied, 'Well, sir, if you would
care to go out and help fight this one I will make sure that
my parcels to you are always the correct weight.' That shut him
up.

While Ian was away and to keep me busy, I decided to go ahead
with plans we had talked about to have an extension built on our
home. The original idea had been to convert the integral garage into

a sitting room, but once the question of children came up, we thought we might just need the extra space for other reasons.

I organised the whole thing as usual, the builders and decorators, even the Home Office, whose security advisers had to return to my little cul-de-sac and extend the existing security arrangements to include the extension. Their reappearance and their talk of panic alarms and bombproof glass brought back unhappy memories of the previous year and the feelings I had then when the scare had taken over my life. But somehow now, with Ian on the other side of the world and facing a very different danger, I took it all in my stride. Better the devil you know, I thought.

After the extension was completed, the security advisers invaded and took over, making a terrible mess. It took three days and the house was even colder than it had been last time, as they constantly left doors and windows open, showing a blatant disregard for heat conservation.

'You've just got to choose a nice new carpet now,' said the last workman as he left the house. In their installation of the cabling under the floorboards for the new panic alarms, the pink fitted carpet we had only had for two years had been ripped up and ruined. It lay back in place now, lumpy and soiled.

'Right,' I thought. 'Carpetland, here I come.'

The next day in my lunch hour at work I went to the carpet shop in Hereford and chose a nice oatmeal berber for the whole ground floor of the house. At several pounds a square yard, the bill was to come to over £2,000. It was to be fitted the following Saturday and I told them to send the Home Office the bill.

Three days later the telephone rang. It was a senior civil servant from Home Office Accounts, who had just received the bill.

'There seems to be some mistake here, Mrs Simpson,' the pen-pusher said. 'The total amount for the carpet you have ordered is well over the budget allowed for the redecoration of your house after the upgrade work. I am afraid that we are simply not able to settle for the full amount. You and your husband will have to meet the difference.'

I pulled myself up to my full five feet two inches and gripped the receiver. 'Now you just listen to me, pet,' I said, in my broadest Geordie. 'In the last year I have had my life turned upside down by a security leak, and my house turned upside down by your lads, putting the fear of God into me about it. My husband is off in the Gulf about to fight yet another war for your Government and you are quibbling over a few quid. Too bloody right you will pay that bill and don't let me hear another word from you about it.'

I put the phone down triumphantly and gave myself a self-satisfied smile. I never heard another murmur and they settled the full account.

Friends and family tried to keep our morale up, calling me regularly and taking me out now and again, and writing to Ian to let him know I was fine. One of his closest friends, Tim, an ex-member of the Regiment, wrote him a letter which Ian really loved and carried with him to cheer him up.

It said:

> Dear Ian
>
> Just a quick note from your sponsor. How's the tan coming along? I hope you remember to take your Ray Bans off long enough to tan your eyes or you'll start to look like a Panda.
>
> Well, mate, it seems very odd writing one of these to some-one who is out there doing it while I am sat on my fat arse talking about it. We don't get very clear ideas of what is going on as it is all reported like a football match. The Yanks have got their wagons in a circle, we've identified the baddy, soon *The Sun* will serialise the script.

Ian also received dozens of letters from strangers back home, people who responded to an Army appeal to send letters and parcels to 'our boys at the front'. Many of the letters were addressed simply, 'Dear soldier', and came from grandmothers, housewives, fathers, sons and schoolchildren, sending their best wishes.

They arrived in the desert by the sackload and neither Ian nor anyone from the rest of the squadron had the time to read them all, although they each grabbed a handful. Of those that he did read, the ones which meant the most to him were from the children, and often came with drawings of planes and helicopters and soldiers fighting each other. Ian neatly folded several of his favourite ones and kept them in his bergen throughout the war.

One letter he kept read:

> Dear soldier
> My Daddy was a soldier but he was killed by a bomb in Belfast when I was five. My Mummy and I have been on our own ever since and miss him a lot. We heard about Saddam and the Gulf crisis and my teacher said I should write and say hello. I hope you are OK and come home safe.
> Love from Tom. XXX

Another was from a woman of seventy-three who had lost two sons to the Army, one who died in a car accident while he was stationed in Germany and another who was shot dead by a sniper in Crossmaglen, Northern Ireland. She wrote:

> I know you will have parents and wives and loved ones praying for your safe return, but without anybody left to pray for myself, I will add to those prayers and wish you well with all my heart. God bless.

One day in mid-December, Ian telephoned out of the blue to tell me he would be coming home for Christmas. It was more than I had hoped for and just what I needed to hear. I was over the moon. In all the years that we had been together and in spite of all the travelling he had done, we had never spent a single Christmas apart and I simply couldn't have coped if that year had been the first. We both knew that he would soon be going back to the Gulf, full-scale war now seemed inevitable, but at least we would have a special few weeks alone together first.

He flew into Brize Norton and I was there to meet him. I hardly recognised him when he walked through the Arrivals gate, one of the last, of course. He was so tanned and, well, Arab-looking, which was the whole point I suppose. His moustache was enormous and, although he had recently washed, two months of living in the desert had caked the creases in his skin with sand dust and grime.

Regardless of an overwhelming desire to scrub him clean, it was wonderful to hold him in my arms once again and know he was safe. I held his face in my hands and kissed it over and over as if the very taste of it would eradicate my fears.

Christmas has always been a very special time for us and that year was one of our best ever. I made all his favourite meals and decorated the house so that it looked truly festive and welcoming. I bought him the camera he had wanted from Santa and he gave me a set of suitcases from the Middle East, and we spent those few weeks together as happily as if we were on honeymoon.

Neither of us spoiled it by discussing when he would have to go back to the Gulf or what might happen when he got there. Neither did we mention children. There seemed little point. How could we know what was around the corner for either of us with a war hanging over our heads?

I had finished decorating the new extension as a sitting room in time for his homecoming and had secretly put away the samples of nursery wallpaper I had brought home a few months earlier when the future had looked so very different. I told myself that this war must have happened for a reason, that parenthood just wasn't meant to be for Ian and me, not just yet anyway, and that we weren't to be greedy. We had each other and that was more than enough. What more did we want?

That New Year's Eve, we decided not to go anywhere too noisy or crowded, so we had a quiet meal at home and then walked down to a nearby pub for a few drinks with some of the locals. It was a very low-key evening and just what we wanted. I couldn't have coped with another night like the one at The Swan before the Falklands. This felt just right.

As midnight approached, the landlord switched on the television so we could watch the traditional celebrations in Trafalgar Square and see Big Ben strike the hour. I held myself together as best I could, even when the first strains of 'Auld Lang Syne' struck up and everyone started to wish each other a Happy New Year.

Fighting to stop the tears from falling, I kissed Ian hard on the mouth and clung to him as if I would never let him go.

'Happy New Year, angel,' he whispered as he held me in his arms. 'Let's hope so, babe,' I said silently, biting my bottom lip. 'Let's hope so.'

# 9 | Love, Honour and Keep Him

AS EACH DAY DAWNED in that week after New Year, I thanked God that Ian was still by my side. The military build-up was complete, the news was full of war-talk, and yet here he was, still with me. I could hardly believe it. Maybe he was right. Maybe it wouldn't be his squadron that was sent in after all. Maybe he would stay home this time although, God knows, he would be unbearably restless at home if the others were seeing some action without him.

I set daily deadlines in my mind, planning one day at a time and giving thanks each time we reached them. Please just let him be here for my birthday in January, I prayed.

It wasn't a big one, I was thirty-nine, but it suddenly felt hugely significant and I got it into my head that I wanted him there for it. It was not to be. His bergen was in the hall on 5 January after a call that morning. He was off the following day. I couldn't be cross when I looked at his face. In spite of everything he ever told me about his feelings for the Regiment, regardless of all the heartaches and the disappointments and the hardships, he loved it more than anything else in the world, even me sometimes.

It was just like the night before the Falklands. The smell of adrenaline on him, the infectious feeling of excitement and fear. He was going to do what he had been training all his life for, fight for Queen and country in a foreign land. This was the face of the little boy who had first seen the SAS solider bury his matchstick in the dirt, of the teenage recruit who had worn his uniform to school every day, of the professional soldier whose moment of glory had come once again. I couldn't help but feel proud of him and pleased that he was so fulfilled. It was time to put my own feelings aside once more and to let him go.

It seemed that I had stood in the doorway waiting to say goodbye to him a thousand times before. Was it ever going to get any easier? I wondered, as I watched him running down the stairs, his belt kit in hand. When would the hurting stop?

He fussed and fiddled, ticking off his checklist, as I stood, watching him, my back against the wall. There was a lot of grey in his hair now, and the years of open-air living had weathered his face. His back had rounded slightly over the years from taking the full weight of his kit, and there was a small thinning patch on the very top of his head as he bent over his bergen. But as he raised his head and looked up at me, those piercing green eyes were still on fire, and they still made my heart beat faster.

His face creased into a smile, the laughter lines deeply furrowed around his eyes. His mouth, that mouth I yearned for when he was away, opened to speak.

'What's going through your head, babe?' he asked, coming to me. I reached my arms up around his neck and let him lift me off the ground momentarily in a bear hug.

'Oh, I was just wondering how many times I've watched you go like this in the last eleven years. And how little you have changed really, in that time – apart from your bald patch that is.'

'I haven't got a bald patch!' he complained, putting me down and glancing in the mirror. 'I am just growing too tall for my hair, that's all.' He reached for me again and held me tight. 'What else were you thinking?'

'Oh, soppy stuff, really. How much I love you, how much I have always loved you and known you were right for me. I've never been a great feminist, as you know. I know what I need and what I want and that has always been you, whatever.'

'I am enjoying this, say some more,' he said, nibbling my ear.

'No, that's quite enough flattery for one day, and anyway if you don't get going, you'll be late for your date with Saddam,' I said, reluctantly pulling his face away from my neck.

'We'll continue this conversation just as soon as I get back,' he promised mischievously. Then, more seriously, he added, 'You do know that I will be coming back, don't you?'

I felt the tears, lining up in their ducts, and fought to keep them where they were. 'Yes, of course I do, babe,' I said. 'You are far too much of a bad penny. No matter where I try and send you, you always keep turning up.'

He picked up his things and heaved them onto his back, rounding his shoulders to bear the weight. We kissed each other goodbye, a long, lingering, melt-your-heart kiss that I never wanted to end. Then he stepped away from me and headed for the driveway and his mate Jim's waiting car.

'Give Saddam a kick in the balls for me,' I called after him but he didn't hear me. My last image was of him blowing me a kiss through the windscreen of the car as it pulled away.

It was later that night that the fear and loneliness really hit me. After putting away the shopping and giving my dinner to Annie, I poured myself a large gin and slumped into bed. My heart was full of sorrow and my head was reeling with the words and images of Iraq that we had been watching for weeks on television.

There were the pictures of the Kurds lying gassed on the ground after an Iraqi offensive a few years earlier, mouths open in a last gasp for breath, mothers cradling their dying children in their arms. There were visions of the imprisoned human shields, the oil workers and their families, whose luxurious lifestyles had been cut dramatically short by the invasion. Their haunted expressions as they looked fearfully at the television cameras said it all.

The Iraqis had already hanged Farzad Bazoft, the British journalist they had accused of spying. What would they do to an SAS soldier they found behind enemy lines?

My mind started to lose all reason. 'He's never coming back from that place,' I heard myself say out loud. 'He is going to be killed or taken hostage and I will never see him again, nor bear his child.' I even tried to prepare myself for it mentally, but only managed to work myself into a terrible state, which was exacerbated by the gin I was drinking.

Drink was never the solution but in the past I had found that it sometimes dried the tears. On this occasion, however much I drank I could not numb the pain.

By the following morning, I was a mess. I phoned work to tell them that I would be late and I drove to my parents' house for some comfort. My relationship with my father was not particularly good when I was a child, but he was there for me in later life and he could not have been kinder during the Gulf War. He could see I was upset and he knew why, but there was little he could do but tell me to be his strong girl. He reminded me what he had said after the helicopter crash – that there would be a lot more and I should have prepared myself for it. I knew he was right and I listened to his advice as he told me to remain strong for both Ian's and my sake.

'Fill your days and nights doing things for Ian out there,' he told me. 'Don't just sit at home feeling sorry for yourself, do something about it. We'll be here for you when you need us but this strength has got to come from within you.'

I left feeling better and drove to the church where Ian and I had married. This time the doors were open. Stepping inside and kneeling in front of the altar, I prayed that God would keep Ian safe and me strong. I promised to try to get Ian's faith back if only He would help him now and bring him home safe.

'If you are up there and listening,' I prayed aloud, 'please hear me now. This is important and I need you to give me the strength I need.' I came away feeling refreshed and drove to work.

Operation Desert Storm began in earnest on 17 January 1991 with an Allied offensive on Iraq, the likes of which had never been seen before. Along with the rest of the world, I watched it all on television from where it seemed like a real-life video game. I knew that Ian was somewhere out in the desert watching the fighter planes flying overhead and guiding the missiles into their targets.

It was extremely frustrating, having a ringside seat and yet not knowing exactly where Ian was in the middle of it all. It was almost better when, as in the Falklands, there had been no news at all and hardly any visual images to frighten the life out of me. This was terrifying, watching the tracers light up the sky over Baghdad like some spectacular light show, hearing the explosions as bombs found their mark, knowing all the while that Ian was out there somewhere underneath it all.

The news bulletins were full of George Bush and the American generals showing off their new weapons, praising their men for the pinpoint accuracy of their missiles and revelling in the Iraqis' lack of response. The television and newspapers reported only the air offensive and said the land offensive was yet to start, but I knew Ian was already in Iraq and I desperately wanted to know more.

The camp did all it could to keep morale high despite the lack of news, and several of the rupert's wives set up social clubs and meetings so Gulf wives could get together and chat. As ever, I felt somehow alienated from it all, as if to sit drinking coffee and knitting socks with the other wives would be an admission of defeat. It wasn't that I didn't think that it might do other people some good, it just wasn't my scene. I was happier sitting at home alone, watching the news and sending my love to Ian across the airwaves.

After one phone call the night before he crossed the border into Iraq, I had no direct news from Ian for weeks. I had no idea if my letters and parcels were getting through, and, unusually, I had nothing back from him for ages, which bothered me tremendously. When I went to the camp to enquire why not, the new Families Officer said there had been some 'logistical problems' that were being ironed out. He asked me to be patient.

The truth was that by this time, Troop Staff Sergeant Ian Simpson and his sixteen men had left 'Victor', the codename for their operational base, and were deep behind enemy lines, having very limited contact with anyone, least of all the Army postal service.

Part of the vast Operation Granby, and with the call-sign (a signal which identifies a particular transmitter) 'Delta One Six', Ian's troop had been briefed to live in the western Iraqi desert, sleeping in scratched out LUPs (lying up positions) by day, moving only at night, attacking any Iraqi positions they found and watching for significant movements of Iraqi troops or SCUD missile launchers.

After telling his men, 'We are all going in together and we are all coming out together,' Ian led his troop in, the first to cross over into the western desert as part of an extraordinary convoy of 110 camouflaged military Land Rovers. They crossed into their particular 'Scud box', as they called their respective areas, while a massive Allied air raid took place on an airfield north of where they were, partly as a diversionary tactic for their benefit. Ian had never seen anything like it, it seemed to him like something out of movies of the Vietnam War. The night sky was filled with the lights from dozens of B52 bombers. Even though the attack was several miles away, the ground where they were shook as the mass pounding continued.

The information Ian and his men had about where they were going and what they would be up against was minimal. Many of their maps were out of date or didn't even relate to their area. The terrain was much harder going than they had been used to and the weather closed in on them. It was the worst winter in living memory.

They were to rely largely on their wits and the five pieces of gold they had each been given with which to barter for their freedom if they were caught or compromised. Each coin, a British sovereign of solid gold featuring the Queen's head, was kept in a small cloth pouch and hung around the neck for safety, along with a promissory note in English and Arabic, each with its own serial number to identify which man had been given it.

I still have a copy of the note at home. It reads, 'H M Britannic Government promises to pay the bearer of this note the sum of £5,000 Sterling providing that you do not harm the person issuing it and that you assist him to either evade capture or return him to either Saudi Arabia or to neutral territory. To claim the reward you should take this note to any British Embassy or Consulate and ask to speak to the defence attaché or one of his assistants. He will then give you the sum of £5,000.'

Ian, as troop sergeant, had also been given a pack of body bags by his superiors – one for each of his men and himself – something he found deeply demoralising. He hid the bags from his men so as not to disturb them as well, and had an argument with the Head

Shed about why he was given them. 'We don't bloody need them,' he told him angrily. 'We are all coming home.'

The weather closed in at home too, in sympathy perhaps. Herefordshire was all but cut off in the deep snow drifts though the local council did all it could to get the gritters and snow ploughs out on the roads. I managed to get to work only with the help of a friend who had a four-by-four vehicle, but on several occasions, even that couldn't get through.

I relied on the telephone and the television to keep me in touch with the outside world. All the news media seemed to be in Saudi with the troops or in Baghdad itself. There was nothing much happening in Saudi at that stage, I was tired of watching Kate Adie chatting up all the bored soldiers, and the Baghdad news was confined to the view from a hotel room window. Where was Ian? What was he doing?

I would lie awake at night, my eyes pressed tightly shut, trying to imagine his circumstances, trying to send him my love and best wishes. I took to having Annie on the bed with me at night, and sometimes she would sit up in the night and howl and I would worry that she had felt something about Ian.

He was already very busy. Within days of crossing the border, the twenty or so vehicles in his convoy had split up into groups of four vehicles each and only had a few hours to get to their LUPs before dawn. The idea was that they would rendezvous three or four days later at the MSR (main supply route).

Shortly after splitting from the main group, Ian's troop encountered what they believed to be Iraqi soldiers on the move behind them, and speeded up into the night to get away from them. In so doing, one of the vehicles broke a track rod on a rock and couldn't be repaired or towed. They took what 'toys' and equipment they could from it, loaded its passengers into other support vehicles and set timer devices to blow it up at first light. By the time they heard the bang at dawn, they were over twenty kilometres away.

They spent the first day in enemy territory lying up in the rocks, watching and waiting in case of attack or compromise. That night they set off again, once more it was very hard going and they knew that if they continued at the rate they were moving they would miss their rendezvous. The following morning, the troop commander suggested they take a risk and move by day as well. The men shouted him down, feeling the danger was too great, and instead they lay up in a dried-up wadi.

Just as Ian started to think about what the troop commander had said, and talk it through with the lads, a goat herder came down the track towards the wadi and spotted them. Ian ran up after him, shouting in Arabic for him to come back, but he legged it fearfully and Ian didn't have the heart to shoot him. He looked about the same age as his son David. The boy ran to a truck that the men hadn't realised was parked over the other side of a small cliff, and drove off.

The rest of that day was spent anxiously waiting for the assault they believed was imminent after they had been spotted. But the hours ticked by and nobody came. Ian persuaded the troop to hang fire until nightfall and, fortunately for them all, the boy did not return with reinforcements as anticipated. Ian told the lads, 'I bet he just thought we were Iraqi soldiers who wanted to screw the life out of him.'

Night drew down and they moved off an hour before last light, covering forty kilometres that night. They kept going even after dawn broke, and within three days they were a few kilometres from the MSR, 250 kilometres from the Saudi border, and ready to start work.

Kate Adie was really starting to get on my tits. Why was she wearing earrings anyway? I thought, as I sat sipping my gin in front of the Nine O'Clock News. When were they going to get to the real news? There was endless talk about how comprehensive the media coverage of this war was, but apart from a few bombing raids around Baghdad, we hadn't seen a thing of value yet. There was plenty of analysis, certainly. There were maps and sand pits and frenetic people prattling on about the politics and the terrain and the problems facing the armed forces. Enough hot air, in fact, to fly the whole squadron out to the Gulf by balloon. But where were the hard facts?

LOVE, HONOUR AND KEEP HIM

I didn't like Schwarzkopf much either. He looked too fat in his uniform as he reached out with his pointer to demonstrate the accuracy of the all-singing, all-dancing American weapons show. I hoped his buttons would burst and show everyone how much he was eating while the real soldiers were out there, laying their lives on the line. I wondered what Ian was eating, or if he was eating at all. How he longed for my Sunday roasts when he was away. I wished more than anything in the world that I could be making one for him.

On his fourth night in the desert, moving fast across the bumpy terrain, Ian was involved in an accident which nearly claimed his life. His vehicle – which had its roll-bars removed to reduce its silhouette – was leading the way when it overturned suddenly in a dip, rolling ten tons of Land Rover on top of him and his driver. The driver was wearing night vision goggles but hadn't seen the dip. They were only saved from being crushed to death by the special machine gun mounts which acted as roll-bars. It took his men four hours of precious moonlight to dig them out and upturn the vehicle. Fortunately, Ian was only winded.

They had had no real sleep for five days, and were tired, cold and physically battered by the time they reached the MSR. There was little more rest when they got there. Ian spent a lot of his time on the radio, talking to the boss and the remainder of the convoy, planning the next move. The weather turned again and as well as the unexpected cold, the rains began, soaking them to the skin. They had waterproof kit with them, but nothing thermal or quilted and the cold and wet started to become a problem day and night.

Within a couple of days, Ian was suffering from frostbite once again and several of the other lads were starting develop health problems. One man suffered terrible backache from never being able to get comfortable, another had a bad knee and a third had a serious cough. By the sixth day they were still laid up in a wadi, their vehicles camouflaged with nets, sand and rocks. They had covered the net pegs with their Arabic shemaghs (headdresses) when banging them home, but they still felt as if the noise could be heard all the way to Baghdad.

At first light, Ian sent out two men to do a recce and they crawled over the ridge to discover an observation tower 400 metres away from their position, and a small fort in a village to the other side. Neither had been marked on their maps. There was nothing the men could do but stand to all day, guns at the ready, waiting once more for the compromise they expected. But again, it never came. My prayers back home must have been working.

It was another freezing day and this time they couldn't even cook up anything hot, so they had to eat cold food from their Army general purpose rations – baked beans and meat stews in sealed aluminium bags. Ian used to bring his spare ones home after every mission, I had a cupboard full of them, and I found myself eating them up when he was away and the weather was too bad to go to the supermarket. Sitting alone at the kitchen table, tucking into Army-issue beef casserole, I wondered if Ian was sitting somewhere eating the same thing.

That night, the troop packed up their site and moved very carefully and quietly away, ten kilometres back into the desert, away from the observation tower. They set up a safe camp, where they could brew up and have a smoke and stay clear of danger, and still move to the MSR when they needed to. They stayed like that for several days, moving back and forth, watching vehicles and planning ambushes if a Scud missile launcher were to come along.

They were waiting for another troop to meet up with them, but – unbeknown to them – that troop had been compromised just a few kilometres away on their first night by an Iraqi force of some strength. One man had been shot as they scattered. They all escaped by running into the desert or hijacking vehicles to take them back to Saudi and blew up a petrol tanker as a diversionary tactic, but it was a close call.

Ian and his troop came across the burnt-out petrol tanker the following day and realised something had taken place, but had no idea what. When the rendezvous with the other troop didn't happen, they feared the worst and radioed in. They were told the others had had a contact and that three were still lost on foot in the area and they should start looking for them.

In the middle of the search, in the early hours of the morning as they were calling out recognition signals near the road, a Scud convoy with twenty accompanying vehicles suddenly loomed at them out of the darkness and they were nearly run over by it. As they all hit the deck either side of the MSR, Ian heard the rupert in charge of them suddenly shout, 'Attack!'

It would have been certain death for them all, and Ian knew that, so he shouted back, 'Fuck off!' and nobody moved. The huge convoy trundled past and disappeared into the night, before Ian jumped up and went over to bollock the rupert.

'If we had started shooting, one of those bloody Scuds would have exploded and killed the lot of us,' he told him, bristling. 'The armour they had around it would have taken us all out in minutes and none of us would have been alive long enough to radio HQ and tell them that the Scud was there. Think next time.' The rupert apologised.

Before daylight, the three missing men from the previous contact had been located and Ian's troop had radioed HQ to tell them of the convoy. It was up to the American and British fighter pilots to do their bit.

The days passed and their routine continued much the same – watching and waiting, reporting back, intelligence-gathering. Ian wrote to me when he could and sent the letters out by the helicopters which flew in occasionally to resupply them. After about two weeks in the desert they ordered in a Chinook helicopter to resupply them with ammunition, petrol, oil and rations, which would be his chance to send his letters off.

Ian was always hugely impressed with the courage of the RAF pilots who were extremely vulnerable flying into Iraq at night and who would land at their designated rendezvous site without lights on and with only the beam of Ian's infra-red torch to guide them in. The crew would often be accompanied by someone from Ian's forward operating base in Saudi who would give them their latest orders.

The helicopter crew would throw out boxes of equipment, the officer would give them their orders and take any mail and within minutes the aircraft would lift off, the clatter of its rotor blades fading into the distance.

Ian and his men would then be left to sort out and load up fifty-gallon drums full of water, oil or petrol, guns, ammunition, ration boxes and any special luxuries they had ordered via signal, like cigarettes or chocolate. While sentries stood guard around the site, the men would hand pump the liquids into jerry cans and then burn everything they left behind that identified it as British, like a Ministry of Defence stamp or a label reading 'British 24-hour ration pack'. The oil drums and other debris they could leave behind because there were so many Bedouins out in the desert that no one would think anything of it if they were found.

No mail was allowed to be delivered to them for operational reasons, which was a major blow for morale and meant that none of my dozens of letters waiting at base camp were getting through to him, but he could hand his letters to me over to the rupert and send them back with him, which made him feel that some contact at least was being made.

As they unpacked the boxes on that first resupply, they tore open one enormous parcel which was unmarked and fell upon the contents excitedly. It was full of heavy camel-hair Arab coats, thick and warm, sheepskin-lined, designed specifically for the cold, damp conditions they were having to endure. Someone back at camp had been thinking for a change, Ian thought as he grabbed a full-length, dark brown Bedouin coat complete with gold trim, for which he was to become eternally grateful.

It was the best thing that had happened to them since they got out there. It was almost good as receiving mail. They felt instantly warmer and able to function better. Dirty, smelly, unshaven and only able to brush their teeth once a day by way of personal hygiene, they looked for all the world like the Bedouins they kept coming across in their travels, but at least they were no longer cold.

The coat helped Ian with his intelligence-gathering as well. He had already spent many a night squatting on his haunches with the Bedouins around an open fire, asking what they had seen and sharing any information about troop movements and convoys, but now he looked more the part. They were generally happy to trade information, as most of them were smugglers and had no more love of the Iraqi authorities than Ian.

They did find the stranger in their midst rather strange, however. He looked and smelt like a Bedouin and dressed like them, but he had light green eyes and spoke best British Foreign Office Arabic, which wasn't exactly the guttural dialect they were used to.

He, equally, found some of them unusual. Many lived as their ancestors had done for centuries and didn't even know there was a war on, but increasingly Ian came across ones who were very clued up and had brand new Toyota jeeps, televisions and generators next to their traditional camel-hair tents. He would sit with them watching the Iraqi military propaganda programmes accompanied by tinny Arabic music, while drinking sweet Arabic tea, and wonder if I was sitting at home watching 'Coronation Street'.

I tried to fill my days and nights with projects to keep me busy. Just as I had when Ian was in Northern Ireland, I kept a scrapbook of newspaper cuttings about where he was. I thought he might be interested in seeing it when he got home. I also bought a dozen blank video cassettes and started to record some of the news bulletins and documentary programmes about the Gulf War. Just because Miss Adie and Co were infuriating me, it didn't mean to say that Ian wouldn't be enthralled on his return.

Rifling through the videos we had to see which ones I could record over, I came across a tape of *Lawrence of Arabia* Ian had bought for himself years before, a memento of his childhood cinema outing to see it with his father and a reminder of his happy weeks spent in the Jordanian desert where it was filmed. I put it on and wondered at my husband's film preferences. I thought Peter O'Toole looked ridiculous in all that garb and make-up, and it seemed to go on for hours and hours, but I felt closer to Ian somehow just by watching it. I remembered the nights he had made me sleep in the garden with him to appreciate the stars and I sat through that film time and again in the following weeks.

\*　　　\*　　　\*

The helicopter resupplies became a vital lifeline to Ian and his men as they continued to monitor movements along the MSR and ambush the odd Iraqi military vehicle. When the second resupply flight dropped another mystery box off, they were intrigued and wondered what other useful item they had been sent from HQ. When they opened it, they could hardly believe their eyes. It was full of Minolta automatic cameras, one for each troop, complete with reel after reel of film.

The Regiment had long used cameras for intelligence-gathering in places like Northern Ireland and even in the Falklands, but the use of cameras behind Iraqi lines had been discussed back at Victor and the lads had decided between themselves not to take any for security reasons. Those who were going in by foot were planning on claiming that they were search and rescue patrols if they got caught. How would that work if they were found with cameras full of pictures of Scud missile launchers?

Along with the box of cameras came the signal from Victor that they should be used to take photographs for 'historical documentation'. It was a command decision, made at the highest level and transferred to them, and the lads all thought it highly unusual in the circumstances.

All their training for the trip had been about secrecy and keeping things from the enemy if they were caught. They weren't even allowed any personal mail, for goodness' sake. Their maps were printed on wafer-thin pieces of silk that could be folded and folded into the smallest packages, so as not to be easily found. They were allowed to carry nothing that could identify them or the Regiment directly.

Now they were being asked to lug cameras all over the place and take photographs. Cameras which could, if found on them, severely compromise their positions and refute any claims that they might make to be non-Regiment.

There was no time to argue, or reason why. They took the cameras and duly photographed almost everything they came across, as well as taking dozens of light-hearted snaps of each other in their Arab coats, in convoys and in their makeshift camps. God help us if we are ever caught with this lot, Ian thought, as did his colleagues, but they were far too busy at that stage to ponder the consequences too deeply.

Because the Gulf was such a high-profile war and anyone who watched the latest developments on television felt almost personally involved, our friends and relatives were very good at keeping in touch and letting me know they were there if I needed them. One of the accountants at work had access to the Reuters news service on his computer and he would tell me the news long before it made the lunchtime or evening bulletins. Everyone tried to make light of the situation to keep me from worrying, and friends at work protected me from any misplaced comments or ill-advised words, but I was still desperate for Ian to be home safe with me and I knew I wouldn't settle until he was.

Ian continued to write to me twice a week, hiding the letters deep in the pockets of his filthy coat until the next Chinook dropped in. Writing to me and telling me what he was feeling and thinking (without, of course giving anything away in case the letters got into the wrong hands) helped him to share what he was experiencing, and to feel that we were somehow keeping in touch.

His letters eventually started to get through to me and it was wonderful to receive that first batch. I took the phone off the hook, curled up on the sofa and stroked and smelt and touched the letters that had been in his hands not all that long ago. I felt that I could smell him on them, even after they had travelled so far across the world. I took them to work and to bed with me and read them over and over, until I had nearly worn the ink off in my hands.

What he wrote was often pretty sentimental but much spoke of his hopes and dreams for the future and how he wished I was with him to see the fantastic starry nights, the likes of which he had never seen.

'When all this is over, babe, I am going to take you to a desert country somewhere and drive you and Annie out into the middle of it. We'll have an open fire and a bottle of scotch under the stars and I'll show you a good time, Bedouin-style,' he wrote.

One of his first letters home was dated the day war began and a week before his birthday, for which he had taken his cards from me into Iraq. His letter said:

> Just to let you know all is well. Busy as always. But no doubt you would have guessed, after today's world event, that many people will be busy for a while to come. That is the way it is so we must all just get on with it. Just like '82.
>
> I hope you received my letter by now asking for news etc to be recorded? As yet to date I have not received any mail from you or anybody else. Don't worry about that, just keep it coming, OK? I believe there was a meeting of the wives up at the camp on the 15th or so? Did you go? I'd suggest you keep in touch with a couple of girls to keep you updated on that end, if you are interested. You probably aren't. Please try not to worry. That may be easy for me to say and not so easy for you to do. I wonder if you will be as grey as me by the time I am home!
>
> Remember what I said about the family. Don't please isolate yourself out there, OK? You have lots of friends who do care so keep busy and stay in touch. That's an order. Well, I'd best finish for now and get on with the business of the day. When I get home I want the biggest Sunday roast since Christmas. Thanks again for the wonderful Christmas we shared. I have some lovely memories. We will have a lot more. Have no fear of that.

Once I started to receive his letters, I was spurred on to write to him even more. I wrote at least one letter every night, even though I never really knew if my letters were getting through or making any impact. It kept me busy, sitting up in bed with my pen and the comforting pile of blue airmail letters, pouring out my heart and soul to the man I loved.

I would place items of his clothing under my pillow each night and clutch them to me as I wrote, as if they were somehow part of him. I would even kiss them goodnight, leaving lipstick marks all over them, whether it was a pair of socks, pants or a T-shirt. Anyone watching me would have thought I was mad, but it gave me some solace and that was all that really mattered.

Ian's letters home had always been upbeat and they were a tremendous comfort, without which I think I would have gone under. Never in all the years he had been away had I heard him say or seen him write anything which might suggest that he would be might not come home safe and well, but I guess the Gulf was the turning point for him. How many wars can you go to as a front-line SAS soldier and expect to survive?

As the fighting continued and as more and more stories of colleagues being killed or injured in action trickled through, all around him he saw men writing 'blood letters' home to their loved ones, telling them what to do 'in the event of'. He started one to me, but found himself weeping in the middle of writing it, so he tore it up. Two days later, in another letter from the desert, half-way through Operation Desert Storm he tried to express his feelings on the subject again, adding a few throwaway lines to an otherwise ordinary letter.

> No matter what may occur in the future ... I love you to death. It makes me strong. It keeps my hopes alive. We will talk to each other in our dreams or reach out across this space of time. *I will leave you to explain to David if necessary.*
>
> Thank you for being with me and making our lives so happy together. I am happy, have no doubt about that. Say hi to my Mum and Dad. Tell them they are on my mind. I love you angel eyes.
>
> Always yours, Ian

I had just walked in from work and had been delighted to find two letters waiting for me. Not even bothering to take my coat off, I sat in an armchair and tore open the airmail seal. The first letter was bright and breezy and I got up and put the kettle on before I opened the second.

I read the penultimate paragraph in shock. I felt numb and completely unable to take it in. After all those years of us both putting on a brave face and waving each other goodbye with a smile, there he was, lying in the middle of the desert 3,000 miles away, thinking about death and telling me that this could be it, the end. He was admitting that my worst fears were secretly his worst fears too.

I felt shattered, as if all my carefully laid defences had been torn down in one moment. It sapped the strength from me. I slumped in the armchair and wondered at the gossamer veil of valour we had been hiding behind all these years.

Unable to face the moment alone, I got up and walked round to my neighbours, Tim and Lynne. The look on my face as they opened the door and saw me standing on their doorstep with a letter in my hand made them both assume the worst.

They took me inside and sat me down, their sympathy releasing my tears. When I showed them what he had written and they realised the reason for my distress, they couldn't have been more sympathetic, which made matters worse.

'I'm so sorry to come here like this and make a scene, but I just couldn't take it any more on my own,' I wept.

As I registered their shock at my outburst, I realised how clever I had become at deceiving people over the years. Jenny Simpson, the stoic Regiment wife, the jolly Geordie, never letting anyone see the real pain. I had locked myself away in my castle keep, pulled up the drawbridge and dealt with it all by myself, and with the help of a drink or two.

'You must be going through hell,' people would say to me, but I would shake my head defiantly and smile. 'No. I'm fine. I knew what he did when I married him,' I would say. 'Someone has to do the job, why not him?'

I realised that Ian had succeeded in making me believe so whole-heartedly in him that I had always kept my fears about his mortality to myself. Now here he was showing me that he felt them too and probably had all along. It was a moment of truth I would never forget. It felt as if part of our marriage had been a sham, a flimsy façade designed simply to bolster us through the worst times.

My neighbours were sweet and very kind and did all they could to make me feel better but it wasn't something I could easily explain.

'But we thought you were coping so well, Jenny,' said Lynne. 'Why didn't you tell us before? We had no idea.' That was the problem. Nobody had, and it was entirely my own fault. I felt slightly embarrassed at having let my guard slip in front of these good people, but

I also felt better for getting it off my chest. It was the first time I had spoken to anyone other than my doctor in ten years of marriage and I was surprised at how good it felt.

My most immediate problem, it seemed to me, was how best to respond to Ian's letter. How to make him feel less vulnerable in such a dangerous place, yet at the same time acknowledging that his letter was a cry for help. I should have joined the Samaritans with my experience in how to handle delicate situations over the years, and yet this time I didn't know what to say.

When the crying stopped and the worst was over I thanked my neighbours, went home and poured myself the first of several drinks before sitting down to write a reply.

By the time I put pen to paper, I was pretty angry. I wrote:

> Are you in trouble . . . You're not going anywhere but home so why suggest otherwise? I hear what you're saying, babe, but wind your neck in. I'm bloody furious at you, you upset me terribly, the things you said, i.e. David. I won't have to explain or say anything to anyone, Simpson, you can tell them your bloody self how it was when you get home. If you ever dare to think bad things I will personally cut your balls off. I know you think that is harsh, but believe me, my love, cut the Vietnam stuff and just get your beautiful arse back here where it belongs.
>
> PS. Is this the right time to ask you to leave the Regiment? I guess not. I always knew that it was your life.

Later that same night, when I had mellowed, I continued the letter, apologising for my anger and pleading with him not to give up. I hoped what I had written would do some good but I didn't even know if it would get to him. It worried me terribly that he was isolated out there without even a word of comfort from me, but though he did not receive my letter until some time later, Ian snapped out of his mood. He never wrote me another letter like it again, and his next one was positively chipper:

> February 3: The cold weather equipment I asked for will be much needed. It snowed here last week. Needless to say my toes are bearing the brunt of things again. As long as I don't

> end up like I did in '82, I will be happy. Keeping well and
> morale is very high so no need to worry on that scale. Everyone
> is fine.

He even went on to apologise for not sending me any flowers for a while, and to tell me he was going to try to make me a Valentine's card – in the middle of the Iraqi desert. Soft git.

Though he seemed to quickly overcome the fears he had expressed, Ian's letter left a permanent mark on me. I had never thought that he would be involved in another war after the Falklands. What if there was another one after the Gulf? What were the chances of him coming home from that? I decided there and then that if he ever got out of Iraq alive, I was going to do all I could to make sure that it was his last war, and that we should start looking to a future away from the Regiment for us both and possibly for our children, a life where death was something years away and not a daily probability.

The war in Iraq escalated when the Allied ground offensive rolled in from Saudi Arabia, tank after tank crossing the border. The news bulletins continued to feature the ongoing precision bombing against key targets, as one by one the missiles found their mark. The repetitive destruction became almost boring and people started to ask how much longer the devastating humiliation of Iraq had to continue as the Americans showed off their latest weapons and lined up prospective buyers.

Ian was still deep in the desert doing his Omar Sharif impersonation. He and his troop were scoring great successes against Iraqi positions, with hardly a life lost or a threat of compromise, but with so many SAS men feared dead or missing elsewhere, they felt that it was only a matter of days before they would be pulled out and sent home.

World events overtook them once again. Saddam Hussein launched a series of Scud launches on Israel, killing civilians and damaging property, and locating the missile launchers became a top

LOVE, HONOUR AND KEEP HIM

priority for the Allies. They were worried that Israel would be dragged into the war and then other Arab League nations would feel honour-bound to come out fighting on behalf of Hussein.

I watched the television images from Tel Aviv as weeping and wailing Israelis mourning those killed by the Scuds and realised immediately that Ian's job might be made that much harder by external political pressure.

As I had suspected, it became Ian and his men's new mission to concentrate on nothing but finding the Scud launchers and then – using TACBE message signals (he was issued with his own this time) and AWACS (Airborne Warning and Control Systems) – help British and American fighter pilots locate the launchers and destroy them. Having heard on the BBC World Service about the success of the precision bombing by the Allied 'sky jockeys' and the supposed clarity of the US satellite pictures, Ian and his men did wonder if there was a role for them on the ground.

They had also heard the bulletins about the thousands of Iraqis who were fleeing the country into Jordan, including many of Saddam's military commanders, and felt that it was only a matter of time before a coup overthrew Saddam and the war was over. They also realised that there was an internal political battle going on at Army HQ that they were merely pawns in, as each division of the armed forces tried to get one over on the other and claim their hour of glory.

They had their orders which they would try to carry out, even if it would be like trying to find a needle in a haystack while blindfolded. Having almost bumped into one Scud convoy already, Ian believed that there was little likelihood of coming across a second. But he was wrong.

In their search for the Scuds, the men had to leave the area they had spent most of their time in so far and traverse new terrain for which they had no maps or information. One night they suddenly came across an area which had recently been used to hide Iraqi tanks. They spent the night there, deciding to carry out a full recce of the area the following morning.

Looking over a nearby ridge the next morning they thought at first that they had come across a Bedouin camp, which annoyed them like hell because it was right in the way of their planned route north. It was only when they crept like Indians up onto the ridge and looked down that they realised it was a Scud and launcher protected by small anti-aircraft guns and armoured personnel carriers. Watching the site from the ridge, Ian called for help on the radio – using the coded flash signal 'Jungle Jungle' signifying a Scud sighting.

It was mid-morning when they first opened fire to keep the convoy engaged. The TACBE, which Ian tried first, didn't work, so he threw it to one side. He eventually got through to Victor on the high frequency radio, which takes much longer and is a much more complicated process. HQ told him it would take two or three hours to dedicate an aircraft from Baghdad or Kuwait, by the time the plane had refuelled. So Ian and his men spent the next three hours badgering the beleaguered Scud in broad daylight, waiting either for the air strike or for reinforcing Iraqi forces to attack them, whichever came first.

It was almost nightfall by the time they received a call telling them that two F15 American Eagles were on their way and would need to be given the correct co-ordinates. What happened next was probably Ian's greatest moment in history and he still talks about it with a childlike sense of euphoria and wonder.

Captured forever on film and audio, recorded in the American pilot's cockpit, the moment Ian directed the pilot and his 500-pound bombs towards the Scud was later broadcast around the world. Ian's troop rupert is heard interrupting him frantically to remind the pilot that he and his men have surrounded the Scud 200 metres away and are not to be fired upon.

The impact, when the bomb blew the Scud sky high, would have blown Ian and his men off their feet too, had they not taken cover underneath their vehicles. The damage done, they didn't hang around to see who was left. They had exposed themselves for quite long enough in that area and needed to get the hell out of there.

Ian's was the first SAS troop to make a positive contact with a Scud in the western desert and his commanding officer was awarded the Military Cross for his troop's part in keeping the missile launcher and its guard engaged in action for several hours until the fighter planes could come in. Ian was Mentioned in Despatches and the troop received a personal commendation from their CO. It was the pinnacle of his time in the desert.

At home we were told nothing. As far as the camp was concerned, we weren't even supposed to know where our men were. All the post I sent had to be addressed to Sgt Ian Simpson, Operation Granby, and a PO Box number. That was it. They could hardly phone us up and tell us of the latest successful contact in Iraq, when the official line was that the men were training 'somewhere in the Middle East'.

The weather in England improved slightly and I didn't feel quite so cut off as I had before, but then the snows came back with a vengeance, and Annie and I were holed up in the country with nothing to do but watch the television or make the occasional snowman with the neighbours' children.

I was bored with the news, I was bored with *Lawrence of Arabia*, the freezer was full to bursting and all my household chores were done. I was in desperate need of a holiday after my intensive period with the new computer at work, and I was missing Ian dreadfully. When would he be coming home?

He, too, was tired by now and hoping for an end to it all. Looking for the Scud launchers continued to be a daily chore for him and his men, although they all genuinely believed they wouldn't be so lucky as to find a third.

They had been warned that they could be hidden in anything, from oil tankers to school buses to ambulances. One day in late February, Ian received a signal that a Red Cross convoy was going to pass through his area. Bearing in mind the urgent quest for Scuds, a rather cheeky message came through from HQ, 'Don't shoot them, they are the ones with the big red cross on the side of their vehicles'. Ian was not amused.

Sure enough, later that day, the convoy passed through, the Western volunteers on board waving their acknowledgement to the small group of 'Arabs' sitting by the side of the road. '*Salaam, salaam alaykum*,' Ian waved back, all the while muttering under his breath, 'Yes, guys, we are not only on your side but could end up having to save your silly arses unless you get a bloody move on.'

A few days later, the desert was plunged into a no moon phase which meant little or no visibility at all at night, but it also offered the SAS the opportunity to deal with an ongoing problem in a most unusual way. HQ decided to organise a supply column to a place called Wadi Tubal, to service all the vehicles that were by then in desperate need of repair and servicing. Ian described it as a 'Kwik-Fit in the Desert'.

Over a period of five days, a mobile workshop serviced column after column of military vehicles, replacing engines, changing oil and stripping and servicing weapons. As sentries stood guard at key positions around the extraordinary natural dust bowl they had identified as the perfect spot, the vehicles were driven in at one end, serviced, fixed and cleaned and driven out at the other end.

A makeshift mess was set up to feed all the men arriving from the four corners of the desert, facilities for the first significant wash any of them would have had were laid on, and they even found time to take group photographs, have a sketch done for a painting, and hold an extraordinary meeting of the Warrant Officers' and Sergeants' Mess.

Items on the agenda, all of which were recorded in minutes, included a vote of thanks for the Hereford Christmas party, the arrangements for the next mess dinner, the provision of a washing machine and new chairs in the Hereford mess and a vote of thanks to the retiring RSM. They all signed the minutes, which the President of the Mess Committee promised to eat if he was compromised.

It was at Wadi Tubal that Ian was told that Bravo Two Zero, the patrol headed by his friend Andy McNab, was among those which had been compromised and scattered. Ian was extremely concerned for the missing men, including Andy, and was further devastated to hear that a good friend of his called Bobby Mason, a sergeant in A Squadron, was missing presumed dead after yet another compromised mission.

Bobby's men told Ian that they had been suddenly fired upon during a reconnaissance. Their Land Rover overturned when they tried to drive away as quickly as possible and Bobby was shot in the leg. His men dragged him to some bushes but as the Iraqis closed in they had to leave him for dead after they had half filled him with morphine. They assumed that he had bled to death from his severe leg wound or had been killed by the Iraqi soldiers. It was a terrible blow for Ian, he mourned the loss of someone he had known and respected throughout his career.

'What the hell are we doing here if we end up losing good people like Bobby?' he wrote to me. 'And Andy too. I mean I've known them forever and now they're probably both gone. It's all gone to jackshit.'

I read his words and thought back to the times that Andy had been a guest at our house. Andy has always been a joker. There was one late summer barbecue when the weather had turned unexpectedly cold but we were all still standing outside, freezing to death but getting on with the barbecue like the English idiots that we were. Suddenly, we heard a shout from the shed. It was Andy. We all rushed over and opened the door and there was the idiot, lying full-length in the chest freezer, hands behind his head, saying, 'Come on in guys, it's a lot warmer in here.'

On another occasion, just after he had passed Selection, he turned up on our doorstep with a mate and I invited them in for Sunday lunch. He had come to tell Ian his news and thank him for his support and encouragement during training. We all drank far too much, Andy especially, and then, unbeknown to me, he threw up all over my bathroom. He did a terrible job at clearing it up, and then legged it by climbing out of the window, leaving me to discover the mess.

The fear of the Iraqis was obviously nothing compared to the fear he had of me. To make matters worse, the following day he dropped a bunch of flowers and chocolates on my doorstep with a note apologising for what had happened. Only he signed it from his mate, not him. Some hero.

\* \* \*

Ian was some considerable distance from where it was thought the missing men might be but he was told to keep a look out for them anyway. They would be in a pretty bad way if they had tabbed that far south-west. He and his men were also warned to be extra careful, as their own positions could be compromised during the Iraqi search for prisoners.

Their task at Wadi Tubal completed, Ian and the rest of the men parted company with a considerable sense of emotion. Not only had it been the most remarkable example of camaraderie in the face of adversity, but they were now all in no doubt whatsoever that the chances were that at least some of them would never make it back alive.

Embracing each other roughly, they parted company and each troop disappeared off into the desert night to continue being what General Norman Schwarzkopf had described as 'his eyes and ears'.

Our friends and family continued to keep in touch and support me as best they could. I was invited out regularly and, although I didn't always feel up to accepting the invitations, I was always very glad to receive them. My father started turning up at my house every day when I was at work. He would walk the dog and lay a fresh coal fire for when I got in. It was a small but significant gesture and one that I appreciated above almost anything else.

When Ian had still been home, the next 'deadline' I had set to keep him with me after my birthday had been Valentine's Day. Ian had always spoiled me with flowers and cards and I wanted us to celebrate it together. When 14 February arrived, however, I was alone with my thoughts and fears, with six inches of snow outside the house.

That morning I got a call from Audrey and Paul, good friends, who asked me if I would go round for a barbecue.

'A barbecue?' I said. 'Give over, it's the middle of winter.'

'It might be cold here but it's probably bloody hot in Iraq and we're holding a Valentine's Day barbecue in honour of you and Ian,' they said. They wouldn't take no for an answer and sent someone to pick me up in a four-wheel drive vehicle. When I got there, the house was full of friends. I was deeply touched. Audrey presented me with a huge bouquet of roses she had grown specially in her conservatory because she didn't think Ian would be able to arrange my usual bouquet from Iraq.

I had a lovely day and came home with my bouquet to find another one waiting on the doorstep for me. It was from Ian who – along with a couple of his mates at Wadi Tubal – had sent a signal from deep behind enemy lines asking the Regiment to organise Valentine's Day bouquets for their wives. The card read: 'Missing you, my Valentine. Always yours, Simpson.' I sobbed my heart out.

I also got a lovely Valentine's day card from Lisa because she, too, didn't think Ian would be able to mark the day in any way. Dear Lisa, she has always been there for me at times of crisis. She was there when the helicopter crashed, she was living with me much of the time Ian was across the water and being a bastard and she knew I needed her thoughts now. I don't know what I would have done without her over the years.

She wrote in the card:

> I hope you don't feel too sad this week. I'll be thinking of you and Ian and I know that he'll be thinking of you, especially on this day of love. You are his life. I pray each night that you two will be together very soon, as you should be. Keep your chin up, I know you will, but I want you to know that I realise how much it costs you sometimes.
>
> Love, Lisa.

Even on such a poignant day, I still appreciated the value of humour in helping us get through all that we faced and when I opened the local evening paper I had to laugh. I cut out the cartoon I saw and sent it to Ian. It showed Saddam and his generals sitting round an operations table in a war room, and Saddam was saying, 'Aircraft carriers. Stealth bombers. What are the Americans going to send next?' Bursting in through the window behind them was a masked troop of Teenage Mutant Ninja Turtles in full SAS kit. My note to Ian said, 'Thought this might amuse you. Pizza's waiting. I love you Simpson. XXX'

*     *     *

After Ian's success with the Scud, his next mission was to capture some Iraqi prisoners of war. Word came from above that they should ambush some Iraqi military vehicles or attack an installation and grab a couple of Iraqis, sending them back in helicopters so that the Allied military intelligence could interrogate them.

They could not find any suitable targets but later that day, they met up with another troop who had captured an Iraqi prisoner of war, a sixteen-year-old Iraqi lance-corporal, whose foot had been all but blown away. The boy told Ian in Arabic that he had been at his post for twenty-two days with little food and no socks or boots. He hated Saddam Hussein, he said, and he was happy to have been captured. They gave him some food and Ian tended to his injuries as best he could, knowing the boy would almost certainly lose the bottom part of his leg. Then they called in a helicopter to take their only POW back to HQ.

The moment Ian and a colleague helped the limping boy to the helicopter was captured on film by the RAF gunner in the aircraft and later featured in the BBC's Gulf War series, as the only film footage of the SAS in action behind enemy lines.

The boy was delighted at being sent out of Iraq and grateful that someone spoke Arabic. He thanked Ian again and again, repeating 'Shukran, shukran' smilingly, and told him he would try to get all his family to England to meet him one day.

The helicopter duly arrived back at HQ with this grinning, toothless teenager who knew very little of any importance that could help the Allied forces but who was nonetheless in need of urgent medical treatment and a decent meal.

A terse message came back to Ian from the Ops officer at Victor which read, 'Very disappointed with POW. Had hoped for five-star general, not sixteen-year-old boy.'

Ian's reply read, 'Very difficult to find a five-star general in Iraq. Suggest you search Jordan.'

By the time the war was officially over at the end of February, Ian had spent forty-six consecutive days deep in the Iraqi desert. He eventually crossed back over to Al Jaouf on 3 March as a flight of A10s did loop the loops in the sky overhead.

The moment was recorded in a painting which hangs on our lounge wall. The caption reads, 'D Squadron Special Air Services Regiment, re-crossing the border from Iraq to Saudi Arabia 4/3/91 following Operation Granby'. Ian can be seen clearly, sitting in the passenger seat of the lead vehicle.

No sooner had they arrived back at Victor base when, instead of offering a word of thanks or even congratulations, the Ops officers marched up to them and demanded two things – their cameras with all the film, and their gold coins. The RSM told them that unless they handed everything over immediately, they would be RTU'd (Returned To Unit). Unless you had a cast-iron alibi that you had spent your gold coins legitimately in the desert, you couldn't keep them, even though the men would have liked just one each as a memento.

Ian duly handed his back, along with his camera and film and asked the RSM what would happen to the pictures. 'All the films will be processed and you will then each be allowed to choose three photographs that you would like to keep as tokens of your time in the desert. The remainder will be kept on file for historical purposes,' he was told.

Months later, when they were back in Hereford, they were indeed allowed to look at the processed negatives and each choose three, but they never received the prints. The next time they saw any of the photographs was when they appeared in a number of books about the Gulf War, including one by their commander, General Sir Peter de la Billière.

The war was over, but word went out that one of the squadrons would have to stay on a few more weeks in case of any further trouble. Fortunately for Ian, A Squadron was chosen and he was allowed to fly home. Once he had taken a shower and had something decent to eat and a bit of proper sleep at last, he caught a C130 flight out of Saudi Arabia.

The flight was jam-packed with men and equipment and he spent the journey sitting on the roof of a Land Rover to open two huge mail sacks that had been waiting for him full of letters and parcels from me, his family, friends and strangers under the 'Dear Soldier' scheme.

The rest of his squadron were severely pissed off because he had three times as much mail as anyone else and the sacks were so full of parcels of food, socks, gloves and mints that he was giving the unwanted stuff away.

Reading the 'Dear Soldier' letters from complete strangers made Ian realise for the first time how personally involved the British people had become in the war. He had had no idea that his countrymen were rooting for him so much and it made him feel quite emotional. He wondered what the response would be when he eventually got home.

When Ian had telephoned me from his base in Saudi to tell me he was coming home, I had never felt so pleased to hear his voice.

'Hello, babe,' was all he had said when I picked up the phone.

'Ian!' I cried, and burst into tears. 'Ian, is it really you?'

He assured me it was and that he was on his way home. It was a Friday and he said he would be home that Sunday evening. I could hardly wait. I am a great Country and Western fan and the song 'Tie a Yellow Ribbon Round the Old Oak Tree' sprang immediately to my mind. I decided to arrange something special for Ian's home-coming. I told my neighbours what I had planned and they promised to help me. We spent the whole weekend getting everything ready.

On Sunday evening I went to collect Ian from the camp. He had been flown to Brize Norton and driven on to Hereford. It seemed to take forever for the truck to pull into camp and then he was taken off for a quick debrief before being stood down. As I sat in the car I could hardly wait to see Ian's smiling face, whatever state it was in.

It was well worth the wait. When the men emerged from the debriefing room Ian pushed through the crowd towards me, his wind-tanned features beaming from ear to ear.

I buried my face in his neck and wept. It felt so good to be held in his arms again. I clung to him as if I would never let go. Neither of us could speak, we just hugged and kissed, crying and laughing all at once. It felt as if we were the only people in the world. Nothing else mattered.

When we eventually managed to prise ourselves away from each other and get into the car, I drove him slowly home, his hand in my hand, his lips kissing my neck. It felt as new and exciting as a first date and I almost regretted what I had planned for him.

As we rounded the corner and pulled into our cul-de-sac, I stopped the car to watch his reaction to the sight before him.

'What the . . . ?' was all he could say, his mouth agape at the dozens of yellow and gold ribbons that lit up the Close, the bunting across the lane, Union Jacks and banners in all the windows. Before he could say any more, the friends who had been waiting inside piled out of our house, their wine glasses raised.

'Welcome home, soldier,' I said as they all cheered.

# 10 | 'Til Death Do Us Part

LIFE RETURNED TO NORMAL when Ian unpacked his bergen. The men were all given the chance to have their kit washed for them before they came home, but, oh no, not my husband, he told them that his wife would be proud to wash it for him. He has one weird sense of humour. His clothes virtually got out of the bag and walked to the washing machine by themselves. I diverted most of them to the dustbin.

He even brought home the filthy old Arabic coat that he had worn out there as a disguise. I took one look at it and threw that out as well. Emotionally attached to the garment that had offered him such good protection and warmth in the desert, he retrieved it from the bin almost immediately.

'Hey,' he said, crestfallen. 'I love this coat.'

'All right,' I said, giving in. 'I'll give it a wash and the dog can have it as a bed.'

He cheered up a little, hoping that the dog would reject it and then he could claim it back, but the dog loved it and slept on it for months afterwards very happily. I often caught Ian looking at the coat longingly.

I had got my man safely home and could, at last, stop worrying. But would he settle?

He seemed to reacclimatise quite quickly. There were no immediate nightmares and seemed to be little of the post-Falklands, post-Northern Ireland angst. He had turned down an offer of counselling from the Regiment – the first time it had ever been formally offered to any of them en masse – and he seemed to be coping well.

He was still very anxious for news of Andy McNab and his patrol, and of Bobby Mason, and he eventually heard, to his great delight, that Bobby was alive and had been handed over to the Red Cross. After being captured by the Iraqis and cared for very well by a doctor who had managed to save his leg, he had been handed over to Saddam's secret service men who repeatedly jumped on his shattered thigh. Even though Bobby was to be crippled for life, he was alive and was later awarded the Military Cross, one of thirty-nine medals and awards given to the members of the SAS following Operation Granby.

Of Andy's patrol, Ian heard that Chris Ryan – a man he had known from Selection days – had made it across to the Syrian border, and that McNab and his friend Dinger had been taken prisoner but were expected to be released to the Red Cross. Three men – Bob Consiglio, Legs Lane and Vince Phillips – were all dead. There but for the grace of God, we both thought. I added them and their families to my bedtime prayers.

I couldn't get over how well and happy Ian seemed. He had had a good war and felt he was fully back on track within the Regiment after his Scud successes. No one terribly close to him had been lost and the lads who had been missing were on their way home.

There was only one evening when he showed any signs of stress after the Gulf. He had gone out on the piss with the lads and had a few too many, then came home and started drinking some more. Without any prompting on my part, he sat down on the sofa next to me and started to talk a little bit about what it was like in the desert.

'It was bloody freezing at night, I was permanently knackered and my feet were giving me terrible gyp,' he slurred. 'It wasn't all starry nights and camels you know.'

I said nothing as I slid to the floor and sat at his feet. I wanted him to continue. But almost as soon as I did that, his face darkened and he held his head in his hands, close to tears.

'What is it, babe?' I asked, kneeling in front of him and holding his hands in mine. He was incoherent with a combination of drink and grief.

'I didn't want to kill them,' he said, weeping openly now. 'I didn't mean to, honestly Jenny, I didn't. It just happened. It wasn't my fault.'

'I know, love, I know,' I said, wondering who on earth he was talking about and whether he would tell me any more.

'It was pathetic,' he went on. 'Pathetic. They were old men and they were frightened and I had to slot them because they would have slotted me and the rest of the troop otherwise. But I didn't want them to die.'

As gently as I could, I asked, 'Who were they, babe? Iraqi soldiers?' He nodded speechlessly, wiping his nose with the back of his hand.

'Old men, old Iraqi men,' he said, his eyes full of tears. 'They would have been all right if they had just come out with their hands up but some idiot threw in a grenade and it frightened them, you see.'

I didn't see at all, but I nodded and in the absence of any further sense from him I helped him to his feet and up to bed. He was still sobbing – big, gasping sobs like a child's – as I turned off the light.

He slept like a baby all night and woke up early to go for a run. At breakfast he could remember nothing of the previous night's conversation and dismissed it as the rantings of a drunk. As usual, it was only weeks later that he felt able to tell me what had happened.

We had taken Annie for a long walk up Dinedar Hill after a big Sunday lunch one summer's afternoon, and we were strolling along arm in arm and talking about the events of the past few years.

'It's been a pretty shitty time for you, hasn't it, Jen,' he said. 'I mean, all the lonely times and the fear and then the nightmares and all that other crap.'

I squeezed his hands and smiled. 'It's certainly had its moments.'

'At least the Gulf wasn't too bad in the end, and I didn't have any trouble afterwards, did I?' he commented.

'No, not really. Only that one night when you got upset. You never did tell me what that was all about.'

He sat down by a fallen tree and pulled me onto his knee.

'The trouble is, I never know how much I should tell you,' he said. 'I mean, if it upsets me to think about it, then isn't it going to upset you if you know about it too? And I think you've got enough on your plate without taking on my horrors as well.'

I cupped his face in my hands. 'Ian Simpson, when I married you, I took a vow. I know you might not have heard me say it, but I did. It was "for better or worse". Now is the better. This is the time that makes up for the rest. But that doesn't mean to say I shouldn't share the worse with you too. And unless I know what you're feeling in here . . .' I tapped his head . . . 'then I can't help you here . . .' I pointed to his heart.

We sat and talked for over an hour as he told me what had happened in Iraq. It was during his final week, when they had been asked to take some Iraqis prisoner. They had decided to target the observation tower that had dominated their time in the desert. Going in by foot, they planned to knock on the door and ask the four men manning it to come out.

But the men inside, who had seen the patrol coming, jumped down from the tower fearfully and hid themselves in an accommodation hut on the ground. There were dogs barking all around the camp and the men inside could have been in no doubt that they were surrounded, but still they wouldn't come out.

Ian, in his best British Arabic, told them not to be frightened and to come out and surrender with their hands up, but still they wouldn't budge. Finally, Ian told one of his younger men to go round the back and see if there was a way in there. The young firebrand, seeing an open window, decided to liven things up by throwing a phosphorous grenade into the hut. The four Iraqis, believing they were being attacked from the rear, came bursting through the corrugated iron front door, guns blazing.

One ran off screaming into the desert, but the rest were mortally wounded, chiefly by Ian, who was directly in their line of fire and had no choice but to shoot them. When one of them then moved on the ground as if to reach for his gun, another member of the troop shot him dead. It was senseless carnage and Ian regretted it very much at the time. He gave the soldier who had thrown the grenade a serious bollocking.

When the men entered the hut afterwards and looked at the Iraqis' weapons and supplies, they felt even guiltier. These men were in their late fifties, poor and very badly served by their Army. Most of their weapons and equipment was extremely outdated and rusty and they had virtually nothing to eat. It was pathetic.

Ian was haunted by the sight he saw when he looked back as they were leaving. He had killed many times before but when he saw the men lying dead on the ground, their life's blood seeping into the sand, he knew the image would remain with him forever.

With the Gulf War over and just a few years left to serve, Ian and I started to talk more and more about the future, about a life outside the Regiment and away from all the bad memories. The Gulf had put everything on hold, and Ian was still waiting to hear about the Northern Ireland job he had applied for and hadn't yet summoned the courage to tell me about.

He believed that after his successes in the Gulf it was almost certainly his. I, too, was more than happy with his accolades from Iraq. I wholeheartedly believed that the sergeant major's badges I so desperately wanted for him were now tailor-made for his arm. I wanted nothing more.

I raised the question of children again one night, as delicately as I could, fully expecting him to shoot me down in flames. But he didn't. He was amazingly in tune with my thinking and I was relieved. We talked about the possibility of adopting, he seemed very keen to give a home to an unwanted child, but we both knew in our hearts that no adoption agency would even consider us when they looked at our ages and lifestyles.

A vasectomy reversal was the only option. We didn't know if it would work or not, but we knew there was only one way to find out. We were also aware that it would probably cost a considerable amount of money.

'I bet it's a lot more than the £101, inclusive of the cup of tea,' Ian joked, but in the same breath he told me it didn't matter how much it cost, if that was what I wanted.

I was delighted. I started to try to prepare myself mentally for the possibilities that lay ahead of us. A family at last. Me, Ian and our child. Not forgetting Annie, of course.

Now that it wasn't just a dream, a faraway thought, I realised that it was probably what I had wanted all along but had been denying myself. It wasn't that I had been bullied or even cajoled, I had certainly believed in my decision at the time. Even as a nervous sixteen-year-old working at my firm's computer department, I remembered thinking I never wanted to be married with kids when I looked around at the women working with me who were.

Yet nearly twenty-four years later, there I was, approaching forty and considering motherhood for the first time. I must be completely off my rocker, I thought, as I flicked open the Yellow Pages for the number of the clinic. Now what the hell do I look under? Plumbers or Antique Repairs?

The appointment made for the following month, I was reminded of another appointment I should make. The doctor. Since just after Ian had come home, I had not been feeling quite myself. There wasn't anything particular to put my finger on, just a general feeling of tiredness and malaise. I was probably just a little run down and needed some vitamins, I thought, but the Seven Seas multi-vitamins I had started to take didn't seem to make any difference.

I had been putting off going to the doctor for a few weeks, hoping it would go away, but it hadn't. I didn't like doctors much, I never had, and there was a new man I hadn't yet met at the surgery. Oh well, I thought, while I am sitting by the telephone, why not make the appointment now? After all, I wanted to be in top shape for when Ian had the snip reversal, didn't I?

Buttoning up my blouse after my examination, I heard the doctor tell me there was nothing to worry about and that he would send away my blood and urine tests.

'Go home and take it easy for a couple of days. Take time off work if you feel like it, you've probably just been under a lot of pressure lately and need time for your body to recover. I'll give you a call and book you back in when the results come through.'

Just what I thought, I mused as I left his surgery. Right, I would take his advice. I rarely took time off sick from work, I was always struggling in with whatever cold, cough or minor ailment I had while others stayed at home. Ian was home for a few weeks, so why didn't I take a few days off to spend with him quietly at home. Feet up in front of the telly, his favourite cheese and pickles laid out on our laps, watching some movie from the video shop. God knows, if we were about to have our lives turned upside down by a baby, there would be precious little time for all of that.

After three days of slothful bliss with my man at home, I had almost forgotten about the doctor when he rang shortly after five o'clock one night.

'Can you come in and see me so that we can discuss these tests?' he said. 'Tomorrow at eleven a.m. would be fine.'

Ian asked me who was on the telephone. 'Oh, just the doctor,' I told him distractedly. 'He's got my test results back and he wants me to go and see him tomorrow.'

Ian lifted his feet down from the sofa and looked at me.

'Everything's all right, isn't it? I mean, you're not ill?'

I smiled at him. Ever the medic, he was always thinking the worst.

'No, silly,' I said, throwing a cushion at him. 'He probably just wants to tell me that he can't find any blood in my alcohol!'

I drove alone to the surgery the next morning. Ian offered to accompany me but I knew he had a Gulf debriefing class to attend that day so I told him not to bother.

'I'll see you tonight at home,' I said. 'I'll make us a nice steak salad.'

The doctor ushered me into his room and was all smiles. I sat down in front of him, relieved by the look on his face.

'Well, Mrs Simpson, I've got some surprising news,' I heard him say jovially. I held my breath as I wondered what he was going to say.

'You are quite young for this, but all the indications are that you may be going through an early menopause.' He looked up from his test results and smiled.

I had watched his mouth open and close as he spoke, and I had heard the words he uttered clattering around inside my head, but there did not seem to be any correlation between the two. My body and brain seemed to be having some sort of seizure and I sat staring at him, waiting for the pain in my chest to stop.

We were too late, by maybe just a few months. The family we had talked and dreamed about wasn't to be. If Saddam Hussein hadn't interrupted our plans or if we had investigated a vasectomy reversal earlier, we just might have been in time. There was nothing but white noise in my head and I wanted it to stop.

I don't know what I said in reply to the doctor's news, but I left his office as soon as I could without appearing rude and rushed to the car, clutching leaflets he had handed me about hormone replacement therapy and the importance of diet in middle age.

I started up the car and drove across town and out towards our home. As soon as the houses stopped and the open fields started, I looked around for a place to stop and pulled into a country lane less than half a mile from my house.

Sitting in the car with the doors locked, I clasped my arms around my body and rocked backwards and forwards, to and fro, in a comforting motion that seemed to ease the pain. So that was it. Chance gone. Go Directly to Jail and do not pass Go. I stared and stared at the steering wheel, concentrating on the small golden lion symbol in the middle of the horn, focusing all my mind and energy on it until I thought I would burst.

Lunging forward, I crashed my head against it with all my might, pushing harder and harder so that the screaming, continuous blaring would not stop.

Ian came home from camp that night and walked into the kitchen to tell me he had just heard that he was off to the Middle East again for a three-month mission.

'It'll be OK though, babe,' he said. 'I'm not going until two weeks after the appointment at the clinic, so we've got a fortnight to try and make a baby. Yum yum.'

I stood with my back to him at the kitchen worktop, chopping onions furiously and trying to stop my knees from buckling under me.

Struggling to maintain the pitch in my voice, I told him breezily, 'I am afraid that doesn't matter now, babe. I went to the doctor today and he said it was too late for me to have children. I am afraid we've missed the boat.' I stopped chopping and listened for movement behind me, but there was none.

When I turned slowly to look at him, my face streaked with tears that had nothing to do with the onions, he peered at me out of a pale face. His expression was of shock, pity and confusion. We stood silently at opposite sides of the kitchen, both of us taking in what I had just said, neither of us able to respond.

Finally, I broke the silence and raised my empty glass. 'Pour me another drink, babe. Supper will be ready in ten minutes.'

We never mentioned it again.

It took me months, but I was eventually able to convince myself that it was quite right and proper that we should never have children. Ian might have made a good father, but together we would have been lousy parents. God wasn't so much punishing me as telling me I couldn't have it all. Hadn't He brought Ian home from all those dreadful, dangerous places, hadn't He kept His side of the bargain? And now here I was asking for more? No, it was too much. Go Directly to Jail. Do not collect £200. If you are not ordained to have children, then you are not ordained to have them. Simple as that.

Ian went off to the Middle East as planned and left me alone to come to terms with my loss. Once again, I felt as if I was mourning the death of a real child, a child I had never carried and now never could. Ian was as affected as me, in his own way, and he lay out under the desert stars contemplating life's twists and turns and wishing there was something he could do to ease my grief.

Just as in a genuine bereavement, time proved a great healer and before Ian returned the brave front I had come to prepare for his homecomings was dusted off, polished and stuck to my face with make-up. When he walked in the door, all sun-kissed and super-fit, I was there to greet him with a smile. His very own Angel Eyed

Blondie, thirty-nine and a little past it, maybe, but still his loving wife.

Almost as soon as he returned, Ian made enquiries about the Northern Ireland job he had been after. It seemed that not all the disappointments were to be mine, because he learned within a few days that the job had been offered to someone else. It was, he believed a political decision and had everything to do with the fact that he and one of his ruperts over there didn't get on. In the same breath, the Head Sheds also told him that he would not be getting the new command appointment I had wanted and, he suspected, never would.

He told me about it all at once, when he walked in the door from the camp one Saturday afternoon, and I knew that it was as hard for him to give me that news as it had been for me to tell him what I had learned from the doctor those few months earlier.

The news wasn't altogether unexpected. We had experienced several setbacks and disappointments during his time in the Regiment, everyone had. There were just too many heroes and not enough gongs to go around. And the competitive streak that got those men into the SAS in the first place never left any of them, so they all took it very seriously. As I told Ian, why should two wars, a gallantry medal and a few heroic weeks in the Iraqi desert make any difference? There were others with even more medals, even greater service to the nation. At the end of the day it was, it seemed, still a question of who you knew and Ian had steadfastly refused to make a special effort to ingratiate himself with those he knew could further his career.

The question was, what was he to do for his final four years in the Regiment? It was late 1991 and he didn't feel he would be able to sit in Hereford for the rest of his career, watching the new racing dogs coming up on the inside track and overtaking him. However old he was getting, he still exhibited the competitiveness that had got him through Selection in the first place.

I think he honestly still thought of himself as a young man of twenty-five with his hair on fire. It would have been too much for him to hang on, slowly coming to the realisation that he was no longer wanted or needed.

He had always loved the jungle and had not been given that many opportunities to return there in recent years, so he started to explore the possibilities of going back as jungle training instructor and taking me with him. I wasn't that keen but I knew I wouldn't really have a say. I had heard about all those creepy crawlies, I had seen the mosquito bites and the leech scars and knew about the poisonous snakes. He assured me I would be living in a bamboo palace with servants and formidable defences against the wildlife, but it still made my flesh crawl to think about it.

He had always enjoyed the training side of his work, teaching the young lads doing Selection how to get through it, tabbing up on the Brecon Beacons with them and taking great personal pride in their successes. Maybe he could go back to Training Wing in some capacity, and put all that hard-earned experience to some practical use. He decided to put out feelers about a couple of jobs and see what was on offer.

In January 1992, I was to be forty years old. It was not a birthday I was looking forward to or particularly wanted to celebrate in any special way, but – unfortunately for me – Ian was home twiddling his thumbs at that time and had other ideas.

'I don't want a big fuss made, pet,' I told him. 'Just a quiet family dinner. Something pretty low-key.'

'Fine,' he said. I should have suspected that the grin on his face was a mischievous one. So many of our birthdays and anniversaries had been spent apart over the years, he decided that this was the perfect opportunity to make up for all those lost celebrations.

My birthday fell on a weekday but as I didn't want any great brouhaha, that suited me fine. On the Saturday night before the big day, we decided to go out for a meal with our friends Ruth and Jerry.

'I just want us to pop round to your brother's new house on the way to the restaurant and pick up some of those architect's plans for our conservatory,' Ian said.

'Do we have to, tonight?' I complained, but he told me it would only take a minute and it was on our way.

My brother and his wife had had a house built for them by my other brother in Hereford and it was almost complete. We were using the same architect to design a conservatory and Ian said he had left the plans with him.

We pulled up outside the empty house and walked up the drive-way. Ian put the key in the door and opened it onto a dark and empty hallway. Squeezing my bottom suddenly, he said, 'Hey, how about having a quickie on your brother's new kitchen floor, to celebrate your birthday?'

'Give over,' I cried aloud. 'I am not fucking you on my brother's kitchen floor!'

At that moment, a light switch flicked on and I looked up in embarrassment to see two dozen smiling faces all waiting for me.

'Surprise!' they all shouted and a camera flashbulb went off. I have never been so mortified in my life. The house was full of family and friends, balloons, posters, flowers, the works. Fortunately, only a few of them heard me so my reputation was saved. I had a wonderful evening, thanks to Ian. So much for a low-key birthday.

Great, I thought. That was just right. Now no more surprises, please.

On the morning of my birthday, Ian brought me breakfast in bed.

'Happy birthday, chooch,' he said, and gave me a kiss. 'Presents later, OK?'

I opened my cards, had a shower and got dressed for work.

'I think you should wear your raincoat today, babe,' he said, holding it up for me to slip into. 'It looks like the weather might turn.'

I put it on and got in the passenger seat of the car, while he got in the driver's side to drop me into work. We set off towards Hereford along the main A-road and chatted about the dinner we were having at a favourite restaurant that night. Half-way through the journey, we came to a huge roundabout where the ring road meets the main street and my mouth fell open at the sight before my eyes.

Six foot high and as bold as brass in the middle of the round-about was an enormous black and white photograph of me as a six-year-old child, with the caption, 'Happy Birthday, Jenny Simpson. Love Ian. XXX.'

Ian said nothing and carried on around the roundabout as I pointed agape at the poster and said, 'What the . . . did you . . . but . . .'

He looked askance at me and said, 'Sorry, babe, is anything the matter?'

'You bloody nutcase!' I yelled, belting him. 'You put my picture on the roundabout, in the middle of the bloody roundabout. Are you mad?'

He did his best to look innocent. 'Sorry, babe. I don't know what you're on about.'

Minutes later, we pulled into my firm's car park and my mouth fell open once again. Plastered all over the front of the office block were a dozen copies of the same photograph with the message 'Happy Birthday Jenny (Wages)' four feet high. I was gob-smacked.

'What the hell do you think you're playing at?' I asked him.

'Well, there's another Jenny at your firm, so I thought I'd better put wages in brackets afterwards. Did I do something wrong?' he asked. Grinning cheekily, he virtually pushed me out of the car. 'See you tonight, chooch,' he said.

His antics were far from over. I walked into the office to find all the girls waiting for me giggling. 'You can wind your bloody necks in,' I told them. 'That's quite enough tomfoolery for one day.' But they turned me round and made me look in the mirror and I realised for the first time that the entire back of my raincoat was plastered with photographs of me and birthday messages from Ian. 'That bastard!' I cried.

The rest of the morning passed without event, thank goodness, and I left the office at lunchtime to go to the local pub with the girls. When I walked in the door, I couldn't believe my eyes. Ian had obviously got there before me. The walls of the bar were plastered with pictures, banners and messages.

To add insult to injury, he had placed a half-page ad in the local newspaper, featuring the same photograph and the message, 'Happy 40th Birthday Pig!' There was no getting away from it, the whole of Hereford seemed to know I was forty.

I had a riotous lunch with the girls and staggered back to work in the afternoon. When Ian came to pick me up that night, I attacked him, smacking and punching him and laughing all at the same time, as the girls stood watching from the windows. He protested his innocence and claimed he didn't know what I was talking about. By the time he took me home a different route and we came across yet another roundabout with my poster and birthday message on it, I had forgiven him everything.

'That is absolutely it now, isn't it? I asked him. 'No more practical jokes?'

He promised me that was the end of it, that we were just going out for a quiet meal together. We showered and changed, poured ourselves a few pre-dinner drinks and then he led me to my present.

Sitting in the middle of the utility room was a brand new dishwasher with streamers and helium balloons attached to it. I smiled and kissed him and made all the right noises, but secretly I was quite disappointed. I hadn't wanted a dishwasher, I hadn't asked for one and I was upset that he hadn't thought of anything more romantic.

Still, you can't have everything, I thought, as we set off for the restaurant. The meal was lovely, the evening was very romantic and we sat chatting by candlelight, laughing about my day. Suddenly, he grabbed hold of his napkin and gave the most almighty sneeze, making a great fuss of blowing his nose.

'Ian!' I scolded. 'Do behave!'

'I can't help it, babe,' he said. 'There was something horrible in my nose, look,' and he held out his napkin for me to inspect.

'Give over!' I cried, shying away.

'Go on, babe. I'm serious, it could be something terrible. I'm worried.'

Ignoring the scowls of the waiters and other diners, I leaned forward and peered into the napkin, not expecting to like what I would find. There, nestling among the folds of material, was the most beautiful blue topaz and diamond ring I had ever seen. I looked up at his grinning face and burst into tears.

Later that month, Ian came home and told me he had been offered a new job which seemed to fill all the criteria he was seeking, as well as giving him the chance to make the most money he had ever earned. It was a full-time posting at a military barracks in central London, as training commander for the SAS Territorial Army. It was an initial posting for two years, but as he was due to come out of the Regiment in spring 1996 when he was forty, they asked him if he would stay there until he left.

Along with the job would go a promotion to warrant officer, the highest rank he ever attained and the best paid. He was to be based in London, but would take the lads to the jungle camps in Belize for training, out to the Brecons for exercises, and to camps in the States and all over Britain.

I was delighted for him. I had never lived in London before and I was excited by the prospect of a change of lifestyle and the opportunity of spending more time with Ian. 'Eh, we're going to be dead posh,' I joked in my best Geordie accent. 'Living down in the big city with all the Royal Family. We can pop in and see the Queen again!' But my vision of a life in London was to be thwarted.

Ian, it seemed, had no intention of taking me with him. He had it all worked out, he said. He would be living in lodgings most of the time or at his parents' house in west London, and claiming his full living allowance. Our finances weren't in a brilliant state for a couple facing retirement, not after all we had spent on holidays, houses and cars. It was, he said, the best opportunity we would have to build up some real savings and prepare for our future once he had left the Regiment. I was to stay in Hereford and he would come home and see me most weekends, he promised.

I knew, in my heart of hearts, that he was running away from

Hereford and all the problems he had experienced there, and – to a certain extent – that he was also running away from me. He seemed to want to put a distance between us deliberately and I was bewildered and confused by that, after all the years we had come through relatively intact.

Was this it? I thought. Now that we had the chance to have a normal marriage, was it suddenly something that he no longer wanted? I understood all his anxieties about the change in lifestyle, I shared them too. I was as scared as he was about whether we would survive in such close proximity to each other, without the constant breaks of his trips away, but I wanted to try to make it work.

So many members of the Regiment use the pressures of coming to terms with their final years in service as an excuse to leave their wives and families and branch out on their own. Call it male menopause, change of life or just sheer bloody selfishness, I had seen it a dozen times. The shattered wives are left behind like nothing more than a cast-off item of clothing, after so many years of loyal devotion, while the men run off with younger women and spend the rest of their lives telling everyone how they used to be heroes in the SAS.

Was this what was going to happen to Ian and me? I wondered, as I looked in the mirror. After all those years, all those tears? I didn't know the answer, and that scared me even more. But I knew Ian, I knew his determination and I instinctively felt that unless I allowed him to go to London on his own, I would never know if he had made his choice because of his love for me or in spite of it.

It was going to be tough, facing all that uncertainty alone. I knew that I would have to make the most of it, put on a brave face and do whatever I could to get him, and me, through this final trial.

We arranged a holiday in the States, to spend some quality time together in our favourite place and prepare ourselves for the big change in our lives. I went over and over the plans for the future in my head, wondering if I could keep it all together. I woke up one morning during the holiday, after yet another restless night, and decided that I had too much on my plate. I no longer wanted to have to go to work each morning, smiling and joking, pretending that everything was fine, not while all this was going on.

Ian was going to be earning the money in London, so I decided to give up my job. After twenty-five years at the same firm it would be a big emotional wrench to leave, but I felt sure I was doing the right thing. On the day we got back I handed in my notice and worked only until the end of that week.

Within a few weeks I knew I had made the right decision. I felt enormous relief at the freedom not working gave me. It allowed me to concentrate on preparing myself for what lay ahead.

Ian loved it in London. He was away from all the politics of Stirling Lines and doing something he really enjoyed in an environment he hadn't known since he was a child. The spring in his step returned, the smile that I missed so much lit up his face and the fire returned once more to his eyes.

It was a new challenge for him and he rose to it. Some of the young men he taught the basics of Selection training went on to leave their civilian jobs and become fully badged members of the Regiment. Chris Ryan entered the SAS that way. Ian divided his time between London, the jungle camps and Hereford, and was largely independent of anyone or anything, including me.

For me there were some blessings to the new posting. When the fighting started in Bosnia, Ian wasn't among the SAS men who were sent there, which he almost certainly would have been had he still been on team in Hereford. My view was that he had more than done his bit and I was not at all sorry that he missed yet another senseless war. How many more were there going to be?

The worst aspect was that for his final four years, we only saw each other at weekends, although we spoke on the phone daily. The separation took time to cause its damage, but, needless to say, it did.

Once I had got used to the idea that it wasn't really a viable option for me to move to London with Ian, I convinced myself that it was for the best. We would have had to sell or rent out our home, give up the dog and I would be living miles away from my family and friends. He was right, it simply wasn't sensible.

But that didn't make the loneliness any easier to bear. It didn't keep me warm at night, or help me fold the sheets or lay a fire or chop the wood. It didn't ease the misery I felt each time I sat down at the dinner table on my own, or walked the dog alone, or watched the television without someone to talk to.

Those four years alone really took their toll on me. Ian was having a great time with all his mates in London, reliving his youth, enjoying new responsibilities, while I felt as if I were wasting away slowly at home, wondering what the future might hold.

I stopped eating, I drank too much, I lost weight and spent hours alone in my fortress home with just Annie and my fears for company. I made myself ill through self-neglect and sometimes wondered if I was going mad.

When Ian came home for the weekend it was often an anti-climax. I prepared for it all week, I looked forward to it, but once he was with me I couldn't help but allow some of my resentment to bubble to the surface. Not surprisingly, perhaps, he started to find reasons not to come. The training exercises seemed to fall more and more on a weekend, the periods in jungle camps seemed suddenly longer than they had ever been before, and the demands of the barracks ruperts seemed unreasonably high.

I could feel him slipping away from me but I knew that the time wasn't right to make a scene. No theatrics, Jenny. I had to hang on, to see if he got through this on his own, to see if he wanted me to be part of his life when he came out the other side.

Sometimes we would be fine. I would cook the big Sunday roast he loved, he would invite a few friends over and we would all have a riotous time until he had to go back to London again. Other weekends, we would spend quietly, rediscovering each other, walking, talking and making love, reminding ourselves how great we could be together when we both made the effort.

But increasingly, the strains of having a long-distance marriage began to show and we both began to wonder what it would be like when Ian eventually retired from the SAS and we had to live together again. The prospect frightened me, though not as much as the prospect of life without him.

Gradually, we found our own space and we slowly acclimatised. It took much of the four years, but we each found our levels and it enabled us to prepare ourselves for what was to come, Ian's eventual departure from the Regiment. The four-year separation was undoubtedly painful, but as preparation for the forthcoming divorce from the Army, it was also invaluable.

After all his time in London, Ian lost the feeling for the Hereford camp altogether, making his parting from it so much easier. I knew the transition had fully taken place when some senior ruperts arranged to dine him out and asked him if he wanted the dinner in London or Hereford. 'Where's Hereford?' he replied. I hoped then that the worst was over for him.

Hard as it was, the four years prepared me for the worst case scenario, the unacceptable risk mission, the thought of life without Ian. However out-dated and anti-feminist it sounds, I have always been just an old-fashioned girl with one thing in mind – a lifetime love affair with the man of my dreams. Ian had been that for me for nearly seventeen years, in spite of everything or even, perhaps, because of it. He was all I ever wanted in a childlike, simplistic sort of way and I couldn't bear the thought of a life without him. For me, that would be no life but four years largely alone steeled me for that, if it were to happen.

We had our fair share of rows in the final eighteen months before Ian left the SAS, as we went through the fear, sorrow and frustrations of cutting the Regimental umbilical cord. It was as painful as a physical withdrawal after so many years of addiction and dependency.

How would we cope on our own? Could we survive without the stresses and strains that had been the oxygen of our marriage? Was it the fears and uncertainties that had adhered us all these years? What would it be like when we didn't have them to blame for any problems we encountered? Would we fall apart without the SAS to bind us together?

We both knew instinctively that things were going to be very different. We would be thrown together, husband and wife and yet complete strangers in so many ways. What if one of us pulled the plug? Decided that the other person really was a stranger? That they had only been in love with the idea of the other for all these years? That the reality was a terrible letdown?

It was nothing short of hell, psyching ourselves up for the final event, limbering up our hearts for the stay or split scenarios. But, as ever with Ian, it also had its endearing moments. He scanned the world atlas looking for countries in need of an ex-member of the SAS, and would come home at the weekends full of it, bursting in on me when I was in the bathroom or the kitchen, to ask what I thought about living in this country or that republic. I told him that I really didn't mind as long as we were together and happy, and I meant it. I was just pleased and relieved that he was including me in his plans.

What I didn't want was for him to go back to the sort of work that brought out the worst in both of us. It was nearly the end of us before and I didn't want to have to go through all that again. That is one of the reasons why I was secretly delighted when the job in Northern Ireland didn't work out. I would have hated living in such a pervading climate of fear.

What do old SAS soldiers do after a lifetime of service and devotion, if not more of the same? Work that is often twice as dangerous, even if it is four times as well paid.

There is not much call for 'pilgrims' in civilian life and little or no opportunity for them to carry on saving the world. Few would be able to handle returning on commission to their old regiments after the sort of lifestyle that is unique in the Army. In the SAS everyone calls everyone else by their first names, even officers, and the level of autonomy and responsibility for oneself is second to none. Orders have to be given and taken but the way in which that is done is based very much on the 'Chinese parliament' system of talking it through at every level first. How difficult it would be to go back to being barked at by some sergeant major, with no oportunity to bark back.

The police force and Customs and Excise are always interested in employing SAS men as training officers, but once again the strict discipline and regimentation required doesn't suit those who have been left largely to their own devices in between missions and even sometimes on them. Some ex-SAS men become outward bound instructors, or try their hand as bodyguards, stunt men or even polar explorers. But they all miss the Regiment badly and spend much of their retirement down Memory Lane.

These are men who, for more than two decades, have been bound together by a common bond, a way of life which demands a particularly high emotional and physical resistance. It is the only life they know and no one ever prepares them for the insecurity and isolation they feel on leaving it.

Instead they are pitched out of the front gates of Stirling Lines with their pensions, like old lags coming out of prison after more than twenty years, blinking in the sunlight and wondering how they should go about earning a living now.

Is it any wonder some of them are so frightened that they swallow their pride and ask for some sort of continuance work within the Regiment, staying on well beyond their sell-by date, or others still feel so much a part of it that they try to get on the Task Force ships during fresh conflicts, or fly out independently to offer their services as mercenaries.

'I'm your mother now,' the sergeant major barks at a young recruit in the old black and white war movies, and nowhere is that more true than in the SAS. The Regiment becomes mother, father and brothers to its men and to expect them just to walk away from that extended family and camaraderie after a lifetime and not look back or feel bereaved is too much to ask.

I think that is why the spate of SAS books started. Those who have criticised the books as a betrayal of all the Regiment stands for have got it all wrong. These men love and respect the Regiment above all else. They had to, to have remained loyal to it for all those years and stayed the course. To have endured the fear and torture and death.

After de la Billière (whose initials have a meaning in the Regiment which I cannot repeat) wrote his book, it was as if someone had shown those men blinking at the prison gates the way, given them the answer they were seeking. They could earn their crust by writing